# BLOOM'S

# HOW TO WRITE ABOUT

# *Tennessee Williams*

JENNIFER BANACH

Introduction by
HAROLD BLOOM

BLOOM'S
LITERARY CRITICISM
*An imprint of Infobase Publishing*

Bloom's How to Write about Tennessee Williams

Copyright © 2010 by Infobase Publishing
Introduction © 2010 by Harold Bloom

Bloom's Literary Criticism
An imprint of Infobase Publishing
132 West 31st Street
New York NY 10001

**Library of Congress Cataloging-in-Publication Data**
Banach, Jennifer.
    Bloom's how to write about Tennessee Williams / Jennifer Banach; introduction by Harold Bloom.
        p. cm.—(Bloom's how to write about literature)
    Includes bibliographical references and index.
    ISBN 978-1-60413-346-2
    1. Williams, Tennessee, 1911–1983—Criticism and interpretation. 2. Criticism—Authorship. 3. Report writing. I. Bloom, Harold. II. Title. III. Title: How to write about Tennessee Williams. IV. Series.

    PS3545.I5365Z798 2009
    812'.54—dc22      2009006653

Bloom's Literary Criticism books are available at special discounts when purchased in bulk quantities for businesses, associations, institutions, or sales promotions. Please call our Special Sales Department in New York at (212) 967-8800 or (800) 322-8755.

You can find Bloom's Literary Criticism on the World Wide Web at
http://www.chelseahouse.com

Text design by Annie O'Donnell
Cover design by Ben Peterson
Composition by Mary Susan Ryan-Flynn
Cover printed by Art Print, Taylor, Pa.
Book printed and bound by The Maple-Vail Book Manufacturing Group, York, Pa.
Date printed: November, 2009
Printed in the United States of America

10 9 8 7 6 5 4 3 2 1

This book is printed on acid-free paper.

All links and Web addresses were checked and verified to be correct at the time of publication. Because of the dynamic nature of the Web, some addresses and links may have changed since publication and may no longer be valid.

# CONTENTS

# SERIES
# INTRODUCTION

**B**LOOM's How to Write about Literature series is designed to inspire students to write fine essays on great writers and their works. Each volume in the series begins with an introduction by Harold Bloom, meditating on the challenges and rewards of writing about the volume's subject author. The first chapter then provides detailed instructions on how to write a good essay, including how to find a thesis; how to develop an outline; how to write a good introduction, body text, and conclusion; how to cite sources; and more. The second chapter provides a brief overview of the issues involved in writing about the subject author and then a number of suggestions for paper topics, with accompanying strategies for addressing each topic. Succeeding chapters cover the author's major works.

The paper topics suggested within this book are open-ended, and the brief strategies provided are designed to give students a push forward in the writing process rather than a road map to success. The aim of the book is to pose questions, not answer them. Many different kinds of papers could result from each topic. As always, the success of each paper will depend completely on the writer's skill and imagination.

# HOW TO WRITE ABOUT TENNESSEE WILLIAMS: INTRODUCTION

## by Harold Bloom

THE MAJOR influences on Tennessee Williams were not the dramatists Anton Chekhov and August Strindberg but the poet Hart Crane and the novelist-poet D. H. Lawrence. This helps to account for the highly original genre Williams created—lyrical drama, in which the protagonists speak and cry aloud in an idiom that transcends them.

I recommend writing about Williams by noting and analyzing this lyrical context his plays inhabit. His masterpiece, *A Streetcar Named Desire*, allows Blanche a diction and rhythm in her utterances that carry us back to the visions of the broken world of desire by Crane and Lawrence. No hero or heroine in *Streetcar* or elsewhere in Williams can subdue his or her vitalism to even a minimal acceptance of what Freud called the reality principle. They refuse to make friends either with the necessity of dying or of living with mere death-in-life.

Attempt the experiment of juxtaposing some of Hart Crane's most intense lyrics, such as *The Broken Tower* and the *Voyages*, with Williams's plays. The yield for your insights will be considerable. Williams told me once that his Sacred Book was *The Collected Poems of Hart Crane*. We ought to employ that in writing about the best plays yet composed by any American.

# HOW TO WRITE
# A GOOD ESSAY

*By Laurie A. Sterling and Jennifer Banach*

WHILE THERE are many ways to write about literature, most assignments for high school and college English classes call for analytical papers. In these assignments, you are presenting your interpretation of a text to your reader. Your objective is to interpret the text's meaning in order to enhance your reader's understanding and enjoyment of the work. Without exception, strong papers about the meaning of a literary work are built upon a careful, close reading of the text or texts. Careful, analytical reading should always be the first step in your writing process. This volume provides models of such close, analytical reading, and these should help you develop your own skills as a reader and as a writer.

As the examples throughout this book demonstrate, attentive reading entails thinking about and evaluating the formal (textual) aspects of the author's works: theme, character, form, and language. In addition, when writing about a work, many readers choose to move beyond the text itself to consider the work's cultural context. In these instances, writers might explore the historical circumstances of the time period in which the work was written. Alternatively, they might examine the philosophies and ideas that a work addresses. Even in cases where writers explore a work's cultural context, though, papers must still address the more formal aspects of the work itself. A good interpretative essay that evaluates Charles Dickens's use of the philosophy of utilitarianism in his novel *Hard Times,* for example, cannot adequately address the author's treatment of the philosophy without firmly grounding this discussion in the book itself. In other words, any analytical paper about a text, even one that seeks to evaluate the work's cultural context, must also have a firm handle on the work's themes, characters, and language. You must look for and evaluate these aspects of a work, then, as you read a text and as you prepare to write about it.

## WRITING ABOUT THEMES

Literary themes are more than just topics or subjects treated in a work; they are attitudes or points about these topics that often structure other elements in a work. Writing about theme therefore requires that you not just identify a topic that a literary work addresses but also discuss what the work says about that topic. For example, if you were writing about the culture of the American South in William Faulkner's famous story "A Rose for Emily," you would need to discuss what Faulkner says, argues, or implies about that culture and its passing.

When you prepare to write about thematic concerns in a work of literature, you will probably discover that, like most works of literature, your text touches upon other themes in addition to its central theme. These secondary themes also provide rich ground for paper topics. A thematic paper on "A Rose for Emily" might consider gender or race in the story. While neither of these could be said to be the central theme of the story, they are clearly related to the passing of the "old South" and could provide plenty of good material for papers.

As you prepare to write about themes in literature, you might find a number of strategies helpful. After you identify a theme or themes in the story, you should begin by evaluating how other elements of the story—such as character, point of view, imagery, and symbolism—help develop the theme. You might ask yourself what your own responses are to the author's treatment of the subject matter. Do not neglect the obvious, either: What expectations does the title set up? How does the title help develop thematic concerns? Clearly, the title "A Rose for Emily" says something about the narrator's attitude toward the title character, Emily Grierson, and all she represents.

# WRITING ABOUT CHARACTER

Generally, characters are essential components of fiction and drama. (This is not always the case, though; Ray Bradbury's "August 2026: There Will Come Soft Rains" is technically a story without characters, at least any human characters.) Often, you can discuss character in poetry, as in T. S. Eliot's "The Love Song of J. Alfred Prufrock" or Robert Browning's "My Last Duchess." Many writers find that analyzing character is one of the most interesting and engaging ways to work with a piece of literature and to shape a paper. After all, characters generally are human, and we all know something about being human and living in the world. While it is always important to remember that these figures are not real people but creations of the writer's imagination, it can be fruitful to begin evaluating them as you might evaluate a real person. Often you can start with your own response to a character. Did you like or dislike the character? Did you sympathize with the character? Why or why not?

Keep in mind, though, that emotional responses like these are just starting places. To truly explore and evaluate literary characters, you need to return to the formal aspects of the text and evaluate how the author has drawn these characters. The 20th-century writer E. M. Forster coined the terms *flat* characters and *round* characters. Flat characters are static, one-dimensional characters that frequently represent a particular concept or idea. In contrast, round characters are fully drawn and much more realistic characters that frequently change and develop over the course of a work. Are the characters you are studying flat or round? What elements of the characters lead you to this conclusion? Why might the author have drawn characters like this? How does their development affect the meaning of the work? Similarly, you should explore the techniques the author uses to develop characters. Do we hear a character's own words, or do we hear only other characters' assessments of him or her? Or, does the author use an omniscient or limited omniscient narrator to allow us access to the workings of the characters' minds? If so, how does that help develop the characterization? Often you can even evaluate the narrator as a character. How trustworthy are the opinions and assessments of the narrator? You should also think about characters' names. Do they mean anything? If you encounter a hero named Sophia or Sophie, you should probably think about her wisdom (or lack thereof), since *sophia* means "wisdom" in Greek. Similarly, since the name Sylvia is derived from the word *sylvan,* meaning "of the wood," you might want to evaluate that character's relationship with nature. Once again, you might look to the title of the work. Does Herman Melville's "Bartleby, the Scrivener" signal anything about Bartleby himself? Is Bartleby adequately defined by his job as scrivener? Is this part of Melville's point? Pursuing questions such as these can help you develop thorough papers about characters from psychological, sociological, or more formalistic perspectives.

## WRITING ABOUT FORM AND GENRE

*Genre,* a word derived from French, means "type" or "class." Literary genres are distinctive classes or categories of literary composition. On the most general level, literary works can be divided into the genres of drama, poetry, fiction, and essays, yet within those genres there are classifications that are also referred to as genres. Tragedy and comedy, for example, are genres of drama. Epic, lyric, and pastoral are genres of poetry. *Form,* on the other hand, generally refers to the shape or structure of a work. There are many clearly defined forms of poetry that follow specific patterns of meter, rhyme, and stanza. Sonnets, for example, are poems that follow a fixed form of 14 lines. Sonnets generally follow one of two basic sonnet forms, each with its own distinct rhyme scheme. Haiku is another example of poetic form, traditionally consisting of three unrhymed lines of five, seven, and five syllables.

While you might think that writing about form or genre might leave little room for argument, many of these forms and genres are very fluid. Remember that literature is evolving and ever changing, and so are its forms. As you study poetry, you may find that poets, especially more modern poets, play with traditional poetic forms, bringing about new effects. Similarly, dramatic tragedy was once quite narrowly defined, but over the centuries playwrights have broadened and challenged traditional definitions, changing the shape of tragedy. When Arthur Miller wrote *Death of a Salesman,* many critics challenged the idea that tragic drama could encompass a common man like Willy Loman.

Evaluating how a work of literature fits into or challenges the boundaries of its form or genre can provide you with fruitful avenues of investigation. You might find it helpful to ask why the work does or does not fit into traditional categories. Why might Miller have thought it fitting to write a tragedy of the common man? Similarly, you might compare the content or theme of a work with its form. How well do they work together? Many of Emily Dickinson's poems, for instance, follow the meter of traditional hymns. While some of her poems seem to express traditional religious doctrines, many seem to challenge or strain against traditional conceptions of God and theology. What is the effect, then, of her use of traditional hymn meter?

## WRITING ABOUT LANGUAGE, SYMBOLS, AND IMAGERY

No matter what the genre, writers use words as their most basic tool. Language is the most fundamental building block of literature. It is essential that you pay careful attention to the author's language and word choice as you read, reread, and analyze a text. Imagery is language that appeals to the senses. Most commonly, imagery appeals to our sense of vision, creating a mental picture, but authors also use language that appeals to our other senses. Images can be literal or figurative. Literal images use sensory language to describe an actual thing. In the broadest terms, figurative language uses one thing to speak about something else. For example, if I call my boss a snake, I am not saying that he is literally a reptile. Instead, I am using figurative language to communicate my opinions about him. Since we think of snakes as sneaky, slimy, and sinister, I am using the concrete image of a snake to communicate these abstract opinions and impressions.

The two most common figures of speech are similes and metaphors. Both are comparisons between two apparently dissimilar things. Similes are explicit comparisons using the words *like* or *as*; metaphors are implicit comparisons. To return to the previous example, if I say, "My boss, Bob, was waiting for me when I showed up to work five minutes late today—the snake!" I have constructed a metaphor. Writing about his experiences fighting in World War I, Wilfred Owen begins his poem "Dulce et decorum est," with a string of similes: "Bent double, like old beggars under sacks, / Knock-kneed, coughing like hags, we cursed through sludge." Owen's goal was to undercut clichéd notions that war and dying in battle were glorious. Certainly, comparing soldiers to coughing hags and to beggars underscores his point.

"Fog," a short poem by Carl Sandburg, provides a clear example of a metaphor. Sandburg's poem reads:

The fog comes
on little cat feet.

It sits looking
over harbor and city
on silent haunches
and then moves on.

Notice how effectively Sandburg conveys surprising impressions of the fog by comparing two seemingly disparate things—the fog and a cat.

Symbols, by contrast, are things that stand for, or represent, other things. Often they represent something intangible, such as concepts or ideas. In everyday life we use and understand symbols easily. Babies at christenings and brides at weddings wear white to represent purity. Think, too, of a dollar bill. The paper itself has no value in and of itself. Instead, that paper bill is a symbol of something else, the precious metal in a nation's coffers. Symbols in literature work similarly. Authors use symbols to evoke more than a simple, straightforward, literal meaning. Characters, objects, and places can all function as symbols. Famous literary examples of symbols include Moby Dick, the white whale of Herman Melville's novel, and the scarlet *A* of Nathaniel Hawthorne's *The Scarlet Letter.* As both of these symbols suggest, a literary symbol cannot be adequately defined or explained by any one meaning. Hester Prynne's Puritan community clearly intends her scarlet *A* as a symbol of her adultery, but as the novel progresses, even her own community reads the letter as representing not just *adultery,* but *able, angel,* and a host of other meanings.

Writing about imagery and symbols requires close attention to the author's language. To prepare a paper on symbolism or imagery in a work, identify and trace the images and symbols and then try to draw some conclusions about how they function. Ask yourself how any symbols or images help contribute to the themes or meanings of the work. What connotations do they carry? How do they affect your reception of the work? Do they shed light on characters or settings? A strong paper on imagery or symbolism will thoroughly consider the use of figures in the text and will try to reach some conclusions about how or why the author uses them.

## WRITING ABOUT HISTORY AND CONTEXT

As noted above, it is possible to write an analytical paper that also considers the work's context. After all, the text was not created in a vacuum. The author lived and wrote in a specific time period and in a specific cultural context and, like all of us, was shaped by that environment. Learning more about the historical and cultural circumstances that surround the author and the work can help illuminate a text and provide you with productive material for a paper. Remember, though, that when you write analytical papers, you should use the context to illuminate the text. Do not lose sight of your goal—to interpret the meaning of the literary work. Use historical or philosophical research as a tool to develop your textual evaluation.

Thoughtful readers often consider how history and culture affected the author's choice and treatment of his or her subject matter. Investigations into the history and context of a work could examine the work's relation to specific historical events, such as the Salem witch trials in 17th-century Massachusetts or the restoration of Charles II to the English throne in 1660. Bear in mind that historical context is not limited to politics and world events. While knowing about the Vietnam War is certainly helpful in interpreting much of Tim O'Brien's fiction, and some knowledge of the French Revolution clearly illuminates the dynamics of Charles Dickens's *A Tale of Two Cities*, historical context also entails the fabric of daily life. Examining a text in light of gender roles, race relations, class boundaries, or working conditions can give rise to thoughtful and compelling papers. Exploring the conditions of the working class in 19th-century England, for example, can provide a particularly effective avenue for writing about Dickens's *Hard Times*.

You can begin thinking about these issues by asking broad questions at first. What do you know about the time period and about the author? What does the editorial apparatus in your text tell you? Similarly, when specific historical events or dynamics are particularly important to understanding a work but might be somewhat obscure to modern readers, textbooks usually provide notes to explain historical background. With this information, ask yourself how these historical facts and circumstances might have affected the author, the presentation of theme, and the presentation of character. How does knowing more about the work's specific historical context illuminate the work? To take a well-known example, understanding the complex attitudes toward slavery during the time Mark Twain wrote *Adventures of Huckleberry Finn* should help you begin to examine issues of race in the text. Additionally, you might compare these attitudes to those of the time in which the novel was set. How might this comparison affect your interpretation of a work written after the abolition of slavery but set before the Civil War?

## WRITING ABOUT PHILOSOPHY AND IDEAS

Philosophical concerns are closely related to both historical context and thematic issues. Like historical investigation, philosophical research can provide a useful tool as you analyze a text. For example, an investigation into the working class in Dickens's England might lead you to a topic on the philosophical doctrine of utilitarianism in *Hard Times.* Many other works explore philosophies and ideas quite explicitly. Mary Shelley's famous novel *Frankenstein,* for example, explores John Locke's tabula rasa theory of human knowledge as she portrays the intellectual and emotional development of Victor Frankenstein's creature. As this example indicates, philosophical issues are more abstract than investigations of theme or historical context. Some other examples of philosophical issues include human free will, the formation of human identity, the nature of sin, or questions of ethics.

Writing about philosophy and ideas might require some outside research, but usually the notes or other material in your text will provide you with basic information, and often footnotes and bibliographies suggest places you can go to read further about the subject. If you have identified a philosophical theme that runs through a text, you might ask yourself how the author develops this theme. Look at character development and the interactions of characters, for example. Similarly, you might examine whether the narrative voice in a work of fiction addresses the philosophical concerns of the text.

## WRITING COMPARISON AND CONTRAST ESSAYS

Finally, you might find that comparing and contrasting the works or techniques of an author provides a useful tool for literary analysis. A comparison and contrast essay might compare two characters or themes in a single work, or it might compare the author's treatment of a theme in two works. It might also contrast methods of character development or analyze an author's differing treatment of a philosophical concern in two works. Writing comparison and contrast essays, though, requires some special consideration. While they generally provide you with plenty of material to use, they also come with a built-in trap: the laundry list. These papers often become mere lists of connections between the works. As this chapter will discuss, a strong thesis must make an assertion that you want to prove or validate. A strong comparison/contrast thesis, then, needs to comment on the significance of the similarities and differences you observe. It is not enough merely to assert that the works contain similarities and differences. You might, for example, assert why the similarities and differences are important and explain how they illuminate the works' treatment of theme. Remember, too, that a thesis should not be a statement of the obvious. A comparison/contrast paper that focuses only on very obvious similarities or differences does little to illuminate the connections between the works. Often, an effective method of shaping a strong thesis and argument is to begin your paper by noting the similarities between the works but then to develop a thesis that asserts how these apparently similar elements are different. If, for example, you observe that Emily Dickinson wrote a number of poems about spiders, you might analyze how she uses spider imagery differently in two poems. Similarly, many scholars have noted that Hawthorne created many "mad scientist" characters, men who are so devoted to their science or their art that they lose perspective on all else. A good thesis comparing two of these characters—Aylmer of "The Birth-mark" and Dr. Rappaccini of "Rappaccini's Daughter," for example—might initially identify both characters as examples of Hawthorne's mad scientist type but then argue that their motivations for scientific experimentation differ. If you strive to analyze the similarities or differences, discuss significances, and move beyond the obvious, your paper should move beyond the laundry list trap.

## PREPARING TO WRITE

Armed with a clear sense of your task—illuminating the text—and with an understanding of theme, character, language, history, and philosophy, you are ready to approach the writing process. Remember that good writing is grounded in good reading and that close reading takes time, attention, and more than one reading of your text. Read for comprehension first. As you go back and review the work, mark the text to chart the details of the work as well as your reactions. Highlight important passages, repeated words, and image patterns. "Converse" with the text through marginal notes. Mark turns in the plot, ask questions, and make observations about characters, themes, and language. If you are reading from a book that does not belong to you, keep a record of your reactions in a journal or notebook. If you have read a work of literature carefully, paying attention to both the text and the context of the work, you have a leg up on the writing process. Admittedly, at this point, your ideas are probably very broad and undefined, but you have taken an important first step toward writing a strong paper.

Your next step is to focus, to take a broad, perhaps fuzzy, topic and define it more clearly. Even a topic provided by your instructor will need to be focused appropriately. Remember that good writers make the topic their own. There are a number of strategies—often called "invention"—that you can use to develop your own focus. In one such strategy, called *freewriting*, you spend 10 minutes or so just writing about your topic without referring back to the text or your notes. Write whatever comes to mind; the important thing is that you just keep writing. Often this process allows you to develop fresh ideas or approaches to your subject matter. You could also try *brainstorming*: Write down your topic and then list all the related points or ideas you can think of. Include questions, comments, words, important passages or events, and anything else that comes to mind. Let one idea lead to another. In the related technique of *clustering*, or *mapping*, write your topic on a sheet of paper and write related ideas around it. Then list related subpoints under each of these main ideas. Many people then draw arrows to show connections between points. This technique helps you narrow your topic and can also help you organize your ideas. Similarly, asking journalistic questions—Who? What? Where? When? Why? and How?—can lead to ideas for topic development.

## Thesis Statements

Once you have developed a focused topic, you can begin to think about your thesis statement, the main point or purpose of your paper. It is imperative that you craft a strong thesis; otherwise, your paper will likely be little more than random, disorganized observations about the text. Think of your thesis statement as a kind of road map for your paper. It tells your reader where you are going and how you are going to get there.

To craft a good thesis, you must keep a number of things in mind. First, as the title of this subsection indicates, your paper's thesis should be a statement, an assertion about the text that you want to prove or validate. Beginning writers often formulate a question that they attempt to use as a thesis. For example, a writer exploring the theme of escape in Williams's *The Glass Menagerie* might consider that each of the main characters exhibits a desire to escape from his or her present circumstances. This may lead the writer to ask, What does the play suggest about the ability to escape one's circumstances? While asking a question such as this is a good strategy to use in the invention process to help narrow your topic and find your thesis, a question cannot serve as your thesis because it does not tell your reader what you want to assert about your theme. You might shape your thesis by instead proposing an answer to the question: In Williams's *The Glass Menagerie*, each of the main characters exhibits a desire to escape from his or her present circumstances, but none are able to succeed in achieving this escape. Even Tom, who manages to leave Saint Louis in order to realize his dream of joining the merchant marine and becoming a poet, fails to achieve true freedom. He is unable to escape his past, bound by the guilt of having abandoned his family. The play ultimately suggests that escape is an illusion; it is elusive and unattainable. Notice that the thesis statement does not necessarily have to fit into one sentence. Notice, too, that this thesis provides an initial plan or structure for the rest of the paper. After discussing what each character wishes to escape from and how they exhibit this desire, you could examine how each character deals with this desire and what efforts they make in an attempt to escape. Next, you might begin to theorize about whether or not their efforts are successful. You might start by considering the outcome of Amanda's and Laura's attempts to escape their circumstances and then present the result of Tom's attempt to escape. At this point, you could draw conclusions about what standpoint the play presents on the matter of the ability or inability to escape one's circumstances. Perhaps you could discuss how the play portrays the desire to escape as a symptom of being faced with difficult present circumstances and an inability to recover from the past. You might consider if this inability to escape is an affliction specific to the Wingfield family, or if it is representative of a greater societal condition. Examining how the different elements of the play—plot, structure, narration, and symbolism, for instance—reinforce this view will help you to craft a strong thesis that will serve as a solid foundation for your argument.

Second, remember that a good thesis makes an assertion that you need to support. In other words, a good thesis does not state the obvious. If you tried to formulate a thesis about escape by simply saying, Escape is an important theme of The Glass Menagerie, you have done nothing but rephrase the obvious. Since Williams's play is centered on the characters' desire to escape their circumstances, their means of coping with this desire, and the outcome of their efforts to escape, there would be no point in spending three to five pages supporting that assertion. Once you identify an important theme and pinpoint the primary question that your paper seeks to answer, you might try to develop a thesis from that point by asking yourself further questions: What is each of the main characters seeking an escape from and why? How does each of these characters deal with this desire to escape? How do they attempt to escape their circumstances? Are their efforts productive? What does the conclusion of the story tell us about Tom's ability to escape in particular? Finally, what does the collective outcome of the characters' pursuits tell us about the ability to escape? Is escape a realistic possibility or just an illusion? Such a line of questioning might lead you to a more viable thesis, like the one in the preceding paragraph, while helping you to organize your thoughts and develop a basic structure for your argument, such as the one that appears above.

As the comparison with the road map also suggests, your thesis should appear near the beginning of the paper. In relatively short papers (three to six pages), the thesis almost always appears in the first paragraph. Some writers fall into the trap of saving their thesis for the end, trying to provide a surprise or a big moment of revelation, as if to say, "TA-DA! I've just proved that in A Streetcar Named Desire Williams uses the oscillation between interiors and exteriors to highlight the conflict between fantasy and reality." Placing a thesis at the end of an essay can seriously mar the essay's effectiveness. If you fail to define your essay's point and purpose clearly at the beginning, your reader will find it difficult to assess the clarity of your argument and understand the points you are making. When your argument comes as a surprise at the end, you force your reader to reread your essay in order to assess its logic and effectiveness.

Finally, you should avoid using the first person ("I") as you present your thesis. Though it is not strictly wrong to write in the first person, it is difficult to do so gracefully. While writing in the first person, beginning writers often fall into the trap of writing self-reflexive prose (writing *about* their paper *in* their paper). Often this leads to the most dreaded of opening lines: "In this paper I am going to discuss . . ." Not only does this self-reflexive voice make for very awkward prose, it frequently allows writers to boldly announce a topic while completely avoiding a thesis statement. An example might be a paper that begins as follows: A *Streetcar Named Desire,* one of Williams's most famous plays, dramatizes a visit between Blanche DuBois and her sister Stella Kowalski in New Orleans. The explosive interaction between Blanche and Stella's husband, Stanley, leads, ultimately, to Blanche's breakdown. In this paper I am going to discuss how the play addresses the state of the Old South. The author of this paper has done little more than announce a general topic for the paper (how the play addresses the state of the Old South), and the third sentence does not seem to hold any connection to the first or second sentence. While the third sentence might be the start of a thesis, the writer fails to present an opinion about how the play addresses the state of the Old South and the means by which this view is presented. What, specifically, does the play tell us about the Old South and why is this significant? How does the play convey this viewpoint? To improve this "thesis," the writer would need to back up a couple of steps. The writer should examine the play and draw conclusions about what the play tells us about the state of the Old South before crafting the thesis. After carefully examining key passages in the play, the writer might conclude that the play presents the death of the Old South and the rise of a coarser industrial society. From here, the author could select the means by which Williams communicates this idea and then begin to craft a specific thesis. A writer who chooses to explore the symbolism that Williams employs in order to dramatize the death of the Old South and the rise of a coarser industrial society might, for example, craft a thesis such as this: In A *Streetcar Named Desire,* Williams employs symbolism to dramatize the death of the Old South and

```
the  rise  of  a  coarser  industrial  society.  The  major
characters  function  as  allegorical  representatives  of
these  two  divergent  societies,  while  minor  symbols
support  this  notion  of  the  now  extinct  genteel  way  of
life  and  the  triumph  of  the  rough  ways  associated  with
a  newly  industrialized  society.  The  many  vestiges  of  the
Old  South  presented  throughout  the  play  are  revealed  to
be  nothing  more  than  illusions,  evidence  of  a  way  of
life  that  no  longer  exists.
```

## Outlines

While developing a strong, thoughtful thesis early in your writing process should help focus your paper, outlining provides an essential tool for logically shaping that paper. A good outline helps you see—and develop—the relationships among the points in your argument and assures you that your paper flows logically and coherently. Outlining not only helps place your points in a logical order but also helps you subordinate supporting points, weed out any irrelevant points, and decide if there are any necessary points that are missing from your argument. Most of us are familiar with formal outlines that use numerical and letter designations for each point. However, there are different types of outlines; you may find that an informal outline is a more useful tool for you. What is important, though, is that you spend the time to develop some sort of outline—formal or informal.

Remember that an outline is a tool to help you shape and write a strong paper. If you do not spend sufficient time planning your supporting points and shaping the arrangement of those points, you will most likely construct a vague, unfocused outline that provides little, if any, help with the writing of the paper. Consider the following example.

```
Thesis:  In  A  Streetcar  Named  Desire,  Williams  employs
symbolism  to  dramatize  the  death  of  the  Old  South  and
the  rise  of  a  coarser  industrial  society.  The  major
characters  function  as  allegorical  representatives  of
these  two  divergent  societies,  while  minor  symbols
support  this  notion  of  the  now  extinct  genteel  way  of
life  and  the  triumph  of  the  rough  ways  associated  with
a  newly  industrialized  society.  The  many  vestiges  of  the
```

Old South presented throughout the play are revealed to be nothing more than illusions, evidence of a way of life that no longer exists.

   I. Introduction and thesis

  II. Streetcar named Cemeteries
     A. Elysian Fields

 III. Characters as major symbols
     A. Blanche represents the Old South
       1. Clothing
       2. Jewelry
       3. Other belongings
       4. Illusion
     B. Stanley represents the new industrial class

  IV. Conclusion
     A. Major and minor symbols in the play create the impression of the death of the Old South

This outline has a number of flaws. First, the major topics labeled with the Roman numerals are not arranged in a logical order. If the paper's aim is to show that Williams uses symbolism to convey the death of the Old South, the writer should begin with the strongest examples of symbolism, or major symbols, before showing the relation of minor or supporting symbols, such as the streetcar named Cemeteries, to this death. Second, the thesis makes no specific mention of a streetcar named Cemeteries, yet the writer includes this as a major topic in the outline. Though the streetcar named Cemeteries may well be relevant to the theme of this paper, the writer fails to provide details about its place in the argument. Therefore, though the streetcar named Cemeteries may be significant, it does not merit a major section. Instead, the writer could include this under a subsection entitled Minor Symbols or Supporting Symbols. The writer could then write about the symbolic significance of the streetcar name in this section of the essay along with other relevant examples of minor or supporting symbols that pertain to the thesis. Third, the writer includes illusion as one of the numbered items in section III. Numbers 1, 2, and 3 refer to specific examples of symbols representing the death of the Old South as they relate to Blanche. Illusion does not belong in the list. The writer could argue that Blanche's clothing, jewelry, and other belongings are objects that create an illusion of the existence of a way of life associated with the Old South (therefore, illusion is the concept that links all of the symbolic items in this section), but it itself is not an example of a symbol that portrays the death of the Old South and, therefore, should be omitted. A fourth problem is the inclusion of a section A in sections II and IV. An outline should not include an A without a B, a 1 without a 2, and so forth. Furthermore, in section II, Elysian Fields is not an example of a streetcar name. Like the streetcar named Cemeteries, it is an example of a minor or supporting symbol that refers to the death of the Old South and the rise of a coarser industrial society and, therefore, would find a more suitable place in a subset entitled Minor Symbols or Supporting Symbols. The final problem with this outline is the overall lack of detail. None of the sections provides much information about the content of the argument, and it seems likely that the writer has not given sufficient thought to the content of the paper.

A better start to this outline might be the following:

Thesis: In *A Streetcar Named Desire,* Williams employs symbolism to dramatize the death of the Old South and the rise of a coarser industrial society. The major characters function as allegorical representatives of these two divergent societies, while minor symbols support this notion of the now extinct genteel way of life and the triumph of the rough ways associated with a newly industrialized society. The many vestiges of the Old South presented throughout the play are revealed to be nothing more than illusions, evidence of a way of life that no longer exists.

    I. Introduction and thesis

    II. Major symbols -- The main characters function
        as representatives of the Old South and the

new industrial society, respectively. Each possesses attributes that best characterize the society they represent.

   A. Blanche represents the Old South.

   B. Stanley represents the coarser industrial society.

III. Minor symbols -- Supporting details also refer to these societies and help to heighten the feeling of tension that exists between the two characters. These symbols create a sense of loss, decay, and death.

   A. The streetcar named Cemeteries, taken by Blanche, represents the cultural death of the Old South.

   B. Elysian Fields is Blanche's destination. It is the address of Stella and Stanley's home. The name, which is taken from the final resting place of the blessed in Greek mythology, refers to a real avenue in a poor section of New Orleans. Williams uses it to present the harsh realities associated with a struggling lower class in a newly industrialized society.

   C. Belle Reve, which means "beautiful dream," is another symbol of the fallen culture of the South. It is the family estate, a reference to plantation life as experienced by the families of rich plantation owners. Blanche indicates that Belle Reve has been lost due to the failings of her family.

   D. The implied rape of Blanche by Stanley presents a dramatic portrait of the Old South being overtaken by the new ways of industrial society. The rape leads to her final breakdown and is, therefore, representative of the final

> and irreparable loss of the genteel way
> of life associated with the Old South
> in the face of a newly industrialized
> society.
>
>      IV. Conclusion

This new outline would prove much more helpful when it came time to write the paper.

An outline like this could be shaped into an even more useful tool if the writer fleshed out the argument by providing specific examples from the text to support each point. Once you have listed your main point and your supporting ideas, develop this raw material by listing related supporting ideas and material under each of those main headings. From there, arrange the material in subsections and order the material logically.

For example, you might begin with one of the theses cited above: In Williams's *The Glass Menagerie,* each of the main characters exhibits a desire to escape from his or her present circumstances, but none are able to succeed in achieving this escape. Even Tom, who manages to leave Saint Louis in order to realize his dream of joining the merchant marine and becoming a poet, fails to achieve true freedom. He is unable to escape his past, bound by the guilt of having abandoned his family. The play ultimately suggests that escape is an illusion; it is elusive and unattainable. As noted above, this thesis supplies a framework for how your paper could be best organized: You might start by introducing the notion that each of the main characters exhibits a desire to escape from his or her present circumstances and then examine what they desire an escape from and how we know this about each character. Next, you might consider how each character attempts to escape and, finally, consider the outcome of their attempts to escape. Therefore, you might begin your outline with four topic headings: (1) What each character desires an escape from, (2) How each character exhibits this desire to escape, (3) How each character attempts to escape, and (4) The collective result of the efforts to escape and the realization of escape as elusive and unattainable. Under each of those headings you could list ideas that support the particular point. Be sure to include references to parts of the text that help build your case.

An informal outline might look like this:

Thesis: In Williams's *The Glass Menagerie*, each of the main characters exhibits a desire to escape from his or her present circumstances, but none are able to succeed in achieving this escape. Even Tom, who manages to leave Saint Louis in order to realize his dream of joining the merchant marine and becoming a poet, fails to achieve true freedom. He is unable to escape his past, bound by the guilt of having abandoned his family. The play ultimately suggests that escape is an illusion; it is elusive and unattainable.

1. Introduction and thesis

2. What each character desires an escape from
    • Amanda wants to escape a difficult life as a single mother. She regrets her decision to marry her husband and wants security for herself and her children. She is unable to abandon the romantic notions of a fading way of life.
        ○ Amanda says, "And I could have been Mrs. Duncan J. Fitzhugh, mind you! But -- I picked your *father*!" (404).
        ○ Amanda confesses, "I'll tell you what I wished for on the moon. Success and happiness for my precious children!" (426).
    • Laura does not want to feel different, like a cripple. She wants to escape from a life without love and romance.
        ○ When Amanda talks about the prospect of marriage, Laura cries out, "But mother -- . . . I'm -- crippled!" (410).

○ When Amanda asks Laura if she has ever liked a boy, Laura admits that she did like Jim, demonstrating that she has the same romantic hopes as anyone else (409). We also learn later that Laura kept the program from the high school production of *The Pirates of Penzance* that Jim starred in (409), which serves as another indication of Laura's romantic hopes.

● Tom wants to escape a life without adventure. He despises the warehouse and is tired of his mother's nagging. Some might argue that he wants to escape the responsibilities he inherited as a result of his father's departure.

○ When Amanda questions Tom about why he goes to the movies, he says, "I go to the movies because -- I like adventure. Adventure is something I don't have much of at work" (421).

○ Tom yells, "Listen! You think I'm crazy about the warehouse? . . . I'd rather somebody picked up a crow bar and battered out my brains" (414).

○ Early in the play Tom says, "I haven't enjoyed one bite of this dinner because of your constant directions on how to eat it" (402).

3. How each character exhibits the desire to escape

● Amanda recalls a better past obsessively and nags her children, thinking that it will compel them to be better people and, ultimately, help them to find the success that will help them all out of their current situation.

- ○ "AMANDA. . . . Why, I remember one Sunday afternoon in Blue Mountain -- . . .
  TOM. I know what's coming!
  LAURA. Yes. But let her tell it.
  TOM. Again?
  LAURA. She loves to tell it" (402).
  - ○ Amanda instructs Tom, "Honey, don't push with your fingers. If you have to push with something, the thing to push with is a crust of bread" (401).
- Laura retreats from reality, lives in a fantasy world, paying attention only to her glass menagerie and the wind-up Victrola.
- Tom goes to the movies, drinks, writes poetry, and talks of joining the merchant marine.
  - ○ Amanda says, "I saw that letter you got from the Merchant Marine. I know what you're dreaming of" (422).
  - ○ "Tom fishes in his pockets for the door-key, removing a motley assortment of articles in the search, including a perfect shower of movie-ticket stubs and an empty bottle" (416).

4. How each character attempts to escape
   - Amanda tries to encourage her children to succeed so that the family can have stability. She says to Tom, "I've had to put up a solitary battle all these years. But you're my right hand bower! Don't fall down! Don't fail! . . . Try and you will SUCCEED!" (419).
   - Laura ultimately tries to open herself up to the possibility of a romance. Her use of a nickname for Jim -- "It's no tragedy, Freckles" (457) -- is a departure from her previous behavior, showing that she

> is opening up to him and becoming more comfortable.
> - In addition to his temporary forms of escape, such as going to the movies, Tom finally leaves Saint Louis and joins the merchant marine.

5. The outcome of the characters' attempts to escape and the realization of escape as elusive and unattainable
   - Amanda fails to inspire her children and refuses to abandon the ways of a past that no longer exists.
   - Laura fails to find romance, retreats back into a fantasy world. After Jim lets her down she "rises unsteadily and crouches beside the victrola to wind it up" (460).
   - Tom does leave Saint Louis, but he is unable to truly escape. He is bound by guilt and cannot forget his sister, whom he left behind. He confesses, "I left Saint Louis. I descended the steps of this fire-escape for a last time. . . . Oh, Laura, Laura, I tried to leave you behind me, but I am more faithful than I intended to be!" (465).

6. Conclusion

You would set about writing a formal outline with a similar process, though in the final stages you would label the headings differently and provide much greater detail. A formal outline for a paper that argues the thesis about *A Streetcar Named Desire* cited above—that the play uses symbolism to present the death of the Old South and the triumph of a coarser industrial society—might look like this:

Thesis: In *A Streetcar Named Desire*, Williams employs symbolism to dramatize the death of the Old South and the rise of a coarser industrial society. The major characters function as allegorical representations of these two divergent societies, while minor symbols support this notion of the now extinct genteel way of life and the triumph of the rough ways associated with a newly industrialized society. Any vestiges of the Old South are revealed to be nothing more than illusions, evidence of a way of life that no longer exists.

I. Introduction and thesis

II. The characters function as major representatives of the Old South and the coarser industrial society. Each possesses attributes that are characteristic of the society he or she represents. When the two are paired together, it quickly becomes apparent that the two cannot peacefully coexist. As Stanley says, "the Kowalskis and the DuBois have different notions" (486).

   A. Blanche, a ruined Southern belle, is a symbol of the faded Old South. Everything about her references a way of life that no longer exists, yet presents the illusion of the preservation of a genteel way of life.

      1. At first glance, Blanche's appearance references a well-to-do lifestyle as a daughter of a rich plantation owner, but this image is quickly revealed to be nothing more than an illusion.

         a. When we meet Blanche, she is "daintily dressed in a white suit with a fluffy bodice, necklace and earrings of pearl, white gloves and hat" (471), but

       Williams goes on to compare her to a moth (471 -- a fragile creature known to be found among old, discarded things.

    b. Stanley also makes note of Blanche's clothing, furs, and jewelry, but Stella is quick to point out that they are fakes (485–86).

2. Blanche's way of speaking also seems very proper. She appears well educated and well mannered, and her actions indicate a kind of romance, but this, too, is false.

    a. Blanche is an alcoholic; she drinks throughout the play.

    b. She claims to have "old-fashioned ideals" but rolls her eyes when Mitch buys into this sentiment (525).

3. Through Blanche's stories and recollections about romantic times in the South, she also creates a false history.

    a. Blanche lies about why she is no longer teaching and what she has been up to.

    b. Her fake stories about suitors reference another way of life that no longer exists.

    c. She lies about her age.

    d. We learn that she did not retire but was fired for having an affair with a student.

4. The constant references to Blanche's not wanting to be seen in full light leave no doubt that what we are

seeing is not what actually exists. The romantic way of life associated with the Old South turns out to be nothing more than an illusion.

B. Stanley is a contrasting symbol of a coarser industrial class. His character is in stark contrast to the character of Blanche.

1. He is immediately identified as a member of the immigrant working class.

   a. When Blanche meets Stanley, he is "roughly dressed in blue denim work clothes" (470).

   b. Blanche refers to him constantly as a Polack instead of a Pole, indicating a kind of presumed superiority that Stanley sets out to quash.

2. Stanley bowls, drinks beer, and plays poker.

3. He is crass, has no hesitation about undressing in front of Blanche.

4. He is without restraint and is often compared to an animal. He flies off the handle, and when Stella leaves him he stands outside "like a baying hound and bellows his wife's name" (502).

5. In contrast to the metaphor of Blanche's not wanting to be seen in full light, Stella reveals that Stanley "smashed all the lightbulbs" on their wedding night (505).

III. Minor symbols support this notion of the extinction of the way of life associated with the Old South and the triumph of a coarser industrial society. These symbols reference death, decay, and loss.

  A. The play is set in a poor section of New Orleans. Williams describes it as having an "atmosphere of decay" (469).

  B. The streetcar named Cemeteries also references death and decay. The ride is symbolic of the cultural death of the Old South.

  C. Elysian Fields is Blanche's destination and the home of Stanley and Stella. As an address, it refers to a real avenue in a poor section of New Orleans. By using a real setting, Williams is able to present the harsh realities associated with a struggling lower class in a newly industrialized society more realistically. The name *Elysian Fields* refers to the final resting place after death for the blessed in Greek mythology.

  D. Belle Reve, the DuBois family estate, is the most literal and direct minor symbol. It is a symbol of the fall of the culture of the Old South, but it also represents loss more generally.

    1. It is the family estate, a literal reference to plantation life as experienced by the families of rich plantation owners. Eunice describes it as "[a] great big place with white columns" (472).

    2. The name, which translates to "beautiful dream," indicates that it is something that does not actually exist.

    3. Blanche indicates that Belle Reve had been lost due to the failings of

her family, which she refers to as "epic fornications" (490).

E. Finally, the implied rape of Blanche by Stanley presents a dramatic picture of the Old South being overtaken by the new industrialized society.

    1. The rape is the antithesis of romance. In the face of the new harsh society, there is no room for the romantic ways of the past.

    2. The rape leads to Blanche's final breakdown. It is representative of the final and irreparable loss of the genteel way of life associated with the Old South.

IV. Conclusion

A. Despite the rape scene, the play raises the question of who is really responsible for Blanche's downfall.

    1. Blanche's flaws give us room to consider that Stanley is not solely responsible for Blanche's undoing, just as industrialism is not the sole reason for the loss of gentility and tradition.

    2. Philip C. Kolin argues, "Gone are the days when critics could confidently and simply associate Blanche with the Old South and . . . Stanley with industrialism and barbarism" (52).

B. The play presents an allegory about an important period of time in American history. Through this allegory it questions the survival of romantic ways in modern society.

C. Other works such as *Gone with the Wind* dealt with similar themes. Together, the works form a genre of southern gothic that provokes thought about cultural shifts, American romanticism, and the loss of old ideals.

D. The play ultimately raises the issue of the necessity of a rekindling of true American romanticism.

1. Blanche indicates that "such a thing as art -- as poetry and music -- such kinds of new light have come into the world" (511).

2. Blanche implores Stella not to "hang back with the brutes" (511).

As in the previous sample outline, the thesis provided the seeds of a structure, and the writer was careful to arrange the supporting points in a logical manner, showing the relationships among the ideas in the paper.

## Body Paragraphs

Once your outline is complete, you can begin drafting your paper. Paragraphs, units of related sentences, are the building blocks of a good paper, and as you draft you should keep in mind both the function and the qualities of good paragraphs. Paragraphs help you chart and control the shape and content of your essay, and they help the reader see your organization and your logic. You should begin a new paragraph whenever you move from one major point to another. In longer, more complex essays, you might use a group of related paragraphs to support major points. Remember that in addition to being adequately developed, a good paragraph is both unified and coherent.

### Unified Paragraphs:

Each paragraph must be centered on one idea or point, and a unified paragraph carefully focuses on and develops this central idea without including extraneous ideas or tangents. For beginning writers, the best way to ensure that you are constructing unified paragraphs is to include a topic sentence in each paragraph. This topic sentence should convey the main point of the paragraph, and every sentence in the paragraph should relate to that topic sentence. Any sentence that strays from the central topic does not belong in the paragraph and needs to be revised or deleted. Consider the following paragraph about how the characters' pursuit of dreams in *The Glass Menagerie* is linked to their frustration with their present circumstances and an inability to recover from the past:

> In *The Glass Menagerie*, each of the main characters pursues a dream in an attempt to escape the reality they inhabit. This pursuit is fueled by their frustration with their present circumstances and an inability to recover from their past. Amanda Wingfield expresses regret over marrying her now absent husband. She frequently talks about the extraordinary number of suitors who courted her when she was younger. She seems to expect that her daughter will attract just as many gentleman callers. Laura is more realistic. When her mother announces that it is time for the suitors to begin arriving, Laura says, "I don't believe we're going to receive any, Mother" (404). At the end of the play, Laura does receive one suitor, although he is unaware that Laura is going to be present. He has simply come to the Wingfield residence because Tom has invited him for dinner. Tom and Jim, the gentleman caller, attended the same high school and now happen to work at the same warehouse. Jim recognized that Tom was a poet and nicknamed him Shakespeare. He is the only person in the play to truly acknowledge Tom's aspirations of being a poet. Tom's mother seems to think that poetry is a waste of time. She wants Tom to be a diligent worker because she feels that this will lead to the family's security. The family has struggled since Laura and Tom's father abandoned them, and Amanda sees Tom as their chance for a better future.

Although the paragraph begins solidly, and the second sentence provides the central idea of the paragraph, the author soon goes on a tangent. If the purpose of the paragraph is to demonstrate that the pursuit of dreams is linked to frustration with present circumstances and an inability to recover from the past, the sentences about Amanda's expectations, the suitor, and Tom's relationship to Jim are tangential here. They may find a place later in the paper, but they should be deleted from this paragraph. The author's points need to address more clearly how each character pursues a dream and how, specifically, this pursuit is linked to frustration with present circumstances and an inability to recover from the past. All of the sentences in this paragraph should somehow tie in to this central point.

## *Coherent Paragraphs:*

In addition to shaping unified paragraphs, you must also craft coherent paragraphs that develop their points logically with sentences that flow smoothly into one another. Coherence depends on the order of your sentences, but it is not the only factor that lends the paragraph coherence. You also need to craft your prose to help the reader see the relationship among the sentences.

Consider the following paragraph about how the pursuit of dreams is linked to frustration with present circumstances and an inability to recover from the past in *The Glass Menagerie*. Notice how the writer addresses the same topic as above but fails to help the reader see the relationships among the points.

> In *The Glass Menagerie*, each of the main characters pursues a dream in an attempt to escape the reality they inhabit. This pursuit is fueled by their frustration with their present circumstances and an inability to recover from their past. Amanda wants security for her family. She regrets marrying her husband, who has abandoned the family. She nags her children because she believes that this will drive them to succeed in life. Tom wants to be a poet and also expresses a desire to join the merchant marine. He does not like the warehouse and is bothered by his mother's nagging and the responsibilities that have fallen on him as a result of his father's abandonment. Laura had a difficult time in high school because of her deformity. She believed that people saw her as a cripple and felt as if her leg brace made a loud noise. She liked Jim in high school

```
and invests herself in the possibility of a romance
with him when he shows up at their home as the invited
gentleman caller.
```

This paragraph demonstrates that unity alone does not guarantee paragraph effectiveness. The argument is hard to follow because the author fails both to show connections between the sentences and to indicate how they work to support the overall point.

A number of techniques are available to aid paragraph coherence. Careful use of transitional words and phrases is essential. You can use transitional flags to introduce an example or an illustration *(for example, for instance)*, to amplify a point or add another phase of the same idea *(additionally, furthermore, next, similarly, finally, then)*, to indicate a conclusion or a result *(therefore, as a result, thus, in other words)*, to signal a contrast or a qualification *(on the other hand, nevertheless, despite this, on the contrary, still, however, conversely)*, to signal a comparison *(likewise, in comparison, similarly)*, and to indicate a movement in time *(afterward, earlier, eventually, finally, later, subsequently, until)*.

In addition to transitional flags, careful use of pronouns aids coherence and flow. If you were writing about *The Wizard of Oz,* you would not want to keep repeating the phrase *the witch* or the name *Dorothy.* Careful substitution of the pronoun *she* in these instances can aid coherence. A word of warning, though: When you substitute pronouns for proper names, always be sure that your pronoun reference is clear. In a paragraph that discusses both Dorothy and the witch, substituting *she* could lead to confusion. Make sure that it is clear to whom the pronoun refers. Generally, the pronoun refers to the last proper noun you have used.

While repeating the same name over and over again can lead to awkward, boring prose, it is possible to use repetition to help your paragraph's coherence. Careful repetition of important words or phrases can lend coherence to your paragraph by reminding readers of your key points. Admittedly, it takes some practice to use this technique effectively. You may find that reading your prose aloud can help you develop an ear for the effective use of repetition.

To see how helpful transitional aids are, compare the paragraph below to the preceding paragraph about how the pursuit of dreams is linked to frustration with present circumstances and an inability to recover from the past in *The Glass Menagerie.* Notice how the author works with the same ideas but shapes them into a much more coherent paragraph whose point is clearer and easier to follow. Notice also how the concluding sentences unify the thoughts and reveal the significance of this information.

> In *The Glass Menagerie*, each of the main characters pursues a dream in an attempt to escape the reality they inhabit. This pursuit is fueled by their frustration with their present circumstances and an inability to recover from their past. Amanda, for instance, dreams of security and happiness for her family. We are quickly provided with evidence that this particular desire stems from her disappointment with the way that her own life has turned out. She regrets marrying her husband, who has abandoned the family, and is plagued by the thought that she could have married one of her many other suitors. Likewise, Tom is driven by his frustration with both his past and his present. He pursues a dream of becoming a poet and also expresses a desire to join the merchant marine because he is unhappy working at the warehouse and is looking for a way out. Additionally, he is bothered by his mother's nagging and the responsibilities that have fallen on him as a result of his father's abandonment. Even Laura, who appears to have little ambition, is driven by a similar frustration. Because of her persistent feelings that she does not fit in and her inability to get over the difficult time that she had in high school, Laura hopes for something better -- romance and love. She is eventually able to open herself up to the notion of a better life and invests herself in the possibility of a romance with Jim when he appears at the Wingfield home at Tom's invitation. This motivation that the characters share serves a very important purpose in the play. Their pursuit of a dream fueled by frustration unifies the seemingly disjointed Wingfield family, allowing readers and viewers to see the characters as a single unit. It also allows readers and viewers to sympathize with each

character, despite the single point of view presented
by Tom as narrator.

## Introductions

Introductions present particular challenges for writers. Generally, your introduction should do two things: capture your reader's attention and explain the main point of your essay. In other words, while your introduction should contain your thesis, it needs to do a bit more work than that. You are likely to find that starting that first paragraph is one of the most difficult parts of the paper. It is hard to face that blank page or screen, and as a result, many beginning writers, in desperation to start somewhere, start with overly broad, general statements. While it is often a good strategy to start with more general subject matter and narrow your focus, do not begin with broad sweeping statements such as Everyone experiences desire. Such sentences are nothing but empty filler. They begin to fill the blank page, but they do nothing to advance your argument. Instead, you should try to gain your readers' interest. Some writers like to begin with a pertinent quotation or with a relevant question. Or you might begin with an introduction of the topic you will discuss. If you are writing about Williams's view of desire in *A Streetcar Named Desire,* for instance, you might begin by talking about how desire is presented as a destructive force. Another common trap to avoid is depending on your title to introduce the author and the text you are writing about. Always include the work's author and title in your opening paragraph.

Compare the effectiveness of the following introductions:

1.  Everyone experiences desire. How does desire affect you? In this play, we see Stanley's uncontrollable desire as well as Blanche's desire through symbolism and character development. Through their interactions we see that desire can be a destructive force.

2.  Desire has appeared as a primary subject in works of art and literature for centuries. It has been presented in many different contexts -- as sexual desire, ambition, and even hope -- but most often it is presented as a positive force closely linked

> to love. In *A Streetcar Named Desire*, Tennessee
> Williams abandons traditional definitions of desire,
> depicting it instead as a destructive force and an
> obsession that characterizes the darkest part of
> human nature.

The first introduction begins with a vague, overly broad sentence; cites unclear, undeveloped examples; and then moves abruptly to the thesis. Notice, too, how a reader deprived of the paper's title does not know the title of the story that the paper will analyze. The second introduction works with the same material and thesis but provides more detail and is consequently much more interesting. It begins by discussing the various ways that desire is typically depicted in art and literature, notes how these visions of desire are linked, and then presents Williams's own untraditional view of desire as presented in *A Streetcar Named Desire*. The paragraph ends with the thesis, which includes both the author and the title of the work to be discussed.

The paragraph below provides another example of an opening strategy. It begins by introducing the author and the text it will analyze, and then it moves on to provide some necessary background information before revealing its thesis.

> Tennessee Williams's play *A Streetcar Named Desire* tells
> the story of the dramatic conflict between Blanche
> DuBois, a faded southern belle, and Stanley Kowalski, the
> husband of her sister, Stella. Through the interaction
> of these characters, Williams is able to enter into
> a dialogue about the true nature of desire. Stanley
> embodies a kind of raw, uncontrolled sexual desire that
> Stella is drawn to. Even Blanche, who at first seems
> to represent purity and romance, comes to embody a
> similar unrestrained desire. Despite their different
> backgrounds, it is revealed that each of the characters
> is driven by desire, a destructive force that Williams
> characterizes as one of the darkest components of human
> nature.

# Conclusions

Conclusions present another series of challenges for writers. No doubt you have heard the old adage about writing papers: "Tell us what you are going to say, say it, and then tell us what you've said." While this formula does not necessarily result in bad papers, it does not often result in good ones either. It will almost certainly result in boring papers (especially boring conclusions). If you have done a good job establishing your points in the body of the paper, the reader already knows and understands your argument. There is no need to merely reiterate. Do not just summarize your main points in your conclusion. A boring and mechanical conclusion does nothing to advance your argument or interest your reader. Consider the following conclusion to the paper about the symbolic presentation of the death of the Old South in *A Streetcar Named Desire*:

> In conclusion, Williams presents the death of the Old South and the rise of a coarser industrial society by creating a dramatic conflict between Blanche and Stanley and by implementing supporting symbols that highlight this conflict. The genteel manners and romance associated with the Old South no longer exist.

Besides starting with a mechanical transitional device, this conclusion does little more than summarize the main points of the outline (and it does not even touch on all of them). It is incomplete and uninteresting.

Instead, your conclusion should add something to your paper. A good tactic is to build upon the points you have been arguing. Asking "why?" often helps you draw further conclusions. You might also speculate on other directions in which to take your topic by tying it into larger issues. You might do this by envisioning your paper as just one section of a longer essay. For example, in the paper on the death of the Old South and the rise of a coarser industrial society in *A Streetcar Named Desire*, you might attempt to explain what message Williams ultimately presents about who is responsible for Blanche's demise. In the following conclusion to the paper on *A Streetcar Named Desire*, the author discusses how Blanche's own defects remove the responsibility from Stanley and are a metaphor for the true reasons behind the collapse of the ways of the Old South, opening the door for dialogue about the possibility of a rekindling of American romanticism:

While Williams chooses to employ such a forceful
conclusion, it is imperative that readers and viewers
not let this scene overshadow the architecture of
carefully arranged details found in the play. Stanley
is presented as brutish and crass, but the play also
raises questions about whether the ways of the genteel
South ever really existed and, if so, what truly caused
the demise of the Old South. Careful readers and viewers
will note that Blanche suggests that the Belle Reve
estate was not lost by accident or by force but over
time due to a long pattern of moral decay and death.
Through this suggestion and through the revelation
of Blanche's own defects, Williams gives us room to
propose that Stanley is not solely responsible for
Blanche's demise, just as industrialism is not solely
responsible for the loss of gentility and tradition.
Williams scholar Philip C. Kolin announces that "Gone
are the days when critics could confidently and simply
associate Blanche with the Old South and . . . Stanley
with industrialism and barbarism" (52). This question
of responsibility leads to the suggestion that there
is some choice involved. Perhaps the most significant
piece of dialogue in the play is an exchange between
Blanche and her sister Stella. Blanche reminds her
sister that "such a thing as art -- as poetry and
music -- such kinds of new light have come into the
world" (511). She reminds us that romance may still be
possible. "Don't," she implores, "hang back with the
brutes" (511). Through the interplay of these symbols
and the creation of this allegory, Williams is able
not only to address an important period of time in
American history when the economic landscape shifted
from agricultural to industrial but to question the
possibility of the survival of romanticism in modern
society. Along with works such as Margaret Mitchell's
Gone with the Wind, Williams's work forms a genre
of southern gothic literature that evokes this time

in American history, sparking dialogue about cultural shifts, the loss of old ideals and tradition, and most important, the possibility and necessity of a rekindling of American romanticism.

# Citations and Formatting

## Using Primary Sources:

As the examples included in this chapter indicate, strong papers on literary texts incorporate quotations from the text in order to support their points. It is not enough for you to assert your interpretation without providing support or evidence from the text. Without well-chosen quotations to support your argument you are, in effect, saying to the reader, "Take my word for it." It is important to use quotations thoughtfully and selectively. Remember that the paper presents *your* argument, so choose quotations that support *your* assertions. Do not let the author's voice overwhelm your own. With that caution in mind, there are some guidelines you should follow to ensure that you use quotations clearly and effectively.

## Integrate Quotations:

Quotations should always be integrated into your own prose. Do not just drop them into your paper without introduction or comment. Otherwise, it is unlikely that your reader will see their function. You can integrate textual support easily and clearly with identifying tags, short phrases that identify the speaker. For example:

> Williams describes the Wingfield apartment as "one of those vast hive-like conglomerations of cellular living-units that flower as warty growths in overcrowded urban centers."

While this tag appears before the quotation, you can also use tags after or in the middle of the quoted text, as the following examples demonstrate:

> "Yes, I have tricks in my pocket, I have things up my sleeve," says Tom.

> "Yes, I have tricks in my pocket," says Tom, "I have
> things up my sleeve."

You can also use a colon to formally introduce a quotation:

> Tom's frustration is evident: "I don't want to hear any
> more!"

When you quote brief sections of poems (three lines or fewer), use slash marks to indicate the line breaks in the poem:

> As the poem ends, Dickinson speaks of the power of the
> imagination: "The revery alone will do, / If bees are
> few."

Longer quotations (more than four lines of prose or three lines of poetry) should be set off from the rest of your paper in a block quotation. Double-space before you begin the passage, indent it 10 spaces from your left-hand margin, and double-space the passage itself. Because the indentation signals the inclusion of a quotation, do not use quotation marks around the cited passage. Use a colon to introduce the passage. Here are two examples:

> Williams supplies us with a telling description of the
> Wingfield home at the start of *The Glass Menagerie*:
>
> > The Wingfield apartment is in the rear of the
> > building, one of those vast hive-like conglomerations
> > of cellular living-units that flower as warty
> > growths in overcrowded urban centers of lower
> > middle-class population and are symptomatic of the
> > impulse of this largest and fundamentally enslaved
> > section of American society to avoid fluidity and
> > differentiation and to exist and function as one
> > interfused mass of automism.
>
> By now, the reader should be able to forecast Tom's
> desire to escape.

The whole of Dickinson's poem speaks of the imagination:

    To make a prairie it takes a clover and
      one bee,
    One clover, and a bee,
    And revery.
    The revery alone will do,
    If bees are few.

Clearly, she argues for the creative power of the mind.

It is also important to interpret quotations after you introduce them and explain how they help advance your point. You cannot assume that your reader will interpret the quotations the same way that you do.

**Quote Accurately:**
Always quote accurately. Anything within quotation marks must be the author's exact words. There are, however, some rules to follow if you need to modify the quotation to fit into your prose.

1. Use brackets to indicate any material that might have been added to the author's exact wording. For example, if you need to add any words to the quotation or alter it grammatically to allow it to fit into your prose, indicate your changes in brackets:

    Amanda tells Tom that "[they] have to do all
    that [they] can to build [themselves] up. In
    these trying times that [they] live in, all that
    [they] have to cling to is -- each other."

2. Conversely, if you choose to omit any words from the quotation, use ellipses (three spaced periods) to indicate missing words or phrases:

    Amanda retains the grace of the Old South in
    her gestures: "She spreads the newspaper . . .

```
and sits down . . . as if she were settling into
a swing on a Mississippi veranda."
```

3. If you delete a sentence or more, use the ellipses after a period:

```
The narrator describes the scene of Laura's
transformation:
```

```
Laura stands in the middle with lifted
arms while Amanda crouches before her,
adjusting the hem of the new dress, devout
and ritualistic. . . . A fragile, unearthly
prettiness has come out in Laura: she is
like a piece of translucent glass touched by
light, given momentary radiance, not actual,
not lasting.
```

4. If you omit a line or more of poetry, or more than one paragraph of prose, use a single line of spaced periods to indicate the omission:

```
To make a prairie it takes a clover and one
bee,
. . . . . . . . . . . . . . . . . .
And revery.
The revery alone will do,
If bees are few.
```

## Punctuate Properly:

Punctuation of quotations often causes more trouble than it should. Once again, you just need to keep these simple rules in mind.

1. Periods and commas should be placed inside quotation marks, even if they are not part of the original quotation:

```
Blanche sizes up Stanley: "You're simple,
straightforward and honest, a little bit on the
primitive side."
```

The only exception to this rule is when the quotation is followed by a parenthetical reference. In this case, the period or comma goes after the citation (more on these later in this chapter):

```
Blanche  sizes  up  Stanley:  "You're  simple,
straightforward and honest, a little bit on the
primitive side" (488).
```

2. Other marks of punctuation—colons, semicolons, question marks, and exclamation points—go outside the quotation marks unless they are part of the original quotation:

```
What does Amanda mean when she says that "all
pretty girls are a trap"?
```

```
Stanley's  desperation  is  evident:  "STELL-
LAHHHHH!"
```

## Documenting Primary Sources:

Unless you are instructed otherwise, you should provide sufficient information for your reader to locate material you quote. Generally, literature papers follow the rules set forth by the Modern Language Association (MLA). These can be found in the *MLA Handbook for Writers of Research Papers* (sixth edition). You should be able to find this book in the reference section of your library. Additionally, its rules for citing both primary and secondary sources are widely available from reputable online sources. One of these is the Online Writing Lab (OWL) at Purdue University. OWL's guide to MLA style is available at http://owl.english.purdue. edu/owl/resource/557/01/. The Modern Language Association also offers answers to frequently asked questions about MLA style on this helpful Web page: http://www.mla.org/style_faq. Generally, when you are citing from literary works in papers, you should keep a few guidelines in mind.

## Parenthetical Citations:

MLA asks for parenthetical references in your text after quotations. When you are working with prose (short stories, novels, or essays) include page numbers in the parentheses.

> Blanche sizes up Stanley: "You're simple, straightforward and honest, a little bit on the primitive side" (488).

When you are quoting poetry, include line numbers:

> Dickinson's speaker tells of the arrival of a fly: "There interposed a Fly -- / With Blue -- uncertain stumbling Buzz -- / Between the light -- and Me -- " (12-14).

When you are citing classic drama, such as Shakespeare, your citation should include the act number, scene number, and the line numbers that you are citing separated by periods. For instance, if you were citing lines 24–26 from act 1, scene 2 of a classic play, your citation would appear as (1.2.24–26).

When you are citing modern drama, such as the works of Williams, you should include the appropriate page number or numbers, and you may also add a semicolon followed by any other identifiers, as available. These identifiers might be act numbers, scene numbers, or other forms of division, such as the "Blocks" used in Williams's *Camino Real.* Since works are usually found in more than one edition, this extra identifier will help your reader find the passage you are referring to quickly and with ease in their own edition:

> Gutman announces, "We have entered the second in a progress of sixteen blocks on the Camino Real. It's five o'clock. That angry old lion, the Sun, looked back once and growled and then went switching his tail toward the cool shade of the Sierras" (758; bl. 2).

### Works Cited Page:

Parenthetical citations should be linked to a separate works cited page at the end of your paper. The works cited page lists works alphabetically by the author's last name. An entry for the above reference to Williams's *A Streetcar Named Desire* would read:

> Williams, Tennessee. *A Streetcar Named Desire.*
>    *Tennessee Williams: Plays 1937-1955.* Eds. Mel Gussow

and Kenneth Holditch. New York: Library of America,
2000. 467-564.

The *MLA Handbook* includes a full listing of sample entries, as do many
of the online explanations of MLA style.

## Documenting Secondary Sources:

To ensure that your paper is built entirely upon your own ideas and
analysis, instructors often ask that you write interpretative papers
without any outside research. If, on the other hand, your paper requires
research, you must document any secondary sources you use. You need
to document direct quotations, summaries or paraphrases of others'
ideas, and factual information that is not common knowledge. Follow
the guidelines above for quoting primary sources when you use direct
quotations from secondary sources. Keep in mind that MLA style
also includes specific guidelines for citing electronic sources. OWL's
website provides a good summary: http://owl.english.purdue.edu/owl/
resource/557/09/.

## Parenthetical Citations:

As with the documentation of primary sources, described above, MLA
guidelines require in-text parenthetical references to your secondary
sources. Unlike the research papers you might write for a history class,
literary research papers following MLA style do not use footnotes as a
means of documenting sources. Instead, after a quotation, you should
cite the author's last name and the page number:

> "Despite the remarkable frequency of Tom's trips to
> the movies . . . critics have generally neglected to
> consider how Tom's vision and recollection of events
> in *The Glass Menagerie* are both a reflection of the
> shaping influence of the cinema and, more importantly,
> an articulation of the dominant cultural ideology as
> expressed by the cinematic apparatus" (Crandell 1).

If you include the name of the author in your prose, then you would
include only the page number in your citation. If it is the first time you

are referencing the author, you should include his or her full name as well as a brief identifier. For example:

> According to literary scholar George W. Crandell, "Despite the remarkable frequency of Tom's trips to the movies . . . critics have generally neglected to consider how Tom's vision and recollection of events in *The Glass Menagerie* are both a reflection of the shaping influence of the cinema and, more importantly, an articulation of the dominant cultural ideology as expressed by the cinematic apparatus" (1).

After the first appearance, it is sufficient to reference the author by last name only.

> According to Crandell, "Despite the remarkable frequency of Tom's trips to the movies . . . critics have generally neglected to consider how Tom's vision and recollection of events in *The Glass Menagerie* are both a reflection of the shaping influence of the cinema and, more importantly, an articulation of the dominant cultural ideology as expressed by the cinematic apparatus" (1).

If you are including more than one work by the same author, the parenthetical citation should include a shortened yet identifiable version of the title in order to indicate which of the author's works you cite. For example:

> According to Parker, "*The Rose Tattoo* was Williams's first full-length comedy, and is generally interpreted as his most optimistic play, a Dionysian celebration of sexuality that reverses the desire-death pattern of his preceding tragedies. It is considerably more complex than just this, however, both in tone and experimental dramaturgy . . . and these complicating elements look

forward to plays that were written later, towards the
end of his career" ("Comedy" 1).

Similarly, and just as important, if you summarize or paraphrase the
particular ideas of your source, you must provide documentation:

Brian Parker suggests that the version of *Cat on a
Hot Tin Roof* that Williams called "Cat number one"
best represents the original concept for the play,
containing all of the elements of a true tragedy ("Big
Daddy" 98).

## Works Cited Page:

Like the references to primary sources discussed above, the parenthetical references to secondary sources are keyed to a separate works cited
page at the end of your paper. Here is an example of a works cited page
that uses the examples cited above. Note that when two or more works
by the same author are listed, you should use three hyphens followed by
a period in the subsequent entries. You can find a complete list of sample
entries in the *MLA Handbook* or from a reputable online summary of
MLA style.

### WORKS CITED

Crandell, George W. "The Cinematic Eye in Tennessee
   Williams's *The Glass Menagerie.*" *Tennessee Williams
   Annual Review 1* (1998): 1–12.
Parker, Brian. "Bringing Back Big Daddy." *Tennessee
   Williams Annual Review 3* (2000): 91–99.
———. "The Rose Tattoo as Comedy of the Grotesque."
   *Tennessee Williams Annual Review 6* (2003): 1–8.

## *Plagiarism*

Failure to document carefully and thoroughly can leave you open to
charges of stealing the ideas of others, which is known as plagiarism,
and this is a very serious matter. Remember that it is important to
include quotation marks when you use language from your source, even

if you use just one or two words. For example, if you wrote References to the cinema in The Glass Menagerie draw our attention to the dominant cultural ideology of the time period represented, you would be guilty of plagiarism, since you used Crandell's distinct language without acknowledging him as the source. Instead, you should write something like: George W. Crandell points out that repeated references to the cinema in The Glass Menagerie reveal the "dominant cultural ideology as expressed through the cinematic apparatus" (1). In this case, you have properly credited Crandell.

Similarly, neither summarizing the ideas of an author nor changing or omitting just a few words means that you can omit a citation. Crandell's essay "The Cinematic Eye in Tennessee Williams's The Glass Menagerie" contains the following passage about evidence of the influence of the cinema in the narrative style of The Glass Menagerie:

> The cinematic influence in The Glass Menagerie is most clearly evident in the figure of the narrator. . . . Williams's narrator functions in ways analogous to those of the camera in film. Most obviously, the narrator and the camera both operate to provide the spectator with an orienting point of view, one with which the viewer is then compelled to identify. . . . By making the narrator an integral presence in the play, Williams not only facilitates identification with a particular point of view, thus duplicating one of the most important functions of the camera in film, he also addresses and anticipates one of the difficulties inherent in theatrical production: the organization and control of both identification and point of view (2–3).

Below are two examples of plagiarized passages:

> In The Glass Menagerie, Williams employs a cinematic style of narration to help direct his audience. Readers and viewers are compelled to relate to Tom because, as narrator and protagonist, he is an important character. By having Tom function as a camera, presenting things from his own unique perspective, Williams is able

to present a controlled point of view, allowing the author to better manage how the audience relates to the characters in the play and the action onstage.

In *The Glass Menagerie,* the influence of the cinema is most evident in Tom. As narrator, he acts as a camera would, providing readers and spectators with an orienting point of view which controls how the audience ultimately identifies with the action of the play (2–3).

While the first passage does not use Crandell's exact language, it does list the same ideas he proposes about the influence of cinema as evidenced in the narrator of *The Glass Menagerie* without citing his work. Since this interpretation is Crandell's distinct idea, this constitutes plagiarism. The second passage has shortened his passage, changed some wording, and included a citation, but some of the phrasing is Crandell's. The first passage could be fixed with a parenthetical citation. Because some of the wording in the second remains the same, though, it would require the use of quotation marks, in addition to a parenthetical citation. The passage below represents an honestly and adequately documented use of the original passage:

According to Crandell, "the cinematic influence in *The Glass Menagerie* is most clearly evident in the figure of the narrator . . . [who] functions in ways analogous to those of the camera in film" (2). Crandell goes on to say that this particular style of narration "provide[s] the spectator with an orienting point of view," helping Williams to maintain some control over how his audience perceives and relates to the action of the play (2–3).

This passage acknowledges that the interpretation is derived from Crandell while appropriately using quotations to indicate his precise language.

While it is not necessary to document well-known facts, often referred to as "common knowledge," any ideas or language that you take from someone else must be properly documented. Common knowledge generally includes the birth and death dates of authors or other well-documented facts of their lives. An often cited guideline is that if you can find the information in three sources, it is common knowledge. Despite this guideline, it is, admittedly, often difficult to know if the facts you uncover are common knowledge or not. When in doubt, document your source.

## Sample Essay

Victor Chang
Professor Thomas
English II
December 5, 2009

### THE SYMBOLIC REPRESENTATION OF THE DEATH OF THE OLD SOUTH IN WILLIAMS'S A STREETCAR NAMED DESIRE

Tennessee Williams's play A *Streetcar Named Desire* has secured a place in American popular culture, largely because of the memorable delivery of lines such as Stanley's earth-shattering "STELL-LAHHHHH!" and Blanche's disarming "I have always relied on the kindness of strangers" in Elia Kazan's 1951 film adaptation of the play. With such powerful performances, our focus tends to settle on the explosive conflict between Stanley and Blanche, and rightly so, but many readers and viewers may fail to realize that the play is more than the dramatic story of the clash of two individuals. It is also an allegory about loss and a reminder of a deeply significant cultural shift in American history that is still relevant today. In A *Streetcar Named Desire*, Williams employs symbolism to dramatize the death of the Old South and the rise of a coarser industrial society. The major characters, Blanche and Stanley, serve as representatives of these two divergent societies, while minor symbols support this notion of the now extinct genteel way of life and the triumph of the rough ways associated with a newly industrialized society and a struggling lower class. Although reminders abound in the play, any vestiges of the Old South are quickly revealed to be nothing more than illusions, evidence of a way of life that no longer exists.

Almost immediately, we are introduced to Blanche, and it is safe to say that this prompt introduction is well planned, for within the context of this allegory, she is the primary subject. As a ruined southern belle, Blanche functions as a representative of the faded Old South. At first glance, her clothes and jewelry indicate that she is from a class of rich plantation owners, while her way of speaking and her manners suggest southern hospitality and romance. However, upon arriving in New Orleans, it becomes apparent that Blanche's appearance, way of speaking, and background are all in stark contrast to that of the people she is confronted with in New Orleans, and upon arriving in such a setting, it becomes immediately doubtful that she is genuine. Blanche is out of place in the realist and gritty urban world. Although we are presented with the illusion of the preservation of a genteel way of life, everything about Blanche references a way of life that no longer exists. When we meet Blanche, she is "daintily dressed in a white suit with a fluffy bodice, necklace and earrings of pearl, white gloves and hat" (471), but this vision of purity is quickly disrupted when Williams goes on to compare her to a moth (471), a fragile creature commonly found among old, discarded items. Stanley quickly takes stock of Blanche's belongings, but Stella is quick to point out that her sister's designer clothing, furs, and jewels are all fakes (485-86). Similarly, Blanche's way of speaking and manner also lack sincerity. She appears to be well educated and well mannered, but this, too, is revealed to be an illusion. Blanche begins drinking upon her very arrival in New Orleans and continues to drink throughout the play. Furthermore, while she claims to have "old-fashioned ideals" (525), she rolls her eyes at the ridiculousness of anyone buying into this sentiment (525). As if this were not enough, Blanche's history becomes more questionable as the play progresses. We soon learn that she lied about why she is no longer teaching, about her age, and about her past and present suitors. Finally, Blanche's constant reminders that she does not want to be seen in full light leave no doubt that what we are seeing is not what actually exists and cannot be trusted as truth. The falsity associated with Blanche tells us that the romantic way of life associated with the Old South is nothing more than an illusion.

Against Blanche, Williams pairs Stanley Kowalski, her sister's husband, who is identified immediately as a member of the immigrant working class. When Blanche meets Stanley, he is "roughly dressed in blue denim work clothes" (470). He bowls, drinks beer, and plays poker with a handful of men who like to tell dirty jokes. He is crass and without manners, undressing in front of Blanche. Williams is careful to repeat the analogy of Stanley as animal throughout the course of the play. When Stella leaves him, he stands outside "like a baying hound and bellows his wife's name" (502). Finally, in contrast to the metaphor of Blanche not wanting to be seen in full light, we have Stella's revelation that Stanley "smashed all the lightbulbs" on their wedding night (505), a symbol, no doubt, of his dominance and an allusion to the fact that with Stanley what we see is what we get and no tricks of lighting will change that. He is, to put it simply, a dose of reality, and it is suggested that this reality is the emergence of a new society driven by industrialism, lacking in refinement and abandoning all tradition. Although Blanche refers to Stanley repeatedly as a Polack instead of a Pole, indicating a kind of presumed superiority, Stanley sets out to quash this superiority and, ultimately, does so successfully.

In order to heighten the feeling of tension between these two characters and give strength to the notion of the extinction of the genteel way of life associated with the Old South and the triumph of a coarser industrial society, Williams is careful to use supporting symbols that reference death, decay, and loss. The play is set in a poor section of New Orleans, which Williams describes as having an "atmosphere of decay" (469). To get to this place, Blanche must ride a streetcar named Cemeteries, a ride that becomes yet another symbol of cultural death. Blanche finally arrives at Elysian Fields, an avenue in a poor section of New Orleans that takes its name from the final resting place for the blessed in Greek mythology, and immediately expresses shock and disgust at what she sees. She is exposed to the harsh realities associated with a struggling working class.

The setting of the play is not the only significant bit of geography in the play. The fantastic Belle Reve, the lost DuBois family estate, is also central to the play's message. It is immediately recognizable as a symbol of the Old South, a literal reference to plantation life as experienced by the families of rich plantation owners. Eunice describes Belle Reve as "[a] great big place with white columns" (472). However, as with Blanche, the myth of this white purity is quickly dispelled. Belle Reve, whose name translates to "beautiful dream," has been lost due to the failings of the DuBois family, or what Blanche refers to as "epic fornications" (490).

The final and most disturbing reference to moral decay and death is found at the conclusion of the play in the implied rape of Blanche by Stanley. The rape presents a final dramatic picture of the Old South being overtaken by the new industrial society and provides a moment that is the clear antithesis of romance, indicating that, in the face of modern society, there is little room for the romantic ways of the past. Leading ultimately to Blanche's final breakdown, the rape is representative of the final and irreparable loss of the genteel Southern way of life and the triumph of a less-refined modern society.

While Williams chooses to employ such a forceful conclusion, it is imperative that readers and viewers not let this scene overshadow the architecture of carefully arranged details of the play. Stanley is presented as brutish and crass, but the play also raises questions about whether the ways of the genteel South ever really existed and, if so, what truly caused their demise. Careful readers and viewers will make note of Blanche's suggestion that the Belle Reve estate was not lost by accident or by force but over time due to a long pattern of moral decay and death. Through this suggestion and through the revelation of Blanche's own defects, Williams gives us room to propose that Stanley is not solely responsible for Blanche's demise, just as industrialism is not solely responsible for the loss of gentility and tradition in American culture. Williams scholar Philip C. Kolin announces that "Gone are the days when critics could confidently and simply associate Blanche with the Old South and . . . Stanley with industrialism and barbarism" (52). This question of responsibility leads to the suggestion that there is some choice and individual responsibility involved. Perhaps the most significant piece of dialogue in the play is an exchange between Blanche and her sister Stella. Blanche reminds her sister that "such a thing as art -- as poetry and music -- such kinds of new light have come into the world" (511). She reminds us that romance may still be possible. "Don't," she implores, "hang back with the brutes" (511). Through the interplay of these symbols and the creation of this allegory, Williams is able not only to address an important period of time in American history when the economic landscape shifted from agricultural to industrial but to question the possibility of the survival of romanticism in modern society. Along with works such as Margaret Mitchell's *Gone with the Wind,* Williams's work formed part of a genre of southern gothic literature that evokes this time in American history, sparking dialogue about cultural shifts, the loss of old ideals and tradition, and most important, the possibility and necessity of a rekindling of American romanticism.

### WORKS CITED

Kolin, Philip C. "*A Streetcar Named Desire.*" *Tennessee Williams: A Guide to Research and Performance.* Westport, CT: Greenwood, 1998. 51–77.

Williams, Tennessee. *A Streetcar Named Desire. Tennessee Williams: Plays 1937–1955.* Eds. Mel Gussow and Kenneth Holditch. New York: Library of America, 2000. 467–564.

# HOW TO WRITE ABOUT TENNESSEE WILLIAMS

W HEN WRITING about Williams and his body of work, you will use the same tactics that you would use when writing about any other author or work of literature—you identify an important feature or topic, begin gathering information about this topic, draft a thesis, support the thesis with evidence from Williams's texts and other reliable sources, and finish with a conclusion that ties your thoughts together and demonstrates the significance of your observations. While the process remains the same, irrespective of author, time period in which a work was written, or genre, every author's work has its own set of benefits and, likewise, its own challenges that need to be overcome in order to understand the work and write successfully about it.

Williams's works come with some benefits. They are modern. The majority of his works were written between the 1930s and 1983, the year of his death, and his plays are likewise set in modern times. The language in his works is, therefore, easier to understand than the language found in medieval literature or Shakespeare's plays, for instance. The form and genre of most of Williams's major works (with the exception, perhaps, of *Camino Real*) also presents little cause for concern. While these characteristics are to our advantage as we try to understand Williams's oeuvre, his works do, like all other works of literature, present their own unique set of challenges. First, there is the problem of separating the author from his work, recognizing his work as semibiographical rather than autobiographical. Second, the great popularity of film adaptations of the texts can pull our attention away from where it should really be focused—on the original words Williams presents. Third, readers are often overwhelmed by the repetition inherent in Williams's works. Readers can become frustrated by reappearing character types, similar plot lines, and recurring themes. Likewise, the fact that the works were often subject to an ongoing process of revision can be somewhat problematic, as many plays exist in multiple versions. Finally (and perhaps most challenging of all), readers often struggle with the grim thematic concerns that pervade many of Williams's major works. The thematic content can seem depressing and pessimistic, discouraging readers and preventing them from having a clear understanding and positive experience of the work.

While these challenges are significant, being aware of them is half the battle. The second half of the battle lies in knowing how to take our recognition and comprehension of these characteristics and use it to better understand Williams's work. These are challenges that can easily be overcome, and your awareness of them will leave you well prepared, ready to create a strong and unique paper or essay.

Thomas Lanier Williams, better known as Tennessee Williams, became interested in literature early in his life and began writing as a young man. His works were entertaining, but they were also deeply reflective and philosophical. Every play was, in many ways, an act of self-revelation. His plays contained elements that reflected the most intimate details of his own life, including insights into his relationships and revelations about his personal struggles. Williams had a strained relationship with his father, a traveling salesman. Williams's mother, with whom Williams spent most of his childhood, has been described as an emotional, smothering woman preoccupied with southern gentility. Williams also had a brother and a sister, Rose, who was diagnosed with schizophrenia at a young age and who was later completely incapacitated by a lobotomy authorized by her parents. The culmination of Rose's tragic condition and Williams's domestic problems led to a pattern of drug and alcohol abuse throughout his life. Because of Williams's confrontation with these issues in his private life, he understood the complexity of issues such as mental illness and homosexuality in a time before civil rights were attained, when gender roles were still rigidly defined. He understood the problem of addiction, the horror of death, and the struggle to maintain faith and to endure in the face of intense pain and conflict. These subjects became central concerns of Williams's plays. In some works, such as *The Glass Menagerie*, these biographical elements were barely disguised, while in others, such as *The Night of the Iguana*, clever readers found traces of these themes despite an absence of any substantial or literal reference to them. This willingness to offer a window into his personal life and his own existential concerns perpetuated the notion that his works were autobiographical, a characterization that was not wholly accurate.

While Williams took a personal, intimate approach to his work, he also approached his work with a distinct cultural awareness. He was born in Mississippi in 1911 and subsequently wrote, starting as a young man in the 1920s, until his death in 1983. Williams witnessed the effects of two world wars, the struggle for civil rights, and the culmination of a major shift in American culture from an agricultural economy to one ruled by industrialism, changes that had a tremendous impact on the everyday life of Americans. In his own life, Williams was privy to the struggles associated with the lower working class and the stress that was placed on the American family. The loss of gentility and the changes in the southern way of life also had a tremendous impact on him as a Southerner, and these concerns subsequently cropped up as major themes in many of his works. Williams set the majority of his plays in poor urban centers in the South and created characters who were struggling members of the lower class. His work was subsequently linked to a genre of literature known as southern gothic, works of literature unified by their revision of stereotypical southern characters, their treatment of cultural issues and concern with the grotesque, and their ultimate emphasis on reality despite recognition of the supernatural and the unusual. While Williams's work was often placed within this genre, it was not defined by it, defying any strict characterization. Williams experimented with genre and form throughout the entirety of his career, and in these portraits of the American South that included references to his own life, Williams was able to address larger, more universal themes—themes that extended beyond the South, reaching to the very core of human nature.

While these biographical and cultural elements are, of course, integral and important elements of Williams's work, there is danger in trying to designate all of the works as thinly disguised retellings of events from Williams's own life. Remember that all authors reveal some part of themselves in their works, and it is important to know where reality ends and fiction begins. If you choose to write about the biographical elements present in Williams's works, you will need to consult a variety of sources. This may mean looking at biographies such as Lyle Leverich's *Tom: The Unknown Tennessee Williams* or Donald Spoto's *Kindness of Strangers: The Life of Tennessee Williams,* for instance, but also you have the benefit of access to Williams's own thoughts. Many of his letters have been published in collections, and his production notes, essays, and memoirs are available for consideration as well. As you approach each of these texts, it will be necessary to keep an open mind, as different authors may have different views of Williams and may be approaching his work from different angles. However, if you are able to navigate this material responsibly, considering the biographical elements of Williams's work has many benefits. Acquainting yourself with more information about Williams will, no doubt, inform you about his works and provide you with fresh insights. It will also make evident the power of self-revelation in writing and provide some answers to questions of why literature is significant and how we can relate to it.

In addition to the problem of casting Williams's work as autobiography, the intimate nature of Williams's works presents another dilemma. The interesting characters and plots, which transformed audience members into voyeurs, made the plays attractive to directors and movie executives. The texts presented the kind of dynamic storylines and passionate characters that audiences enjoyed seeing on the big screen, and many of the film adaptations, especially *A Streetcar Named Desire* and *Cat on a Hot Tin Roof,* had enormous success. Many people who were previously unacquainted with Williams's works could now perform recitations of key lines of dialogue, and these movies still appear today on lists of the best films of all time.

While the popularity of these adaptations demonstrated that there were a great number of people who found these works interesting and relatable, their presence also created a potential pitfall for those studying or writing about Williams's plays. The adaptations created a singular, popular (and often inaccurate) interpretation of Williams's work. In addition to each director's having his own interpretation of the play he sought to adapt, in order to make the works suitable for popular audiences, the works were often significantly altered—censored, in fact—to conform to industry standards. Characters were modified, any references to controversial issues such as homosexuality were typically omitted, and endings were sometimes completely rewritten to present a more optimistic ending that executives felt audiences desired. Therefore, while an analysis of these adaptations can certainly present strong material for an essay, if the topic of your paper is the nature of adaptations or the cultural or social implications evidenced in adaptations, in almost all other cases you should rely primarily on Williams's original text.

As you consider Williams's texts, you will no doubt note that there are a great number of similarities between the works. Williams's plays often presented similar character types, plot lines, and thematic concerns. By the middle of Williams's career, many critics assumed this position, dismissing later works as little more than recycled versions of the plays that preceded them. While it is true that Williams had a preoccupation with certain character types—the outsider, the female in peril, the unchivalrous male, and the artist, to name a few—and certain themes, it is imperative that you consider why Williams focused on these archetypes and topics. How do they unify Williams's body of work? Close readings of the texts will reveal that, while the characters share a great deal in common, they each tell us something new about the themes of the work they inhabit. Noticing shared elements of the works reveals Williams's key concerns and allows us to better understand his work.

Another stumbling block for those writing about Williams and his works has been the evolution of the texts. Williams's works were subject to an intense, ongoing process of revision. This means that it is often possible that multiple versions of a single play exist and are circulated in the public realm. Some plays, such as *Cat on a Hot Tin Roof,* have multiple endings, and other plays were revised and presented as new works altogether, like *Summer and Smoke,* which was later released as *The Eccentricities of a Nightingale,* or *Battle of Angels,* which was revised and presented as *Orpheus Descending.* This characteristic of Williams's dramatic writings presents countless opportunities for research and exposition. The accessibility of the various versions gives us insight into Williams's writing process; it provides us with information that is typically not available to us, giving us unique insight into Williams's concerns and his development as a writer.

Finally, Williams's works address tough issues such as death, isolation, failed relationships, and the destructive nature of desire, and through his characters, he presents startling portraits of the outsider—the alcoholic, the mentally ill, the repressed artist, and the widow. The themes found in his plays are, therefore, often grim and challenging. Before beginning to write about any of Williams's works, consider why he treated the themes that are present in the work and what the play tells us about these themes. You will find that Williams's views are not always clear or conclusive. Like many great authors, Williams often presented more than one view of a single topic. Perhaps appropriately, this text concludes with a look at one of Williams's later works, *The Night of the Iguana*, which best encapsulates this feature of Williams's work. In *The Night of the Iguana*, Williams presented grim themes alongside contrasting themes such as compassion, the search for faith, and human endurance. Remember that an author's presentation of a negative theme or a stereotype is not synonymous with the author's condoning these views. Likewise, a character's view is not necessarily reflective of the author's own stance or position. In fact, these views are often diametrically opposed. Therefore, the treatment of tough themes in Williams's work should not be seen as an indication of the author's pessimism or resignation to these issues but rather as evidence of a will to protest, to create a dialogue, to overcome.

If you are able to surmount these challenges, approaching the works both well-informed and with an open mind, it will make the task of writing about Williams and his works much easier and more rewarding. Opening yourself up to the ideas of someone else and entering into a larger dialogue will give you the chance to ask questions, to learn new things, to grow, and to begin a new dialogue that will not only enrich any essay you write but can teach and inform others as well.

## TOPICS AND STRATEGIES

In the sections that follow, you will find a variety of suggested topics accompanied by questions and observations to assist you in the task of writing successfully about Tennessee Williams and his works. Remember that this is not a comprehensive list of topics, and the statements and questions that appear after each suggested topic are merely a guide to help spark your own ideas about each subject. A successful paper will present a strong thesis based upon your own original ideas and will be supported by relevant examples resulting from close readings of the texts. A wide variety of interpretations will be possible as you consider each topic. Use the strategic questions and observations to stimulate your own thoughts about each subject and to assist you in developing a strong thesis. Remember to read through the texts more than once, making note of those elements of the texts that support your argument. It will be equally important to make note of those elements that contradict your thesis, as this will help you to refine your argument and create a stronger case.

## Themes

While each of Tennessee Williams's works is unique, it is easy to find connections among the themes presented in these works. Williams's primary concern was admittedly the effect of society on the outsider, but in the exploration of this subject we also find discourses on models of love and romance, desire and sexuality, the parent-child relationship and the plight of the modern family, the passage of time, loneliness, mendacity, and illusion versus reality. As you prepare to write about these themes, you will need to look at how Williams presents these themes in his plays. What do his works ultimately reveal about these topics? You may find that, like many great authors, Williams does not necessarily present conclusive statements or clear answers. Rather, he engages us in a dialogue about particular themes. Therefore, it will be up to you to draw your own conclusions, which should consist not of simple speculations but rather careful observations based on close readings of the text or texts. Remember to make note of how Williams's presentation of theme through formal elements brought you to these conclusions.

### Sample Topics:
1. **Illusion versus reality:** Many of Williams's plays treat the theme of illusion versus reality with characters who are unable to distinguish between the two. What do the plays indicate is the source of this problem?

   In answering this question it will be most helpful to consider the main characters of *The Glass Menagerie*, Blanche and Stella of *A Streetcar Named Desire*, the characters of *Camino Real*, and Serafina of *The Rose Tattoo*. Consider where we find evidence in these texts of characters having difficulty distinguishing between reality and fantasy. What causes them to retreat from reality? Is a psychological problem responsible for this problem? How do the characters' histories play a part in this problem?

2. **The passage of time:** In his plays, Williams presents characters of varied ages—children, middle-aged men and women, and people who have reached old age. Why do his characters reflect this variety of age?

Think about why Williams would wish to include characters of varying ages. How does this tie in to a common theme in Williams's work? Consider, for instance, how the characters deal with the passage of time in plays like *The Glass Menagerie, A Streetcar Named Desire, Camino Real,* and *The Night of the Iguana.* Are the characters able to accept the passage of time and the passing of youth? You may find that characters like Amanda of *The Glass Menagerie* and Blanche of *A Streetcar Named Desire* react similarly in their confrontation with time, while some characters from *Camino Real* and *The Night of the Iguana* are able to deal with it more successfully. How do other characters, such as the children in *The Rose Tattoo* and Nonno in *The Night of the Iguana,* reinforce this theme?

3. **Desire:** How do Williams's works present desire? Is it presented as a positive force or a negative force? Or does the presentation of desire vary from work to work?

Desire has commonly been presented as a theme in literature and is often linked to romance and love. Consider how Williams's view of desire compares to or differs from traditional treatments of this theme. As you think about this, remember that Williams's plays present desire in many different contexts. There is physical desire that appears in works such as *A Streetcar Named Desire, Summer and Smoke, Cat on a Hot Tin Roof* and *The Night of the Iguana.* However, the plays also address a broader definition of desire—namely, that which we want to achieve or attain. You may choose to treat one of these definitions of desire or to address desire in its various contexts. Consider examples of desire in the plays. How does desire affect the characters in the plays you have chosen to write about? Does anything good come of desire? How does Williams's presentation of desire in some plays subvert traditional notions of desire? It will also be fruitful to explore what drives the characters' desires. How does this allow us to gain a better sense of the true selves of the characters?

4. **Reconciling spirit and body:** Many of Williams's plays present the problem of the reconciliation of spirit and body or religion and science. What view does Williams ultimately present on this subject? Is it possible to reconcile these two elements?

It will be most helpful to use *Summer and Smoke, The Rose Tattoo,* and *The Night of the Iguana* as your primary texts. Consider what formal elements Williams uses to present this dilemma. What is the result of the characters' attempts to reconcile spirit and body in these plays? Consider the development of the characters and the conclusion of each play.

5. **Escape:** Many of the characters in Williams's plays desire an escape of some kind. What message do the plays present about the attainability of escape?

Plays such as *The Glass Menagerie, A Streetcar Named Desire, Camino Real, Orpheus Descending,* and *The Night of the Iguana* all contain characters seeking an escape. What are the characters in each play seeking an escape from? Do they desire a physical escape? Or some kind of emotional or spiritual escape? What is the result of their attempts to escape? You may find that some characters are able to escape, while others remain stunted. In this instance, you will want to explain why you believe some characters were able to escape while others were not. Ultimately, you will need to explain whether or not you feel that the texts present a conclusive statement about the possibility of escape.

# Character

Williams's works are well-known for the dynamic characters that inhabit them. The main characters are remarkably full, well-rounded characters, and through the course of the works we are presented with the revelation of the inner selves of these characters. While the characters often seem to lack self-awareness—or are aware but choose to repress or deny their true selves—Williams uses the other formal elements of the text to grant us access to the deepest parts of themselves—their thoughts, their fears and regrets, their hopes and their dreams.

Williams's works also carefully employ flat characters who enhance our understanding of the themes of the works—the vendors in *A Streetcar Named Desire*, for instance, or the children who giggle and play in the background of *The Rose Tattoo*. Do not overlook these characters, as they, too, serve an important function. Likewise, it will be fruitful to consider absentee characters, those characters who never actually appear in the text except through the references or memories of other characters. They, too, have a tremendous impact on the characters we do view.

While the range and depth of characters in Williams's work is quite broad, it should be easy to draw connections between the major characters of different works. While great essays can come from an analysis of a single character, it would be just as productive to consider some groupings that seem to crop up in Williams's plays across the board: the mad heroine, the anti-chivalric male, the repressed artist, and the outsider, for example.

## Sample Topics:

1. **The mentally unstable or unbalanced heroine:** Critics often write about the presence of "the mad heroine" in Williams's works. Analyze the appearance of this character in Williams's works.

   Many of Williams's plays include a female who is mentally ill or emotionally distressed. Consider characters such as Laura in *The Glass Menagerie*, Blanche in *A Streetcar Named Desire*, and Alma of *Summer and Smoke*. How do each of these characters function in the play? How are they characterized? Note their similarities. How do these characters help our understanding of the themes of the play? You may also wish to explain why you believe Williams was preoccupied with this character type. Is his motivation linked to his own history or is the use of this character as an archetype suggestive of a greater cultural concern?

2. **Male characters as the antithesis of the chivalrous knight:** Classic literature often presents male characters that are a version of the chivalrous knight. How do the male characters in Williams's play contradict this notion?

   If you decide to undertake this topic, you will need to begin by providing some explanation of how males have typically been treated in literature. If you believe that there is an archetype of the male as a kind of chivalrous knight, provide some examples. It will be helpful to give examples not only from classical literature but also from modern literature. How do characters like Tom from *The Glass Menagerie*, Stanley of *A Streetcar Named Desire*, John Buchanan, Jr., of *Summer and Smoke*, and Alvaro and Rosario of *The Rose Tattoo* undermine this traditional view? How do these characters treat women? Does the play give us the sense that they have a feeling of responsibility toward women or respect for them? If you conclude that this archetype is undermined in many of Williams's plays, what does this tell us about his treatment of gender roles and definitions of masculinity? Consider also what this this might tell us about cultural or societal shifts as they apply to gender.

3. **Outsiders:** Williams has often acknowledged that the goal of all of his works was to show the effects of society on the outsider. How do Williams's works define the outsider? And how are these characters generally affected by society?

   Examine the plays for examples of characters that you perceive as outsiders. You will find that Williams's definition of the outsider is somewhat broad. His plays present alcoholics, the mentally ill, homosexuals, and people from various ethnic groups as outsiders. Do these characters share anything in common? What makes them outsiders? Are they simply defined by cultural biases or do any of the characters isolate themselves? How does Williams treat characters with a certain uncommon sensitivity as outsiders? You will be able to support your answer with evidence from just about any of Williams's plays. Consider if any of the characters are able to overcome their status as outsiders.

4. **The artist:** Why does Williams present an artist in so many of his plays? What do these characters represent and what do we learn from their inclusion in the texts?

Consider characters such as Tom in *The Glass Menagerie*, Val and Vee of *Orpheus Descending*, and Hannah and Nonno of *The Night of the Iguana.* How do these characters differ from the other characters? It may be helpful to consider the notion of the artist as presented in romantic works of literature. How is Williams's view of the artist similar? Consider the concept of the artist from a psychological, philosophical, or cultural perspective. Do the plays suggest that the artist represents a sensitive side of the human condition or a repressed, threatened, or now extinct part of society?

5. **Working class:** How do Williams's plays create a portrait of the working class?

Consider how Williams creates a sense of the working class in his works. You will need to examine the characters and their interactions, themes, plot, and symbolism. How do the characters of *The Glass Menagerie* and *A Streetcar Named Desire*, for instance, inform us about the working class and their everyday life and struggles? How do themes and the treatment of romance, desire, and escape also pertain to an examination of the working class? Think also about why Williams would have been interested in creating a portrait of this class. How does his concern with this class tie in with the cultural atmosphere at the time he wrote these plays? How did his own life perhaps inform his understanding of this class?

6. **Flat characters:** In addition to round main characters, Williams includes many flat characters in his plays. What purpose do these flat characters serve? Can we do without them?

Choose a few plays that contain flat characters. For instance, *The Rose Tattoo* contains children who are present throughout the story but who are not central to the plot. Likewise, *The Night of the Iguana* contains German and Mexican characters who are not central to the plot. Consider why Williams has included them in the play. How do the characters reinforce the themes that Williams is treating in these works?

7. **The family:** How is the family characterized in Williams's plays?

Most of Williams's works present a view of an American family and reveal some type of parent-child relationship. How does the Wingfield family of *The Glass Menagerie* compare to the Winemiller family of *Summer and Smoke* or the Pollitt family in *Cat on a Hot Tin Roof*? Does Williams wish to portray the family as a decaying and fractured entity? Or are the family members ultimately united in their struggles? Consider also the various parent-child relationships in the plays—Tom and Amanda of *The Glass Menagerie* or the characters' relationship to their parents in *Summer and Smoke,* to name a few. What do we learn from these relationships? You may also wish to enter into a broader discussion of how the state of the family became a major concern in American theater during this time period. How is Williams's treatment of the family in line with the treatment of family in these other works?

8. **Absent characters:** Many of Williams's works include references to characters who never actually appear in the plays. Why?

Consider the characters who are referenced but never actually appear in the plays. Despite the physical absence of these characters, they are extremely influential. Consider how Williams uses the absent character as a device for greater revelation. It will be most useful to consider Mr. Wingfield from *The Glass Menagerie,* Blanche's family and deceased husband from *A Streetcar Named Desire,* Rosario of *The Rose Tattoo,* the generalissimo from *Camino Real,* and Skipper from *Cat on a Hot Tin Roof.* What role do these absent characters play? How do they affect the characters that we do see? What do they teach us about loss? Is it fair to say that they inform us about the characters in ways that simple dialogue cannot? If so, explain how.

9. **Interpretation of the characters:** Does Williams present a balanced view of his characters, or does he create distinct villains and heroines in his plays?

Consider the main characters of some of Williams's plays. How do we perceive them? Think about how they are perceived by the other characters as well. Is there typically a clear consensus as to each character's true nature? Or do the supporting characters have varying perceptions of the main characters? We know that all of the characters are flawed, but are we meant to feel generally sympathetic toward them? Or critical of them? Is it possible to react to them both sympathetically and critically? Consider, for instance, Amanda in *The Glass Menagerie* or Maxine and Shannon from *The Night of the Iguana.*

## History and Context

Williams wrote the bulk of his plays between 1930 and 1983 during a tumultuous time in American and world history. Although Williams's works are not overtly political, consider how they reference cultural or historical issues relevant to the time period in which they were written. How do the plays address economic changes, civil rights, and the effects of war? Consider how Williams deals with changes such as the loss of gentility, the rise of industrialism, and the birth of the lower working class through the employment of Southern settings. You will also want to note how Williams's treatment of these themes makes apparent the changes inherent in everyday life, the stress on the American family, and the changes in definitions of romance and love.

## Sample Topics:

1. **The Old South:** What message do Williams's plays contain about the Old South? Why is this a significant theme?

   Consider which plays address the state of the Old South. Look for references to gentility, plantation life, and associated social conventions. You may choose, for instance, to examine *The Glass Menagerie, A Streetcar Named Desire,* and *Cat on a Hot Tin Roof.* What shared message do these plays present about the state of the Old South and the ways of life associated with it? Analyze the formal elements of these texts and explain how Williams is able to present this message without stating it literally.

2. **Tolerance:** Consider Williams's treatment of ethnic groups in his plays. Do his works reflect or challenge the conventional notions of ethnicity that were prevalent at the time the works were written?

   You will need to begin by identifying a few plays that reference this issue. You could use, for example, *The Rose Tattoo* and *Orpheus Descending,* which respectively feature Italian and African-American characters. Next, you will need to do some research about civil rights and tolerance at the time in which these plays were written. How does Williams present these characters? How do the other characters in the play react to these characters or speak about these ethnic groups? Consider Williams's use of stereotypes. You might wish to address this topic by comparing and contrasting the use of stereotypes in these two plays. For example, you might note how the perpetuation of stereotypes in *The Rose Tattoo* is a comical device that draws our attention to the absurdity of stereotypes. From there you might go on to show how the stereotypes in *Orpheus Descending* have far more serious implications. Do these two methods ultimately serve the same purpose? Explain which method you feel is more effective and why.

## Philosophy and Ideas

While many of Williams's works have found a place in popular culture, due in large part to successful film adaptations of the texts, the plays were also able to function on a level beyond simple entertainment. Together the works examine tough philosophical issues such as ethics, free will, faith, and human endurance, but they do not always provide conclusive statements about these topics. If you are primarily interested in Williams's characters, it will be interesting to consider that, while Williams describes in detail those forces that bear down upon the characters, he does not refrain from exposing flaws and exposing self-destruction either. Consider examples of this in Williams's texts. How does the complete exposure of the characters add to or change the course of these philosophical discussions? Do the works indicate that we are responsible for our own fates? Or do they suggest that there are larger forces at work?

### *Sample Topics:*

1. **Free will and choice:** Are Williams's characters responsible for their own actions or is there some indication that there are other forces at work?

   The results of your essay will vary depending upon which plays you choose to work with. You may feel that characters such as Blanche from *A Streetcar Named Desire* and Tom from *The Glass Menagerie* have little control over their fates. However, a consideration of other factors from the same plays may also reveal that Blanche is destroyed by her own flaws and mistakes, and Tom is, in fact, capable of making his own decisions. It is fine to conclude that the plays present an inconclusive treatment of these topics and rather present an open dialogue, but you will need to back up this assertion with even-handed evidence from the texts.

2. **Ethics and responsibility:** According to Williams's plays, how are we to reconcile responsibility and our own needs or

desires? Is reconciliation possible or must we choose one over the other?

Consider characters who have a certain responsibility to someone else. For instance, you might write about Tom from *The Glass Menagerie,* John Buchanan from *Summer and Smoke,* and Shannon from *The Night of the Iguana.* Who are these characters responsible to? Do these characters need to abandon their responsibilities in order to fulfill their own desires? What choice do they make and how does this choice affect them and others?

3. **Paradox:** As Williams progressed in his career, he seemed more intent on examining paradoxes in his work. How does Williams address paradoxes in his works and what do we learn from his use of this device?

   This is a broad topic that you will need to narrow down by concentrating on a few specific examples. In many of Williams's plays, he presents us with seemingly contradictory ideas. Why? How does the presentation of these dual concepts create a larger dialogue? How do these pairings also bring our attention to the notion of duality? Consider how this notion ties in with Williams's goal of more closely approaching reality in his works.

4. **Existentialism:** Williams's plays present us with many existential questions. How do the characters in Williams's plays respond to the unknown? Is there any clear resolution to these questions?

   The characters in Williams's plays have many different ways of dealing with the existential questions that they struggle with. Choose a few plays that present existentialism as a theme and examine how Williams addresses faith and superstition in these instances. Aside from characters who turn to faith or superstition, how do other characters, such as Shannon and

Hannah of *The Night of the Iguana,* deal with these questions? Do they find something in reply to these questions that functions as a kind of answer?

## Form and Genre

Although Williams also wrote short stories and poems, he is best known for his plays. These works function on two levels—as drama meant to be performed on stage and as textual reading versions. Of course, Williams's works have also taken on another life in television, film, and musical adaptations, and any of these can be profitably explored in your paper. Consider how the genres of Williams's works complement his thematic concerns. The majority of his works are viewed as tragedies—subverted or failed romances and family dramas—but Williams also dabbled in comedy, composing at least one tragicomedy, *The Rose Tattoo.* You might decide to compare and contrast these genres, drawing some conclusion about the effectiveness of each.

Consider also how Williams's works challenged the traditional forms prevalent in American theater. His works marked a departure from the strict realism of American theater, but how did Williams's new forms maintain their concern with reality and even complement his goal of more closely approaching reality? Explore Williams's use of expressionistic elements and even the fantastic in *Camino Real.* An exploration of the implementation of his concepts of plastic theater and memory play could also make excellent essay topics.

### Sample Topics:

1. **Narration:** Analyze the narrative methods employed by Williams.

   You may wish to choose one play and analyze the narrative method found in the work, or you may wish to compare and contrast the narrative methods implemented in a few different works. It will be particularly helpful to consider *The Glass Menagerie* and *Camino Real,* which employ actual narrators. How do these characters function as traditional or untraditional narrators? You may also wish to consider how the absence of narration in other plays affects our understanding of the work.

2. **Biographical connections:** How do Williams's plays reflect Williams's own life and personal concerns?

The most important piece of advice is not to depend on what you think you know about Williams and his life. Consult some of the sources suggested herein. Think about Williams's relationship with his parents and his sister, Rose; Williams's sexual orientation; his childhood; and his struggle with addiction. Refer to the texts and consider where we find these elements reflected. How much of Williams's plays are biographical and how much is fiction? Of course this is not a question to be answered literally, but you will need to give some general response to this question. How do the plays differ from autobiography?

3. **Family drama:** Analyze Williams's works as examples of family drama.

Many of Williams's plays can be classified as family dramas. Consider *The Glass Menagerie* and *Cat on a Hot Tin Roof,* for example. How do these plays center on the plight of an entire family rather than a single individual? How are the characters united and what divides them? Is one character's problem more prominent than another's or is Williams even-handed? Consider how Williams's use of family drama perpetuates a genre found in literature for centuries. Why is this genre so popular and why is it still relevant today?

4. **Subverted or unrealized romance:** How do Williams's works function as examples of subverted or unrealized romances? What do the plays tell us about love and romance in modern culture?

Consider examples of love and romance in *The Glass Menagerie, A Streetcar Named Desire, Summer and Smoke,* and *Cat on a Hot Tin Roof.* How is love defined? And how do these models of romance differ from the models traditionally presented in literature? Consider the way the characters live and the problems they face. Are the notions of love and romance presented in Williams's plays indicative of a cultural problem or shift?

5. **Plastic theater:** How do Williams's works embody his notion of plastic theater? Is this a successful form?

   Consider Williams's explanations of plastic theater. Although you will want to explore how the idea of plastic theater is evidenced in *The Glass Menagerie*, you should also consider where we find evidence of this form in Williams's other plays. How is plastic theater defined? Consider your reaction to these plays. How would your reaction or interpretation of the plays differ if Williams adopted a more straightforward realistic approach?

6. **Southern gothic:** Williams's works are often placed within a genre of literature known as southern gothic. Is this an appropriate classification of Williams's work?

   You will need to begin by consulting some literary reference books that define this genre and then review some examples of other works that are categorized within this genre. What do they share in common? Are the plots or the thematic content similar? Do they share a preoccupation with a particular character type? You may observe that, while Williams's work fits under this heading, his work is not defined by it. If you take this approach, you will need to explain what characteristics Williams's work shares with southern gothic literature but, more importantly, what characteristics his work possesses that southern gothic works do not. How does he work beyond the bounds of this genre?

## Language, Symbols, and Imagery

Williams's works are filled with symbolism and imagery heavy with meaning. His choice of language is full of intention, helping to create more authentic characters. Therefore, a consideration of examples of symbolism or a specific use of language—such as an exploration of his use of foreign languages—can serve as an excellent starting point for your essay. Consider how these elements reinforce the themes found in the works.

## Sample Topics:

1. **Language:** Why does Williams choose to employ foreign languages in his plays?

   Consider plays where Williams's characters speak in a foreign language such as *The Rose Tattoo* and *The Night of the Iguana*. Which characters speak in a foreign language? Do the other characters understand this language? How would our perception of the characters be different if they simply spoke in English? Consider if the use of other languages ties in to the themes of the plays. How, for instance, does it create a sense of isolation? Does the use of foreign language create a sense of "other-ness"? If so, why is this significant?

2. **Lyricism:** Before Williams wrote his own plays and poetry, he studied the works of others. He frequently cited the poet Hart Crane as one of his biggest influences. How does Williams's work show evidence of his interest in lyricism?

   Consider the form of Williams's works, including his sentence structure and the rhythm of his sentences and the dialogue. Where do we find evidence of a melodic or poetic quality in the text? How can we find similarities between drama and poetry through an examination of Williams's plays?

3. **Birds:** Birds are presented literally and metaphorically throughout many of Williams's works. Why does Williams use the bird as a metaphor and what might it symbolize?

   You will need to begin by choosing some plays that contain the image or metaphor of the bird. You can find the bird in almost any Williams play—*The Rose Tattoo, Camino Real, Summer and Smoke,* or *The Night of the Iguana,* to name a few. When we think of birds, what do we typically associate them with? Does Williams use these same associations in the text? Where does Williams use the metaphor of the caged bird? Consider how the use of the bird helps Williams to reinforce the thematic concerns of these plays.

4. **Light:** Analyze Williams's use of light.

Williams is very specific about the use of light in all of his plays. Often, he presents instructions for directors on how lighting should be arranged and why it is important. Consider, for instance, the use of light in *The Glass Menagerie, The Rose Tattoo,* and *A Streetcar Named Desire.* You may choose to analyze the use of light in one of these plays or the various uses of light throughout his works. Consider how his use of light creates atmosphere and how it functions symbolically. The symbolic value of light may differ depending on which text or texts you choose to address. Consider also how the characters respond to light. How do their responses reveal their psychological conditions?

5. **Music:** Analyze Williams's use of music.

Again, you may wish to discuss an isolated use of music or Williams's overall employment of music. How does his choice of music coincide with the characters who are presented while the music is playing? You may wish to use *The Glass Menagerie, A Streetcar Named Desire, The Rose Tattoo,* and *Orpheus Descending* as your primary texts. Does the use of music create a greater sense of reality or is it used as a fantastical element? Your answer will depend on which plays you are considering. For example, in *The Glass Menagerie,* we hear jazz being played or music coming from the Victrola, but in *A Streetcar Named Desire,* the polka that Blanche hears is only in her head. This might lead you to explore the contrasting uses of music in these two plays. Of course, this is only one option that is available to you.

# Compare and Contrast Essays

Most of the suggested topics above are, by nature, compare and contrast essays, because you are addressing two or more works at the same time. Of course you might compare or contrast elements from a single play, but there is much that can also be gained from a consideration of Williams's works as a whole. As you prepare to write your essay, remember not to choose too many works for comparison or contrast. You will find that certain works lend themselves to a group comparison better than others. For instance, *The Glass Menagerie, A Streetcar Named Desire,* and *Summer and Smoke* are often classified as a Southern trilogy, while *The Rose Tattoo* and *Camino Real* stand out because they are so different from Williams's other works, serving as examples of Williams's experimentation with genre. Consider how various works share similar themes, characters, and symbols. If works seem very different, ask yourself why this is. What did Williams change? Another option is to consider Williams's work from a broader perspective. How does his work compare to or differ from the work of other American playwrights of this time period? What about international playwrights of other periods? What can we learn from a comparison of his works to works from other genres?

## Sample Topics:

1. **Elements across Williams's works:** Compare a single element across Williams's works.

   Consider the formal elements of Williams's work. Choose one element that you find in more than one text. You might choose a theme that Williams addresses in more than one work—desire, for instance. In this case you could compare how Williams treats this topic in *A Streetcar Named Desire* versus *The Rose Tattoo.* You could also compare or contrast a few characters or the forms of various works. Explain how the element is treated in each text. No matter which topic you choose to explore, remember to explain why these similarities or differences are significant.

2. **Williams's work and other American playwrights:** Compare Williams's works to the works of another American playwright.

It may be helpful to compare Williams's work to that of Eugene O'Neill or Arthur Miller. For instance, you should be able to find similarities between O'Neill's *Long Day's Journey into Night* or Arthur Miller's *Death of a Salesman* and Williams's *The Glass Menagerie* or *Cat on a Hot Tin Roof*. Consider what these works share in common. How do their works share a concern with the everyman, the family, and changes to American life? How do the forms of the plays compare? Compare other formal elements of the plays including characters, plot, and symbolism. What is the significance of these similarities? Why would American playwrights have shared these concerns?

3. **Williams and his influences:** Compare and contrast Williams's work with that of one of his influences.

Scholars and critics have cited Williams's influences as William Shakespeare, Hart Crane, Anton Chekhov, D. H. Lawrence, Marcel Proust, and Jean-Paul Sartre, to name only a few. We also know that Williams was influenced by Greek mythology and romanticism. Choose one of Williams's influences or areas of influence and explore what elements Williams has preserved and what he has discarded or adapted in his own work. You will need to demonstrate where we find these works in Williams's plays. Explain why you believe he made these changes. How do they better serve his thematic concerns and goals?

4. **Adaptations of Williams's works:** Compare or contrast one of Williams's works with an adaptation of the text.

Many of Williams's plays were adapted for film and television. His works also inspired musical adaptations. Choose one of these adaptations and explain how the original text compares to or differs from its adaptation. What is changed or omitted in the adaptation? More importantly, why were these changes made or these items omitted? In the instance of some film adaptations such as Elia Kazan's *A Streetcar Named Desire,* for instance, you might discuss how cultural factors and censorship played a role in the treatment of the adaptation.

5. **Early works and later works:** It is evident that Williams was always changing and trying new things. How do Williams's early works compare to his later works? Do you feel that some progress is evident?

In addressing this topic you could take a number of approaches. You might isolate a single formal element such as theme or form and follow Williams's treatment of it throughout his career, noting if this treatment was more successful in later works. In the case of theme, for instance, you might discuss how Williams's thematic concerns remained steady throughout his career. In the case of form, you might choose to show how Williams experimented with form throughout his career. You could also combine two topics. For instance, you could discuss how, while the form of Williams's works changed and evolved, his thematic concerns remained the same throughout his career. Consider what the works share in common and what Williams changed in the later works. Which do you believe are more successful and why? Although the last play we consider in this text is *The Night of the Iguana*, Williams wrote several other works before his death in 1983. Therefore, you will need to be specific about how you are defining "early" and "late" works. While critics felt that *The Night of the Iguana* was a great success, many critics feel that it was his last great success and that his work declined after this point. It is imperative that you be clear about what period you are addressing.

## Bibliography and Resources

Adler, Thomas P. *American Drama, 1940–1960.* New York: Twayne, 1994.
Asibong, Emmanuel B. *Tennessee Williams: The Tragic Tension: A Study of the Plays of Tennessee Williams from 'The Glass Menagerie' (1944) to 'The Milk Train Doesn't Stop Here Anymore' (1966).* Ilfracombe, Devon: Stockwell, 1978.
Bauer-Briski, Senata Karolina. *The Role of Sexuality in the Major Plays of Tennessee Williams.* New York: Peter Lang, 2002.

Bigsby, C. W. E. *A Critical Introduction to Twentieth-Century American Drama.* 3 vols. Cambridge: Cambridge UP, 1982–85.

Bloom, Harold, ed. *Tennessee Williams.* Bloom's Biocritiques. Philadelphia: Chelsea House, 2003.

———. *Tennessee Williams.* Bloom's Major Dramatists. Broomall, PA.: Chelsea House, 2000.

———. *Tennessee Williams.* Modern Critical Views. New York: Chelsea House, 1987.

Boxill, Roger. *Tennessee Williams.* London: Macmillan, 1987.

Broussard, Louis. *American Drama: Contemporary Allegory from Eugene O'Neill to Tennessee Williams.* Norman: U of Oklahoma P, 1962.

Coronis, Athena. *Tennessee Williams and Greek Culture: With Special Emphasis on Euripides.* Athens, Greece: Kalendis, 1994.

Crandell, George W. *Critical Response to Tennessee Williams.* Westport, CT: Greenwood, 1996.

———. *Tennessee Williams: A Descriptive Bibliography.* Pittsburgh: U of Pittsburgh P, 1995.

Falk, Signi. *Tennessee Williams.* Boston: Twayne, 1978.

Fedder, Norman J. *The Influence of D. H. Lawrence on Tennessee Williams.* The Hague: Mouton, 1966.

Fleche, Anne. *Mimetic Disillusion: Eugene O'Neill, Tennessee Williams and U.S. Dramatic Realism.* Tuscaloosa: U of Alabama P, 1997.

Griffin, Alice. *Understanding Tennessee Williams.* Understanding Contemporary American Literature. Columbia: U of South Carolina P, 1995.

Gross, Robert F. *Tennessee Williams: A Casebook.* New York: Routledge, 2001.

Hayman, Ronald. *Tennessee Williams: Everyone Else Is an Audience.* New Haven, CT: Yale UP, 1993.

Heintzelman, Greta. *Critical Companion to Tennessee Williams.* New York: Facts On File, 2005.

Holditch, Kenneth, and Richard Freeman Leavitt. *Tennessee Williams and the South.* Jackson: UP of Mississippi, 2002.

Jackson, Esther M. *The Broken World of Tennessee Williams.* Madison: U of Wisconsin Press, 1965.

Kolin, Philip, ed. *American Playwrights since 1945: A Guide to Scholarship, Criticism, and Performance.* Westport, CT: Greenwood, 1989.

———. *Tennessee Williams: A Guide to Research and Performance.* Westport, CT: Greenwood, 1998.

————. *The Tennessee Williams Encyclopedia.* Westport, CT: Greenwood, 2004.

————. *The Undiscovered Country: The Later Plays of Tennessee Williams.* New York: Peter Lang, 2002.

Leavitt, Richard F. *The World of Tennessee Williams.* New York: Putnam's, 1978.

Leverich, Lyle. *Tom: The Unknown Tennessee Williams.* New York: Crown, 1995.

Londré, Felicia Hardison. *Tennessee Williams.* New York: F. Ungar, 1979.

Martin, Robert. *Critical Essays on Tennessee Williams.* New York: Simon & Schuster, 1997.

McCann, John S. *The Critical Reputation of Tennessee Williams: A Reference Guide.* Boston: G. K. Hall, 1983.

Murphy, Brenda. *Tennessee Williams and Elia Kazan: A Collaboration in Theatre.* New York: Cambridge UP, 1992.

O'Connor, Jacqueline. *Dramatizing Dementia: Madness in the Plays of Tennessee Williams.* Bowling Green, OH: Bowling Green State U Popular P, 1997.

Pagan, Nicholas. *Rethinking Literary Biography: A Post-Modern Approach to Tennessee Williams.* Rutherford, NJ: Fairleigh Dickinson UP, 1993.

Paller, Michael. *Gentleman Callers: Tennessee Williams, Homosexuality and Mid-Twentieth-Century Drama.* New York: Palgrave Macmillan, 2005.

Pritner, Cal, and Scott E. Walters. *Introduction to Play Analysis.* New York: McGraw-Hill, 2004.

Rasky, Harry. *Tennessee Williams: A Portrait in Laughter and Lamentation.* New York: Dodd, Mead, 1986.

Roudané, Matthew C., ed. *Cambridge Companion to Tennessee Williams.* Cambridge: Cambridge UP, 1997.

Saddik, Annette K. *The Politics of Reputation: The Critical Reception of Tennessee Williams's Later Plays.* Madison, NJ: Fairleigh Dickinson UP, 1999.

Savran, David. *Communists, Cowboys and Queers: The Politics of Masculinity in the Work of Arthur Miller and Tennessee Williams.* Minneapolis: U of Minnesota P, 1992.

Spoto, Donald. *Kindness of Strangers: The Life of Tennessee Williams.* Boston: Little, Brown, 1985.

Stanton, Stephen S., ed. *Tennessee Williams: A Collection of Critical Essays.* Englewood Cliffs, NJ: Prentice-Hall, 1977.

*The Tennessee Williams Annual Review.* Murfreesboro, TN: Middle Tennessee State U, 1998–   .

*The Tennessee Williams Film Collection.* 8 discs. DVD. Warner, 2006.

*The Tennessee Williams Literary Journal.* 1989–   .

Tharpe, Jac. *Tennessee Williams: A Tribute.* Jackson: UP of Mississippi, 1977.

Thompson, Judith J. *Tennessee Williams's Plays: Memory, Myth and Symbol.* New York: Peter Lang, 1987.

Tischler, Nancy Marie Patterson. *Student Companion to Tennessee Williams.* Westport, CT: Greenwood, 2000.

Voss, Ralph F., ed. *Magical Muse: Millenial Essays on Tennessee Williams.* Tuscaloosa: U of Alabama P, 2002.

Williams, Dakin. *Tennessee Williams: An Intimate Biography.* New York: Arbor House, 1983.

Williams, Tennessee. *The Collected Poems of Tennessee Williams.* Eds. Nicholas Moschovakis and David Roessel. New York: New Directions, 2007.

———. *Memoirs.* Garden City, NY: Doubleday, 1975.

———. *Notebooks.* Ed. Margaret Bradham Thorton. New Haven: Yale UP, 2006.

———. *The Selected Letters of Tennessee Williams.* Eds. Albert J. Devlin and Nancy M. Tischler. New York: New Directions, 2000.

———. *Tennessee Williams's Letters to Donald Windham, 1940–1965.* Ed. Donald Windham. New York: Holt, Rinehart and Winston, 1977.

Yacowar, Maurice. *Tennessee Williams and Film.* New York: Frederick Ungar, 1977.

# THE GLASS
# MENAGERIE

## READING TO WRITE

WHEN WRITING about the works of Tennessee Williams, there is, perhaps, no better work to start with than *The Glass Menagerie*. The play, Williams's first major critical and popular success, presents evidence of themes and concerns that recur throughout the author's complete body of work and demonstrates early traces of his signature style and a preoccupation with the character types that would inhabit his later works. In the minute details and major action of the play, there is an autobiographical footprint present that is characteristic of Williams's work. The play also serves as a prime sample of the output that resulted from an intense process of revision and an evolution of forms that Williams's work is well known for. For those who are just introducing themselves to Williams's work, or to this particular type of American drama in general, most reading versions of *The Glass Menagerie* come equipped with Williams's own production notes, which are typically printed alongside the text. The notes function as a kind of cheat sheet that explains his overall thought process, giving us the benefit of some insight into his intentions for the play and providing us with an introduction to a new genre of drama that diverged from the realistic forms that were prevalent in American theater at the time Williams created this work. Finally, the plot of *The Glass Menagerie* is highly approachable due to its simplicity and minimal physical action; it is easy to comprehend and moves at a slow and steady pace, but it is also remarkably memorable and relatable. With all things considered, whether *The Glass Menagerie* is one's introduction to Williams's work or whether the play is considered within the greater context of the playwright's entire body of work, it is a valuable jumping-off point from which to write, providing numerous avenues for research and exposition.

Premiering in 1944 to critical acclaim, *The Glass Menagerie* won the New York Drama Critics' Circle Award in 1945, catapulting Williams to stardom and helping him to achieve the financial security that would allow him to produce his later works. More than 60 years after its debut, the play is still being performed and adapted regularly. It is one of the most highly lauded works of American theater, recognized internationally and, likewise, studied in classrooms all over the world.

It is worthwhile to consider why this is—why the play has outlasted so many others and why it is still considered relevant today. These are valuable questions to ask not only in the case of *The Glass Menagerie* but in the case of all lasting works of literature. Why has the work remained in our consciousness despite the passage of time and the evolution of literary styles? What message or messages does the work contain, and why are these ideas significant and relevant long after their original introduction in the text? When preparing an answer to these questions, many writers naturally turn to plot first, asking themselves what it is that is happening in the work, why it is happening, and why this action is significant. And yet, while the plot may often cast us reliably in the direction of key themes and concerns, authors rely on countless other means to divulge important information. Many modern works of literature are known for their minimal treatment of plot, and therefore, it is necessary for a writer to know where else to turn for information. When considering those works such as *The Glass Menagerie* that do not approach their themes primarily through physical action, one must consider the entire anatomy of the work, including all of its formal or textual elements. These types of works, which exhibit limited physical action, are particularly valuable because they remind us to consider all elements of the work, including those most subtle elements such as language, symbolism, setting, and structure—elements that can fade into the background and be easily overlooked because they seem to be such a natural, inherent part of the work. For instance, while *The Glass Menagerie* may, at first glance, seem to be a simple work centered on the anticipation of a single event and the consequences of the actualization of this event—the moments leading up to the visit of a gentleman caller and the disappointment that results following Jim and Laura's meeting—writers must give equal consideration to each formal element of the play. For example, while Williams's production notes tell us that *The Glass Menagerie* is a memory play, if there was not the benefit of the author's own explanation, the text itself reveals this to us. In considering the form of the play—its structure and Williams's choice of narrative style—we quickly see that *The Glass Menagerie* is actually a unified series of recollections, a story within a story and, therein, it becomes more informative and more complex. The events of the Wingfield household that we bear witness to are the recounted memories of Tom Wingfield, and therefore, there is not only the prominent matter of Laura's disappointment to consider but also the matter of Tom's escape and its effect on him after some time has passed. So while the play is actually presented from a single point of view—Tom's—Williams is able not only to engage us in Tom's situation but also to involve us in the world of Laura and Amanda as well. Through these two strains of the narrative—the revelation of the inner workings of the family in the form of memory and the final retrospective considerations of Tom that conclude the play—not only are we exposed to an external view of the action as voyeurs but also the inner selves of the characters are revealed to us—the memories and regrets of Amanda Wingfield, the insecurities and hopes of Laura, the frustration and guilt of Tom. Williams's choice of narrative method and structure are only two examples of the critical function of the formal elements of the text. Every piece of the story—the structure, narration, characters, symbolism, setting, and even the title—provides readers with the information necessary to draw their own conclusions about the work. The best and most informative passages may often be the most unassuming. Introductory passages, such as the initial description of the Wingfield home, can easily be overlooked as we anticipate the physical, dramatic action of the work, but passages such as the one included below often yield an enormous amount of information for those who are receptive to it. Consider the following passage:

> *The Wingfield apartment is in the rear of the building, one of those vast hive-like conglomerations of cellular living-units that flower as warty growths in overcrowded urban centers of lower middle-class population and are symptomatic of the impulse of this largest and fundamentally*

*enslaved section of American society to avoid fluidity and differentiation and to exist and function as one interfused mass of automatism.*

*The apartment faces an alley and is entered by a fire-escape, a structure whose name is a touch of accidental poetic truth, for all of these huge buildings are always burning with the slow and implacable fires of human desperation. The fire-escape is included in the set—that is, the landing of it and steps descending from it . . .*

*At the rise of the curtain, the audience is faced with the dark, grim rear wall of the Wingfield tenement. This building, which runs parallel to the footlights, is flanked on both sides by dark, narrow alleys which run into the murky canyons of tangled clotheslines, garbage cans and the sinister lattice-work of neighboring fire escapes.*

*Downstage is the living room, which also serves as a sleeping room for Laura, the sofa unfolding to make her bed. Upstage center, and divided by a wide arch or second proscenium with transparent faded portieres (or second curtain), is the dining room. In an old-fashioned what-not in the living room are seen scores of transparent glass animals. A blown-up photograph of the father hangs on the wall of the living room, facing the audience, to the left of the archway. It is the face of a very handsome young man in a doughboy's First World War cap. He is gallantly smiling, ineluctably smiling, as if to say, "I will be smiling forever." (399–400)*

Once you have completed a pass or two through the play, a return to this introductory passage should spark countless ideas for essay topics. There is the matter of the Wingfield apartment as part of a "hive-like conglomeration," the heavy symbolic presence of the fire escape, the introduction of Laura's glass menagerie, and the portrait of the absent father who has abandoned his family. This single passage arms us with information about Williams's choice of themes, symbolism, plot, and characters. It provides readers with significant and revealing information of psychological, philosophical, and social relevance. Therefore, when we consider a play like *The Glass Menagerie*, while we may have the benefit of the author's own character descriptions and production notes, and while the overall action of the play may be informative though minimal, writers must turn to the text itself, making note of the work's most unassuming details. Remember that information is not contained only in plot. It is found in every aspect of the story. Every detail was chosen deliberately and implemented with purpose. As a writer, it is your job to act as a detective would, looking for the clues that will reveal valuable information about the author's choices and the messages of the text.

## TOPICS AND STRATEGIES

In the sections that follow, you will find a variety of suggested topics accompanied by questions and observations to assist you in the task of writing successfully about *The Glass Menagerie*. Remember that this is not a comprehensive list of topics, and the statements and questions that appear after each suggested topic are merely a guide to help spark your own ideas about the work. A successful paper will present a strong thesis based on your own original ideas and will be supported by relevant examples resulting from close readings of the text. A wide variety of interpretations will be possible as you consider each topic. Use the strategic questions and observations to stimulate your own thoughts about the text and to assist you in developing a strong thesis. Remember to read through the text more than once, making note of those elements that support your argument. It will be equally important to make note of those elements that contradict your thesis, as this will help you to refine your argument and create a stronger case.

### Themes

As you read through *The Glass Menagerie*, consider what subjects the author may be trying to address. What issues or subjects are evident in the text? What does the play reveal about the author's preoccupations? Remember that a close reading will confirm that each and every part of the work—the characters, narrative method, setting, symbolism, language, form, and structure, as well as plot—have all been chosen with intention. Together these elements give shape to the themes. The themes found in *The Glass Menagerie* are themes that appear in many of Williams's other works as well as in works of literature by other authors. Consider, however, Williams's approach to these themes. What makes his presentation and treatment of these themes unique? As noted above, a play with minimal physical dramatic action such as *The Glass Menag-*

*erie* may reveal more about its themes through symbolism and setting than through plot. It is a good rule of thumb to consider not only what appears on the paper before you but also those items that the author has chosen to omit. For instance, a character who never appears onstage, such as Mr. Wingfield, may reveal just as much about a theme as one who spends most of his or her time in the spotlight.

Once a general topic is evident, consider how each individual element of the text lends itself to a deeper examination of this subject. It is not enough to talk broadly about a theme. Try to consider how Williams's work engages us in a dialogue about the topic, and think about what messages may be revealed following some reflection on the text.

## Sample Topics:

1. **Escape:** What does the play tell us about the ability to escape? Can this be realized? If so, do the negative consequences outweigh the rewards?

   Many different papers may result depending on your opinion. For instance, you might choose to examine one character's experience of escape, or you might prefer to compare or contrast the experiences of escape for the entire Wingfield family. Do not limit your consideration of this subject to an examination of escape as physical release only. How does the text present the experience of escape as a psychological and spiritual concept? You might examine escape as a means to overcome one's past, to surmount one's present circumstances and to choose one's own fate, to overcome disabilities or obstacles. Read the text closely, paying particular attention to manifestations of the characters' desire to escape. What are Laura, Tom, and Amanda each trying to escape? How do we know this? Are they successful in their attempts to escape? Consider the devices that Williams uses to draw our attention to the characters' struggles to escape their own realities. What symbols does Williams employ to further this notion? How do the setting and the presence of symbols such as the fire escape heighten our ability to recognize escape as an important subject? Remember to read carefully, considering the setting, lighting, music, and symbols. How does the overall dramatic action of the play relate to the theme of escape? Ultimately, you might want to ask yourself whether or not you believe that *The Glass Menagerie* presents a conclusive statement about escape. If so, what is this statement? If not, what might be the purpose of Williams's exposition on this subject? What does the conclusion of the play suggest?

2. **Memory:** What does *The Glass Menagerie* tell us about the nature of memory?

The seemingly contradictory themes of the power of memory and the flawed nature of memory are evident throughout the course of the play. For instance, at the beginning of the play when Williams introduces *The Glass Menagerie* as a memory play, he acknowledges that memory "takes a lot of poetic license . . . [and] omits some details" (399). Meanwhile, at the conclusion of the play, Tom's thinly veiled admission of guilt seems to indicate that memory is a powerful and overbearing force that cannot be conquered. There is no doubt that Williams considered memory a significant subject; he has incorporated the concept of memory into the very structure of the play. He chooses to have Tom Wingfield function as both protagonist and narrator to accomplish this. What does the form of the play and this type of narration tell us about memory? How does memory affect each of the characters? Consider Amanda Wingfield's preoccupation with recounting the days of her youth and Laura's recollection of high school and her past interactions with Jim. Consider also Tom's relationship with memory and, finally, his concluding remarks.

3. **Family:** What kind of family is the Wingfield family? What conclusions are we to draw about the Wingfield family as a whole?

Consider each member of the Wingfield family and their relationship to each other. Depending on your point of view, you may draw different conclusions about the overall status of the Wingfield family. Are they a fractured family? Or perhaps they represent a realistic portrait of the modern family? Before you jump to any single conclusion, consider what unites the family and what divides them. Consider their interactions from a social standpoint as well as an emotional one. You might reveal your thesis about the Wingfield family by choosing to consider how they compare to or differ from another famous family in literature—for example, the Tyrone family in Eugene O'Neill's *Long Day's Journey into Night* or perhaps the Pollitt family from Williams's own *Cat on a Hot Tin Roof.*

# Character

While the plot of *The Glass Menagerie* is straightforward and simple, the characters are deeply complex, round characters. They are not only individuals with their own personalities and flaws, but they are also able to represent something greater. Williams grants his audience insight into each character by carefully crafting their language, their gestures, and their dialogue. While the play is technically presented from a singular point of view, one could argue that Williams's development and presentation of each character is remarkably balanced. When you write about the characters of a work, remember to consider each character not only as an individual but also examine their interaction with the other characters. How are they alike and how are they different? For instance, how does the contrast between Tom and Jim help us to gain a clearer sense of each character? How do the interactions between Tom and Amanda reveal intimate details about their inner selves? Consider what unites the characters and what divides them. Often our strongest emotional response to a work comes from our interpretation of these commonalities and divisions. The most critical dramatic action is also often generated in these unique relationships between characters.

It is a good rule of thumb to pay attention not only to what a character says in dialogues and in monologues but also how they say it. Consider how the author describes their voice, their gestures, and their facial expressions. How does the author use external factors such as the atmosphere to give us a deeper understanding of the characters? Certainly, one of the most revealing passages in *The Glass Menagerie* is Williams's careful depiction of Laura and her surroundings as she prepares for the gentleman caller's visit. While Laura seems to be a guarded and fairly closed-off character, it could be argued that Williams's use of metaphor and symbolism reveals more about her character than some dialogue. A careful reader will pay close attention to the methods the author uses to draw us closer to a character by eliciting our sympathy or how they can cause us to recoil from a character in disgust, and such close attention will be necessary as you begin writing about a character. Finally, do not fail to take note of how our relationship to or interpretation of each character shapes our perception of the overall story and the themes it presents.

## *Sample Topics:*

1. **The absence of Mr. Wingfield:** Analyze the absence of Tom and Laura's father. Why does Williams choose to include in the play a character who will never actually appear onstage? What function does this serve?

   Mr. Wingfield is incorporated into the play only through the characters' remembrances of him, the emotional scars his absence has bestowed upon each character, and a dignified, illuminated portrait that hangs on the wall of the Wingfield family home. And yet, one could conclude that Mr. Wingfield is one of the most influential characters of the play. What is revealed to us about Mr. Wingfield's character, and how does Williams reveal this in lieu of presenting him as a round character onstage? Consider how his absence affects each character. It might be interesting to discuss why Williams chose to have Mr. Wingfield appear in uniform in the portrait of him that remains in the family home. Does this change our perception of him? Would it have been more effective to present Mr. Wingfield as an actual character onstage?

2. **Amanda:** Analyze the character of Amanda. Does Williams want us to be sympathetic toward Amanda or to judge her more harshly? Do you believe that the way that Amanda treats her children is driving them away? Or are her actions justified as a mother? Discuss.

There are numerous ways to address this topic. Answering these questions first involves making a judgment as to whether you believe that Williams wants us to be sympathetic to Amanda or to judge her more harshly. Or is it possible to do both? Once you make a determination, consider Amanda's interactions with both Laura and Tom. Consider what we know of her background and the events of her life. How does her own history affect her interactions with her children? Does this information change how you perceive Amanda? Depending upon the direction of your paper, it may be useful to consider the final scene of the play where we find Amanda comforting her daughter but also driving Tom from the home. What can we conclude from this scene? You might choose to begin your discourse by writing about Williams's description of Amanda in the character list. Is Williams's description of Amanda accurate? How does your own perception of Amanda compare to or diverge from Williams's own characterization of Amanda?

3. **Jim:** The great majority of *The Glass Menagerie* is dedicated to a long wait for a gentleman caller. When he finally arrives, we are presented with Jim, whom Williams describes in the character list as a "nice, ordinary, young man." Is this description of Jim accurate and does it capture his true function in the play?

Some readers may feel that Williams presents an accurate description of Jim, while others might find that the play presents a more in-depth and well-rounded view of Jim than that presented to us in the character list. For instance, Tom characterizes Jim as "an emissary from a world of reality that [the Wingfields] were somehow set apart from" (401), but he also depicts Jim as "the long delayed but always expected something that we wait for" (401). What does Tom mean when he makes these remarks? Is one characterization of Jim more accurate than the other? Do you feel that Jim is a representative of the reality that the other characters fail to conquer? Or does he represent something larger than himself and more fantastical? If so, what?

**4. Tom:** Tom functions as both protagonist and narrator of *The Glass Menagerie*. How can we reconcile these two different roles? How are these two sides of Tom the same? How are the two roles different? What do we learn about Tom through his narration that we are not able to see through his role as a traditional character?

Consider how the Tom we experience as protagonist differs from the Tom we are exposed to as narrator. Which of the Toms presents a closer presentation of the truth? You might choose to tackle this topic by considering Tom's initial reference to himself as a magician. Does this change your opinion about Tom and the possibility of his sincerity? You might consider the other roles that Tom is cast in: poet, dreamer, rebel, abandoned son, brother, and magician, for instance.

## History and Context

All stories must take place within a certain space and a certain period of time. Even science fiction, which may present a world we have never experienced or which does not really exist, is framed within a certain space and time. Whether a setting and time period are fictional or whether they closely resemble reality, they offer us clues to understanding what the author has to say. Authors may write about the time period in which they are living or their view of a time or event of the past, or they may speculate about the future. Like many of Williams's works, *The Glass Menagerie* refers to a specific time of change in America, when social conventions were in flux and a new working class struggled in the face of a new industrialized economy. Williams utilized his own understanding of the changes specific to the American South as a starting place for his exploration of this subject. The play takes place in an urban neighborhood in Saint Louis, Missouri, during the 1930s. Through his use of this setting and time period, Williams is able to address a broad range of topics and concerns. They enable Williams to use the advent of the radio and television and the magic of the cinema as tools to create a unique and powerful work. The play, which depicts the struggles of the lower and middle class during this time, also shows how historical and contextual elements of a work of literature can allow it to function as a social tool. It does not take long to realize that Amanda's old home with its jonquils and gentleman callers is a far cry from the reality she now inhabits and the world of her children. The story is able to contrast the two different cultures, in many ways, by presenting an image of both past and present. The themes revealed in the setting and time period represented—the reconciliation of past and present, the passage of time, and the attempt to preserve or reclaim tradition—are common threads in Williams's works that can be explored profitably in your paper or essay.

## Sample Topic:

1. **Courting in the Old South:** Through Amanda's repeated recollections, Williams presents a picture of the courting process in the Old South. How does it differ from the social world that her daughter Laura experiences? What does this teach us about social conventions and how they have changed? Are the changes cultural or are differences in convention linked more personally to the individual characters?

   Writing about this topic will first require that you make a determination as to whether or not Amanda's recollections are truthful. If you believe that they are truthful, what does this tell us about how social conventions have changed? What does the play suggest caused these changes? Does the difference in social conventions affect the way that Amanda and her children relate to each other? What kind of commentary does this make about modern society and ideals and tradition?

## Philosophy and Ideas

Because *The Glass Menagerie* reveals the inner selves of the characters and deals heavily in an emotional realm, the play opens the door for the consideration of challenging issues such as the existence or absence of free will and questions such as how we should define responsibility and loyalty and where their boundaries lie. The play compels us to consider what choice the characters have, or if there is really any choice involved at all. Tom's decision to leave his family behind in order to pursue his own dreams, and his subsequent admission that he has been unable to reconcile this choice, presents us with an ethical dilemma. Williams concludes the play with Tom's admissions, opting not to provide us with any easy answers. As a writer, it is your job to pick up where Williams left off, engaging in this dialogue, proposing answers, or in the absence of conclusive answers, asking your own questions that will further the debate.

## Sample Topics:

1. **Ethics and responsibility:** Was Tom's decision to leave his family ethical or not? What about his father's decision to leave? Compare and contrast the two choices.

    This paper could be written from a variety of viewpoints. If you feel that Tom's decision to leave was not ethical, you might find similarities between his departure and his father's. On the other hand, you might feel that Tom did what he needed to do. Use examples from the text to support your opinion. What view do you think Williams was trying to present? How does the presentation of the story from Tom's point of view affect our interpretation of these choices? How do Tom's concluding remarks alter our perception of his decision to leave?

2. **Free will and choice:** To what extent is free will, or the absence of free will, a theme of the play? Are the characters truly able to exercise free will or are they bound by circumstance?

    Tom ultimately escapes from his home and begins a new life. His father also escapes. However, Amanda and Laura seem to remain in their current place and often appear incapable of escaping their circumstances. Examine each character's power of choice and the consequences associated with their choices. Ultimately, what view do you think Williams is trying to impart?

3. **Transparency:** Transparency is a motif that recurs throughout *The Glass Menagerie*. Consider the concept of transparency and discuss how Williams creates a sense of transparency in the

work. How does he use this tactic to inform his audience? What information does it give us about the characters and the themes of the play?

There are countless examples of transparency throughout *The Glass Menagerie.* Consider physical examples of transparency, for example, Williams's use of transparency in the set, and note how other elements of the play reflect this same notion. How does the idea of transparency relate to our perception of the characters? Why is the idea of transparency important within the context of this play? Go beyond the obvious by also examining transparency as a metaphor. What does transparency represent within the context of the play?

## Form and Genre

When one is asked to consider genre and form in light of *The Glass Menagerie,* it is easy to begin with the simplest classification of the work. It is, simply, a work of drama—a play consisting of two acts broken down into seven scenes. If one examines the play further, one will see that *The Glass Menagerie* is also a family drama, a tragedy, and a failed or subverted romance. It is also an expressionistic work that diverged from the realistic theater that was prevalent at the time the play was written.

If we consider Williams's production notes, before we even read the play we are armed with the knowledge of Williams's own classifications of the play. He considered *The Glass Menagerie* a form of plastic theater and a memory play that allowed the story to function dually as both reality and fantasy. Those who take the time to become acquainted with the author's own background will notice that *The Glass Menagerie* is also a semiautobiographical work. While Williams makes his intentions clear regarding the form and genre of his work in his production notes, there is more information to be found in the play itself.

It may be useful to consider an anthology of American drama from this time period so that you have a sense of what else was being produced. You may also consider an anthology of drama that covers a broader range of works with respect to place of origin and time period. Give some consideration to Williams's influences and note what he shared in common with other authors and where his work diverges from that of his influences.

When considering the form of *The Glass Menagerie*, there is also the matter of the evolution of the play to consider. Like many of Williams's works, *The Glass Menagerie* was subjected to a long process of revision, and the various forms of the work present different visions with varied conclusions and varied treatment of formal elements. The genesis of *The Glass Menagerie* alone could provide countless topics for research and discussion.

## Sample Topics:

1. **Plastic theater:** In his production notes, Williams reveals his desire to create "a new, plastic theatre" (395). How is this form realized in *The Glass Menagerie*? Would you say that Williams's efforts are successful?

   You might begin by giving some definition to plastic theater. Naturally, someone writing a paper on this subject might refer first to Williams's own production notes, but the bulk of your information should come from the text itself. How do the formal elements of the text evidence a plastic quality? It will be useful to compare and contrast this concept to the form of other drama of the period. What was Williams trying to accomplish and how did he try to reach this end in *The Glass Menagerie*? Was he successful? Use specific references from the text to show how Williams set out to realize this form. How might our interpretation of the play be different if Williams did not utilize this form?

2. **Memory play:** Why did Williams choose to create in *The Glass Menagerie* a memory play rather than a play with a more traditional treatment of time?

   As with the last topic, you might begin by giving some definition to the notion of a memory play. Explain how *The Glass Menagerie* falls into this category. Next you may want to begin noting your observations about Williams's reasons for choosing this form. How does the narration play a part in this form? How does it affect the sense of time in the play? Why would Williams have wanted to create this effect? How does this form reveal things about the characters that we would not otherwise learn? You might compare or contrast *The Glass Menagerie* with another work of literature—one with a traditional treatment of time or, perhaps, a work that also presents a distorted sense of time or a nonlinear story. How do these presentations inform our sense of each work? Does the form tie in to the thematic content of the work?

3. **Autobiography:** How does *The Glass Menagerie* reflect Williams's own life and experiences? Is it fair to say that the play is autobiographical?

A paper on this subject might use the play to determine how biographical elements are used in a work. Many scholars and critics say that Tom is based on Williams himself, while Amanda and Laura were based on Williams's own mother and sister. Consider how the elements of the play compare to the author's own life. You will need to consult some reliable biographical sources. You might refer to some biographies such as Donald Spoto's *The Kindness of Strangers: The Life of Tennessee Williams* and Lyle Leverich's *Tom: The Unknown Tennessee Williams* or Williams's own *Notebooks, Memoirs,* and letters. Where does the play diverge from reality and what do the play and Williams's own life share in common? What does this tell us about the use of biographical material in literature?

4. **The evolution of *The Glass Menagerie*:** Analyze the evolution of *The Glass Menagerie* and its effect on our interpretation of the work.

*The Glass Menagerie* started as a screenplay for MGM and was drafted in short story form before it was presented for the theater or printed in the reading versions we know today. Each of these different forms is unique. Examine, for instance, changes in plot and character in the different versions. You might also consider the omission of the screen device in later versions, which Williams addresses in his production notes. You might choose to single out one change and follow it throughout the various drafts and stages or talk about the changes as a whole and how they affect our interpretation of a specific element of the play or the play as a whole.

## Language, Symbols, and Imagery

*The Glass Menagerie* is ripe with symbolic content from its title to the smallest details of the play. Together these symbols present countless options for essay topics. You might explore the use of glass as a metaphor, the menagerie as a social metaphor, Laura's glass unicorn, or the fire escape, just to name a few. One general concept for your paper might be to consider how Williams uses repetition, or motifs, to make these symbols apparent and to convey their significance. Alternatively, you may want to consider the multiple meanings that one symbol takes on within the play.

### Sample Topics:

1. **The title:** Why do you think that Williams chose to name this play *The Glass Menagerie*? How does the title reflect the concerns of the play? Would another title have been more appropriate?

   Consider the implications of utilizing the image of the glass menagerie in the title of the play. Think about how glass is used as a symbol in the play—its fragility and transparency and its ability to interact with light. Also, remember not to overlook the meaning of the menagerie. In addition to referring directly to Laura's collection of glass animals, what does the menagerie symbolize and how does it relate to the Wingfield family and the conditions in which they live? You might use the answer from this question to segue into a discussion of societal factors represented in the play. You might also choose to discuss the evolution of the title as the work was evolving in form. As a screenplay it was titled *The Gentleman Caller*; as a short story it was called *Portrait of a Girl in Glass*. Why did

Williams ultimately settle on *The Glass Menagerie*? How does it reveal the concerns of the play?

2. **The unicorn:** What is the significance of Laura's glass unicorn and the loss of its horn? Why does Laura give it to Jim?

Consider the symbolic value of this animal from Laura's collection. Why does Laura allow Jim to hold her glass unicorn? What does it represent? What can be said about Williams's choice of material and animal? How does Laura react to its being broken? What are we to think of her allowing Jim to take the broken animal with him? Consider the scene in which it is presented and how this symbolism ties in with the greater concerns of the play.

3. **Music:** What is the effect of Williams's use of music in the play? What kinds of music does the audience hear, and how does this reflect or contradict the action of the play?

Williams uses music carefully throughout the play, whether it is in the repeated glass menagerie theme at Laura's appearance, Laura's presence at the Victrola playing her absentee father's records, or the sound of jazz coming from outdoors. You might contrast the use of music in these various contexts or compare them. What shared purpose does the employment of music serve, or alternatively, how does each distinct appearance of music create a distinct and contrasting atmosphere? You might consider Williams's own notes about music in the production notes that precede the play. Another idea would be to compare Williams's use of music in *The Glass Menagerie* to his use of music in another play, such as *A Streetcar Named Desire*.

4. **Cinema:** The cinema is well-represented in *The Glass Menagerie*. Tom tells his mother that he goes frequently to the cinema. What might the cinema represent for Tom? What does it represent more generally? How and why does Williams use the concept of the cinema as a narrative device?

Consider not only Tom's voyages to the theater and the meaning of these trips in a literal context but also the author's own use of cinematic devices in the play. Examine the formal elements of the play. Where do we find traces of the cinema? You will want to think about narration, point of view, and form. Why do you think Williams chose to utilize the cinema in this way? In addressing this topic, it will also be helpful to consider the significance of the cinema within a historical context. What is the relation of the cinema and the time period in which the play was written and produced?

## Compare and Contrast Essays

The similarities between characters and events create an informative, unifying force within the text. Differences also inform us in ways that similarities cannot. Williams himself utilizes a compare-and-contrast tactic in his treatment of characters in *The Glass Menagerie* and many of his other works, generating sympathy for the characters by uniting them in their struggles.

These differences between characters and events in the play bestow us with greater knowledge. You might compare or contrast a single element within the play, or elements found in *The Glass Menagerie* and another Williams play, or in *The Glass Menagerie* and the work of another author. Williams's work also presents us with the opportunity to compare and contrast a play with a television or film adaptation, a final product with an early draft, or variations of endings within a single work.

### Sample Topics:

1. **Film adaptations:** Compare and contrast a film adaptation with the reading version of the play.

   How do the text and the film version of *The Glass Menagerie* differ? Compare the characters, the plot, and the use of symbols. Do the text and the film have the same conclusion? Why would the director choose to make these changes? Are they creative choices or are they choices dictated by social constraints such as censorship? Does the film version enhance or take away from our own interpretation of the play or does it inform us?

Would you say that the director was true to the text? Explain why or why not.

**2. Tom and Jim:** Compare and contrast these two characters.

Although Tom and Jim work together and attended the same high school, they are very different characters. How are they different, and how does Williams make these differences felt? What effect does the presentation of these differences have on us? How are Tom's and Jim's ambitions similar, and how are they different? Explain how these differences inform us about each character.

## Bibliography and Resources for *The Glass Menagerie*

Adler, Thomas P. "*The Glass Menagerie*." *Tennessee Williams: A Guide to Research and Performance.* Ed. Philip C. Kolin. Westport, CT: Greenwood, 1998. 34–50.

Babcock, Granger. "*The Glass Menagerie* and the Transformation of the Subject." *Journal of Dramatic Theory and Criticism* 14.1 (Fall 1999): 17–36.

Bigsby, C. W. E. "Entering *The Glass Menagerie*." *Cambridge Companion to Tennessee Williams.* Ed. Matthew C. Roudané. Cambridge: Cambridge UP, 1997. 29–44.

Bloom, Harold, ed. *Tennessee Williams's The Glass Menagerie.* Bloom's Guides. New York: Chelsea House, 2007.

———. *Tennessee Williams's The Glass Menagerie.* Modern Critical Interpretations. New York: Chelsea House, 2007.

Cardullo, Bert. "The Blue Rose of St. Louis: Laura, Romanticism, and *The Glass Menagerie*." *Tennessee Williams Annual Review* 1 (1998): 81–92.

Crandell, George W. "The Cinematic Eye in Tennessee Williams's *The Glass Menagerie*." *Tennessee Williams Annual Review* 1 (1998): 1–12.

Debusscher, Gilbert. "Tennessee Williams's Dramatic Charade: Secrets and Lies in *The Glass Menagerie*." *Tennessee Williams Annual Review* 3 (2000): 57–68.

———. "Where Memory Begins: New Texas Light on *The Glass Menagerie*." *Tennessee Williams Annual Review* 1 (1998): 53–62.

*The Glass Menagerie.* Dir. Anthony Harvey. DVD. Broadway Theater Archive, 1973.

Kramer, Richard E. "The Sculptural Drama: Tennessee Williams's Plastic Theatre." *Tennessee Williams Annual Review* 5 (2002): 1–10.

Leverich, Lyle. *Tom: The Unknown Tennessee Williams*. New York: Crown,
1995.

Moschovakis, Nick. "Tennessee Williams's American Blues: From the Early
Manuscripts Through *Menagerie*." *Tennessee Williams Annual Review* 8
(2005): 15–36.

Parker, R. B., ed. *Twentieth Century Interpretations of The Glass Menagerie: A
Collection of Critical Essays*. Englewood Cliffs, NJ: Prentice-Hall, 1983.

Presley, Delma Eugene. *The Glass Menagerie: An American Memory*. Boston:
Twayne, 1990.

Pritner, Cal, and Scott E. Walters. *Introduction to Play Analysis*. New York:
McGraw-Hill, 2004.

Siebold, Thomas, ed. *Readings on The Glass Menagerie*. San Diego, CA: Green-
haven Press, 1998.

Single, Lois Leathers. "Flying the Jolly Roger: Image of Escape and Selfhood in
Tennessee Williams's *The Glass Menagerie*." *Tennessee Williams Annual
Review* 2 (1999): 69–85.

Spoto, Donald. *Kindness of Strangers: The Life of Tennessee Williams*. Boston:
Little, Brown, 1985.

*Tennessee Williams's 'The Glass Menagerie': A Study Guide from Gale's "Drama
for Students."* Vol. 1. Ch. 7. PDF. 23 July 2002.

Thompson, Judith J. "Symbol, Myth and Ritual in *The Glass Menagerie, The Rose
Tattoo*, and *Orpheus Descending*." *Tennessee Williams: Thirteen Essays*. Ed.
Jac Tharpe. Jackson: U of Mississippi P, 1980. 139–71.

Williams, Tennessee. *The Glass Menagerie. Tennessee Williams: Plays 1937–
1955*. Eds. Mel Gussow and Kenneth Holditch. New York: Library of America, 2000. 393–65.

———. *Memoirs*. Garden City, New York: Doubleday, 1975.

———. *Notebooks*. Ed. Margaret Bradham Thorton. New Haven, CT: Yale UP,
2006.

———. *The Selected Letters of Tennessee Williams*. Eds. Albert J. Devlin and
Nancy M. Tischler. New York: New Directions, 2000.

# A STREETCAR
# NAMED DESIRE

## READING TO WRITE

FOLLOWING THE success of *The Glass Menagerie*, Williams began work on a story about the drama surrounding the presence of two women at a men's poker night. The story eventually evolved into *A Streetcar Named Desire*, a work that became one of Tennessee Williams's best-known and best-loved plays. After the success of its original Broadway run from 1947 to 1949, *A Streetcar Named Desire* was awarded a Pulitzer Prize and a New York Drama Critics' Circle award for Best Play. Only a few years later, *Streetcar* had secured its place in the American pop culture consciousness, largely due to the release of Elia Kazan's 1951 film adaptation of the play, which included dynamic and unforgettable performances by Marlon Brando as Stanley Kowalski and Vivien Leigh as Blanche DuBois. Kazan's adaptation of *A Streetcar Named Desire*, which presented a unique vision of Williams's story, struck a chord with viewers. Audiences committed to memory the play's most famous lines and the intense dramatic conflict between Stanley and Blanche as it was reflected onscreen. More than 50 years later, Kazan's film continues to be cited regularly on lists of the best films of all time.

While there is no doubt that Kazan's film helped fuel the success of Williams's work in the popular mainstream by projecting it to a larger audience, the powerful performances and the overwhelming appeal of this adaptation put forth a challenge for those writing about the play. Readers and writers may, consciously or unconsciously, depend on Kazan's vision of the play in their own search for information about the work. This brings to light a problem for those writing about any literary works that have popular film adaptations—namely, the pitfall of drawing ideas from a singular interpretation of the work rather than from an open examination of the original text. An exploration of Kazan's own interpretation of the play or an analysis of his vision of specific individual elements, such as the presentation of the characters or treatment of plot, could certainly serve as interesting essay topics, but for those opting to write about topics not directly related to Kazan's adaptation, having a predetermined notion of the play and the characters means that writers will need to unlearn what they think they know about the play. In fact, choosing to write about Kazan's interpretation of the text would also require the formation of your own opinions of the original text so that you can compare and contrast the two, citing important similarities or differences. In either of these scenarios, it will be necessary to resist the urge to work off the ideas and vision presented in the famous film and focus on your own interpretation of the text.

Relying too heavily on popular adaptations of a text presents a problem—namely, that the creator of a popular adaptation may not necessarily have been faithful to the author's own vision. Those who are familiar with both the reading version of *A Streetcar Named Desire* and Kazan's film may have already recognized this problem, noticing that references to Blanche's husband as a homosexual are omitted in the film. As we witness in Kazan's work, there is always the possibility that censorship of some kind may have hindered accurate representation of the work, and even in cases where censorship is not a concern, someone else's vision of the play may simply differ greatly from the author's own view for any number of reasons.

Reconciling the problem of censorship and resisting the urge to rely on the personal choices of a single interpreter are not the only potential stumbling blocks for those writing about *A Streetcar Named Desire*. Williams's literary tactics present their own challenge. In *A Streetcar Named Desire,* as in many of his other works, Williams makes a habit of building up a particular image and then breaking it down, allowing him to keep some control over our assumptions and presuppositions. Consider the text as a whole. A close consideration of the full text reveals information that gives us a deeper understanding of the themes and characters. In fact, Williams's build up–break down technique allows us access to the inner selves of the characters. Take a look at the paragraphs that introduce us to Stanley and Blanche. First, Stanley: "Two men come around the corner, Stanley Kowalski and Mitch. They are about twenty-eight or thirty years old, roughly dressed in blue denim work clothes. Stanley carries his bowling jacket and a red-stained package from a butcher's" (470). From this single introductory paragraph, we can place Stanley within the working class. He is young. His accessories—a bowling jacket and a package of meat—enhance this view of Stanley as a macho working man. They also indicate his love of sport and signal his overt sexuality, which is revealed to us shortly. Our introduction to Blanche presents an equally vivid picture:

> Blanche comes around the corner, carrying a valise. She looks at a slip of paper, then at the building, then again at the slip and again at the building. Her expression is one of shocked disbelief. Her appearance is incongruous to this setting. She is daintily dressed in a white suit with a fluffy bodice, necklace and earrings of pearl, white gloves and hat, looking as if she were arriving at a summer tea or cocktail party in the garden district. (471)

From this paragraph we see that Blanche is equated with the color white; she seems to represent a kind of purity. Her clothes and jewelry indicate that she is well-off, and the references to her being dressed for a special occasion indicate that she is socially adjusted.

While there is some truth in both of these introductions, a thorough examination of the text provides the warning that we cannot base our opinions of the characters on these descriptions alone or on any singular description for that matter. There is more to the story than what is at the surface, and the play poses the additional challenge of presenting contrasting points of view. Stanley, who seems to be a simple and straightforward character, is actually a deeply complex character. His image as an animal and a brute can be, and has been, challenged by scholars and critics. In Stanley's case, you might consider the part of the play where a contrite Stanley is compared to a "baying hound" (502), calling out his wife's name in the streets. Some might see this as an indication of a more human side of Stanley, a vulnerable and loving side. Certainly some contemporary critics have chosen to work from this viewpoint, supporting a more sympathetic, or at least empathetic, view of Stanley. The same can be said for Blanche. Blanche is presented to us in a manner similar to a slowly unraveling ball of tangled yarn. In this case there is less work to do, for it is Williams himself who challenges the initial depiction of Blanche. In fact, Williams begins to break down our preconceptions of Blanche immediately, concluding his introduction of the character with the following observations: "Her delicate beauty must avoid strong light. There is something about her uncertain manner, as well as her white clothes, that suggests a moth" (471). Our preconceptions of Blanche as a pure lady cannot survive this comparison to an insect that is either found among decaying items or flitting around in the night. Therefore, as we can see from these two examples, just as readers should not rely on a single adaptation or interpretation of the text for information, readers must also be careful not to cling too tightly to any single passage or any preconceptions that the text evokes. An analysis of this single tactic could serve as a valuable essay topic. Why would Williams want to present us with a certain image and then break down that image? What does this tell us about stereotypes and simple classification?

Similarly, many scholars and critics choose to write about the theme of the death of the Old South and the rise of a coarse industrial class in *A Streetcar Named Desire.* It is easy to match up Stanley and Blanche as archetypes of these particular societies. And yet, upon full consideration of the supporting details, writers may begin to see that these characters also resist these archetypes in many ways. Certainly, there is scholarship that extends in both directions. For instance, while Stanley is presented as crass and brutish, contemporary critics have proposed that Stanley is just as much a victim of his circumstances as Blanche, and Williams himself seems to suggest that Blanche's downfall cannot be linked solely to her exposure to Stanley. Williams presents Blanche as a character who, like the others, is equipped with her own flaws. One could argue then that she is capable of contributing to her own demise without Stanley's help. This shows how writing about a very common theme of the text is not a problem, so long as you have fresh observations to contribute about the subject.

If you are particularly interested in Kazan's film adaptation, it could be interesting to analyze the most famous lines of the play. What does Stanley's primal cry of his wife's name and Blanche's final admission of her dependence "on the kindness of strangers" tell us about each of these characters? For instance, Stanley's comparison to a "baying hound" (502) perpetuates the idea of him as animalistic, but how else could this be construed? Some might find this particular gesture to symbolize his true connection with Stella, a deeper connection that we are not able to see elsewhere. Others might see it as an indication of Stanley's desperation and, therefore, an indication of his vulnerability. Consider how these bits of dialogue transcend the characters who give voice to them and how they take on a universal meaning. What is it that has made these lines so memorable when they were translated on-screen?

*A Streetcar Named Desire* presents other challenges for writers to consider as well. In the preceding chapter, we discussed the challenge of minimalistic plots as evidenced in *The Glass Menagerie* and many other modern works of literature. *A Streetcar Named Desire* may present the opposite problem. The play is full of dramatic action, and readers can easily become caught up in the overall action of the play, leading to the pitfall of missing the more subtle elements of the work. Similarly, *Streetcar* has some themes that can dominate the play because of their prominence. For instance, the most prominent subject of the play seems to be desire, as evidenced by the very title of the work. A good writer should be able to resist making obvious observations about desire, considering instead how this prominent theme relates to broader themes such as love, the demise of romance, the effects of a changing society, and even the relationship between desire and death. If you recall these suggestions to resist relying on any single popular interpretation of the text and to reach beyond the most obvious details of the play, you will be able to develop your own original ideas about the work, which will result in a strong and engaging essay.

## TOPICS AND STRATEGIES

In the sections that follow, you will find a variety of suggested topics accompanied by questions and observations to assist you in the task of writing successfully about *A Streetcar Named Desire*. Remember that this is not a comprehensive list of topics, and the statements and questions that appear after each suggested topic are merely a guide to help spark your own ideas about the work. A successful paper will present a strong thesis based upon your own original ideas and will be supported by relevant examples resulting from close readings of the text. A wide variety of interpretations will be possible as you consider each topic. Use the strategic questions and observations to stimulate your own thoughts about the text and to assist you in developing a strong thesis. Remember to read through the text more than once, making note of those elements of the text that support your argument. It will be equally important to make note of those elements that contradict your thesis, as this will help you to refine your argument and create a stronger case.

## Themes

In considering the themes presented in *A Streetcar Named Desire*, as discussed above, the most obvious is undoubtedly the powerful and destructive nature of uncontrolled desire. It is referenced in the work's title and is repeated as a motif throughout the play. It is evident in symbols such as the streetcar and the fallen Belle Reve and is reflected in each of the main characters, who function as examples of the impact of the destructive nature of desire. Williams makes it impossible to ignore the ruling force of Stanley and Stella's relationship, with scenes that function as tongue-in-cheek metaphors, such as the scene wherein Stanley throws his package of meat at Stella and Stella gleefully accepts it. Even Blanche, who seems at first to represent a kind of purity, is deeply affected by her own desires and is battered by the uncontrolled desires of those around her—her family, who squandered their estate, and her husband, whom she caught having a homosexual affair. While desire is certainly a key theme of *A Streetcar Named Desire*, it is important not to become so entangled in this one subject that you miss out on the other major themes of the work. As a matter of fact, an examination of Williams's presentation of desire can lead us to other significant themes such as love and relationships, loneliness, sexuality, need and reliance, and the widespread effects of a changing society, to name only a few.

## Sample Topics:

1. **Desire:** What kind of commentary does the play ultimately make about desire? How are each of the characters driven by desire and what effect does this have on them?

   This topic could be addressed from many different viewpoints. Each of the characters in *A Streetcar Named Desire* is deeply affected by desire. You might consider how desire affects a single character or how it affects all of the main characters, more generally. Consider Stella and Stanley's relationship, and consider Blanche's inability to rein in her desires and its part in her ruination. You might choose to focus on how Williams uses symbolism to create a discourse about desire. As suggested above, try to consider desire as more than a sexual force. How is desire reflected in other variations and what is Williams trying to say about the nature and effect of desire? Is it inherently a bad thing?

2. **Illusion and reality:** Throughout the play Blanche, in particular, seems most incapable of distinguishing illusion from reality. Ultimately, at the conclusion of the play, it becomes clear that the two are, for her, blurred together. Why is this so? What does it tell us about Blanche and about the larger themes of the play?

   While it may be useful to begin by explaining how Williams presents Blanche as divorced from reality, remember not to simply present a list of examples. The methods Williams employs, such as his use of symbolism and character development, are relevant, but use the text to examine why Blanche chooses illusion over reality. Or is it a choice at all? It will be helpful to consider Blanche's various roles—sister, wife, schoolteacher, and southern belle. How do these roles contribute to our understanding of Blanche's separation from reality? Consider why Williams might have created a character like Blanche. What did he hope we would learn from Blanche?

Another interesting way to approach this topic might be to compare Blanche with characters from Williams's other works, such as Laura or Amanda from *The Glass Menagerie*. In terms of their inability to separate reality and fantasy, what do the characters share in common and how does Williams reveal this? Does he use the same method or methods to convey this in both texts?

## Character

*A Streetcar Named Desire* presents us with two of the most memorable and dynamic characters in the history of American theater— Blanche DuBois and Stanley Kowalski. As noted above, there remain few people who are not familiar with Marlon Brando's performance as Stanley and Vivien Leigh's portrayal of Blanche in Elia Kazan's 1951 film adaptation of the play. At first glance, these characters seem diametrically opposed, but by the play's end, one could say that Williams has united the characters through their flaws and their basic human-ness. Comparing or contrasting these characters could lead to interesting insights about the characters and the themes of the play, but while these two characters often steal the limelight, there is much to be learned from the other characters such as Stella, Mitch, and even the vendors selling tamales and flowers for the dead who appear intermittently throughout the play. Like *The Glass Menagerie*, *A Streetcar Named Desire* also utilizes absentee characters such as the DuBois ancestors and Blanche's deceased husband, characters who are revealed only through memory to give us deeper insight into the inner selves of the primary characters. Any of these topics could provide you with the basis for a good essay.

### *Sample Topics:*

1. **Blanche:** Analyze and evaluate this character.

Critics continue to present varied interpretations of Blanche. You might choose to develop your own analysis of Blanche based on your interpretation of the text, or you might choose to analyze a common portrayal of her, such as Vivian Leigh's portrayal of Blanche in Elia Kazan's film adaptation of the play.

You might even compare or contrast multiple portrayals of Blanche. What does Blanche symbolize? Why is she such an important and memorable character? Remember to consider all elements of her character. Do not overlook more subtle elements such as the meaning of her name.

2. **The relationship of Stella and Stanley:** Analyze and evaluate the relationship of Stella and Stanley. What does it tell us about modern society and relationships? And about love? What impact did this depiction have on models of romance in literature?

At the time Williams wrote *A Streetcar Named Desire*, the relationship of Stella and Stanley was somewhat unique in literature, for it challenged conventional notions of love and romance and focused on a primal magnetism not traditionally central to classic literature. What does the relationship of the two tell us about each character? And about relationships as a whole? Is their relationship a product of the society that they live in? Or does it reveal something more basic about human nature that simply was overlooked or censored previously? Perhaps you might consider the effect of the presentation of this kind of relationship in literature and film at the time it made its debut. In this case you would need to compare it to other examples of relationships and romance in literature.

If you disagree with the idea that the relationship of Stanley and Stella serves as an example of a new model of romance in literature, you will need to support this assertion by aligning it with similar examples of romance and relationships in other texts. How can works like Shakespeare's *Romeo and Juliet* support your assertion? Once you have presented your argument, you will want to conclude with some thoughts on the subject of why writers continue to present this vision of romance and relationships in literature. Are Williams and the other authors you referenced promoting the Stella-and-Stanley model as a statement of reality that dismisses fantastical notions of love? Or are they trying to illuminate the problems with this model of "love"? If you believe they are trying to illuminate problems with this model, discuss where the problem lies.

3. **Stanley as the antithesis of the chivalric male:** Many classic works of literature build their story around a male who functions symbolically as a kind of chivalric knight, either literally or symbolically. In *A Streetcar Named Desire,* Williams challenged this notion through the creation of Stanley Kowalski. Why is Williams's presentation of the male protagonist (or antagonist, as the case may be) significant?

You will probably want to begin by explaining what is meant by the idea of a chivalric knight. Give some definition to the term and use examples from other works of literature to back up your assertion that it is indeed a traditional view of the male in literature predating Williams's work. Next you will need to build your case by explaining how Stanley is the antithesis of the traditional male character. How do his appearance, gestures, and manner of speaking support this notion? Finally, consider why Williams would prefer to include a character like Stanley in the play? What is to be gained by abandoning traditional notions of the male character in literature? You might want to conclude by making some larger observations about the way that we are to perceive Stanley. Did Williams mean for us to see Stanley as an animal and a brute? Or is it possible to sympathize with his character, or at least to understand him? You might opt to dispute the notion of Stanley as the antithesis of the chivalric knight.

4. **Characterization of the working class:** Consider the cast of characters as a whole. Was Williams trying to create a portrait of the working class? If so, do you believe he was successful?

If you have chosen to write about this topic, you may want to first refer to some literature about the working class in America following the Industrial Revolution. You will need to have an understanding of what life was like for members of this class in urban areas during the 1940s. What would the experience of being a member of the lower working class have been like? Do Williams's characters represent this accurately? Consider also how the diversity of the cast reflects societal changes of the day. Why would Williams have wanted to create a portrait of the working class? This topic would allow you to consider if Williams's work can be considered a social tool or even a work of protest. If you believe it does fall under this classification, compare it to some other works of protest. How do the means the authors use compare and how do they differ? How do they share a common purpose?

## History and Context

Like *The Glass Menagerie* and many of Williams's other works, *A Streetcar Named Desire* presents a portrait of an important time in American history, when the economic landscape was rapidly evolving, shifting from an agrarian culture to an industrial one. Along with changes in the economy came major changes in the daily life of those struggling to make a living. The urban society was largely formed as a result of industrialization, and the composition of populations shifted as people migrated to these urban centers to find work. The genteel ways associated with southern plantation life seemed to be fading away in favor of the rough ways associated with the day-to-day realities associated with the drive for industrial progress.

The setting and time period that Williams utilizes—a real-life avenue in a poor section of New Orleans in the 1940s—allowed Williams to deal with a myriad of important issues, including the threat of the extinction of American romance and tradition and the need for the preservation of ideals. In fact, the play, in its presentation of a view of the life of the working class and the confrontation of characters like Blanche and Stanley, allows us to question what is meant by progress and how it can be defined. Blanche, who initially appears to be a much more highly evolved human being than Stanley, is ultimately cast in a different light, and this discrepancy raises the question of what is better. Williams chooses to set his characters on a real street in a poor section of New Orleans. The streetcars were also taken from an existing streetcar line. A writer might choose to discuss the impact of Williams utilizing a real-life setting rather than a fictional one. How does this affect our interpretation of the work? Would our perception be different if the setting was fictional?

The condition of Blanche presents another interesting topic that appears throughout Williams's entire body of work, which is the prevalence of diagnoses of mental disorders in women at the turn of the century. This was a very important matter for Williams as his own sister, Rose, was institutionalized and later fully incapacitated by a lobotomy. The prevalence of the idea of hysteria and neuroses as a female affliction is echoed in Williams's other plays such as *The Glass Menagerie* and *Summer and Smoke,* but it is the example of Blanche in *A Streetcar Named Desire* that is perhaps most prominent in the public consciousness. Consider what Williams is saying about this issue—is he confirming it or disputing it?

## *Sample Topic:*

1. **The death of the Old South:** What message does *A Streetcar Named Desire* give us about the death of the Old South?

   Critics have approached this topic from many different standpoints. While there is some consensus that Williams was concerned with creating a portrait of the Old South compared to the new industrial society, do not fall into the trap of simply announcing this in your paper. First you will want to define the Old South and present a picture of the culture associated with it and then discuss how this society changed as a result of industrialization. Consider why this subject is relevant. How do the formal elements of the play reflect this theme and reveal information about this subject? Is Williams actually saying that industrialism caused the downfall of genteel culture?

# Philosophy and Ideas

While *A Streetcar Named Desire* is a dynamic, action-packed play, the work is also able to serve as a catalyst, allowing audience members to consider deeper issues such as the nature of truth, the definition of reality, and our confrontation with it. Considering any of these topics will require you to look beyond the surface of the play, examining the inner lives of the characters, the symbolism, and other formal elements.

*Sample Topics:*

1. **The interior life of characters:** How does the play create a sense of the interior life of the characters and what does this reveal to us? How does this ability to access the inner selves of the characters shape our perception of them and, subsequently, our perception of the play at large?

    You might consider how Williams used his set and the oscillation between interiors and exteriors to show the inner workings of the characters while creating the impression of a voyeuristic view. Consider also how Williams uses other symbols to demonstrate the true nature of the characters and their psychological condition.

2. **Truth:** Each character addresses truth in a different way. What does the play tell us about the nature of truth?

    Stanley claims to seek out truth while Stella disregards it, and Blanche hides from the truth. While you will need to provide examples of how we know this about each character, you will also want to discuss the motivations behind their ability or inability to deal with truth. Why would Williams want to present three different views of the confrontation of reality or the failure to confront reality?

3. **Self-awareness:** How self-aware are the major characters in this play?

    You may want to narrow down this topic by discussing the self-awareness of one character, or you might choose to compare and contrast the self-awareness of more than one character. Consider how well the characters seem to know themselves. Are they aware of their own flaws? Or are their flaws primarily recognized by other characters?

## Form and Genre

The sections above suggested that it might be interesting to consider Stanley as the antithesis of the chivalric knight in literature and to examine Stella and Stanley's relationship as a new model for romance in literature. When considering genre and form in the context of the play, one might consider how these characterizations contribute to the notion of the play as an example of a subverted romance.

## Sample Topics:

1. **Subverted romance:** How does the play function as a subverted romance? And what message does this send about modern society? How does this idea of the subverted romance relate to larger themes about romance in American culture?

   These questions will require you to consider romance not only as a counterpart of love but also as cultural phenomenon. Begin by considering how romances are typically presented in literature and in film. What usually happens to the characters? How do the romances of Stella and Stanley and Blanche and her husband or Blanche and her other suitors compare to traditional depictions of romance? Are they similar or do they present another model of failed or subverted romance? If so, why is this significant? Consider the social implications. Do the characters' backgrounds affect their romances? Explain how, using examples from the text to back up your assertions.

2. **Romanticism:** How does Williams's work function as an example of romanticism?

   First you will need to refer to some works that give an overview of the romantic movement. You might begin by defining romanticism in your essay. Some information with respect to its origins will be necessary. Next consider how *A Streetcar Named Desire* functions as a romantic work. Compare elements of the text to some other romantic works. What do they share in common? How are they united in purpose? Do they share similar themes or character types?

## Language, Symbols, and Imagery

Symbols function as architecture; they give form to themes and provide support for the author's ideas. In *A Streetcar Named Desire*, Williams uses light, streetcar names, Belle Reve, and even the characters as symbols. *A Streetcar Named Desire* is also well known for its distinct use of language. Stanley and Blanche, for instance, have very distinct ways of speaking that allow us to realize their differences more easily. An exploration of symbols or language in the play will lead you to a number of good essay topics.

## Sample Topics:

1. **Streetcars:** Consider how Williams uses the streetcars both literally and symbolically. How does Williams use the streetcar names as a link to important themes? Aside from their role in creating a more authentic setting, what do the streetcars represent? Why does Williams use this image?

   You might consider one of the streetcars, for instance Desire or Cemeteries, or you might discuss how the use of the streetcars function together as a whole within the work. What do the streetcars symbolize? Why does Williams choose to have Blanche arrive in New Orleans on a streetcar?

2. **Blanche's wardrobe:** Why is Blanche's wardrobe significant? How does it tie in to the larger concerns of the play?

   Consider our initial impression of Blanche's wardrobe. Is this impression correct? How do Stanley and Stella view her wardrobe? Does the way each character views Blanche's wardrobe, including Blanche, tell us something about their ability to decipher fantasy from illusion? What does Blanche's wardrobe reveal to us about her true character?

3. **Light:** The characters in *A Streetcar Named Desire* have different reactions to light. How does Williams use light as a metaphor to speak to us about truth and the revelation of self?

   Light is a recurring symbol in Williams's works. Consider the uses of light specific to *Streetcar*. In particular it will be useful to consider Blanche's and Stanley's reaction to light. Blanche covers it up and does not want herself to be revealed in strong light, while Stanley prefers strong light and displays a mastery over it, smashing lightbulbs with the heel of a woman's shoe. How do these scenes where Blanche and Stella interact with light act as a metaphor for something greater?

4. **Music:** Analyze Williams's use of music in the play.

If you decide to undertake this topic, you might choose to isolate and discuss one particular use of music—for instance, Blanche's rendition of "Paper Moon"—and its significance within the context of the play. Alternatively, you might compare or contrast two or more different uses of music in the play. Consider the polka that Blanche hears in her head, the jazz being played in the streets, and Blanche's performance of "Paper Moon" in the bathtub. You might also choose to compare or contrast the various uses of music between Williams's works. For instance, how does the use of music in *A Streetcar Named Desire* relate to the use of music in *The Glass Menagerie*?

5. **Bathing:** Why does Williams choose to have Blanche bathing or speaking of bathing so frequently? What symbolic significance might this action have?

Consider each instance where Blanche talks about bathing or is revealed to actually be in the bathtub or off freshening up. Is her preoccupation with bathing cultural—a reference to her manners as a lady? Or should it be accepted as an obsession with a deeper meaning? What else does bathing symbolize?

## Compare and Contrast Essays

In the case of *A Streetcar Named Desire*, comparing and contrasting elements of the work will serve as a very informative process. You could compare the text to a film version of the play, two or more characters in the play, or an element that is used in similar (or different) contexts within the course of the play. These are only a few of the options that are available to you. Be sure to conclude your essay by explaining why any similarities or differences are significant. Your essay should be more than a simple list of what the works share in common or how they differ.

## *Sample Topics:*

1. **The text and the film:** Compare or contrast the reading version of the play with Elia Kazan's famous film adaptation.

   Remember that you do not want to simply provide a list of how the text and the film compare or differ, although that will comprise a major portion of your essay. This explanation of similarities and differences should lead to a larger, more insightful conclusion. If you choose to compare the two, consider how Elia Kazan maintained Williams's vision of the play. If you decide to contrast the two versions, ask yourself not just what is different but why it is different. Why did Elia Kazan choose to make the changes that are evident in the film? Do you believe that they were personal choices or were they dictated by societal constraints and censorship? Or are they a mix of both? Discuss. This might lead you to a larger conversation about censorship issues in literature or about the variation of interpretation of works.

2. **Stella and Blanche:** Compare and contrast these two characters.

   Although Stella and Blanche are sisters, they are very different. Stella seems to have had no problem assimilating to urban life, while Blanche is shocked by it and seems incapable of adapting. The characters also, however, have much in common. Both are greatly impacted by their inability to rein in their desires. Why is this important? You will also wish to compare the fates of the two characters.

3. **Stanley and Blanche:** Compare and contrast these two characters.

   Countless scholars and critics have explored the dynamic interaction between Stanley and Blanche, so begin by considering how your interpretation of the text can bring something new and insightful to this dialogue. You might choose to discuss the differences between the characters and focus on the clash between them, or you might choose to discuss what the characters share in common, but avoid simply making a list of similarities or differences. The focus of your essay should be on why these similarities or differences are important.

## Bibliography and Resources for *A Streetcar Named Desire*

Adler, Thomas P. *A Streetcar Named Desire: The Moth and the Lantern.* Boston: Twayne, 1990.

Bloom, Harold, ed. *A Streetcar Named Desire.* Bloom's Guides. New York: Chelsea House, 2006.

———. *Tennessee Williams's A Streetcar Named Desire.* Modern Critical Interpretations. New York: Chelsea House, 1988.

Cardullo, Bert. "The Blind Mexican Woman in Williams's *A Streetcar Named Desire.*" *Notes on Modern American Literature* 7 (Fall 1983): Item 14.

Crandell, George. "Misrepresentation and Miscegenation: Reading the Racial Discourse of Tennessee Williams's *A Streetcar Named Desire.*" *Modern Drama* 40.3 (1997): 337–46.

Davis, Walter A. *Get the Guests: Psychoanalysis, Modern American Drama and the Audience.* Madison: U of Wisconsin P, 1994.

Foster, Verna. "Desire, Death, and Laughter: Tragicomic Dramaturgy in *A Streetcar Named Desire.*" *American Drama* 9.1 (Fall 1999): 51–68.

Kolin, Philip C. "Cleopatra of the Nile and Blanche DuBois of the French Quarter: Antony and Cleopatra and *A Streetcar Named Desire.*" *Shakespeare Bulletin* 11.1 (Winter 1993): 25–27.

———. *Confronting Tennessee Williams's A Streetcar Named Desire: Essays in Critical Pluralism.* Westport, CT: Greenwood, 1993.

———. "Roland Barthes, Tennessee Williams and *A Streetcar Named Desire/* Pleasure." *Centennial Review* 43 (Spring 1999): 289–304.

———. "*A Streetcar Named Desire.*" *Tennessee Williams: A Guide to Research and Performance.* Ed. Philip C. Kolin. Westport, CT: Greenwood, 1998. 51–79.

Londré, Felicia Hardison. "A Streetcar Running Fifty Years." *Cambridge Companion to Tennessee Williams.* Ed. Matthew C. Roudané. Cambridge: Cambridge UP, 1997. 45–66.

Manvell, Roger. *Theater and Film: A Comparative Study of the Two Forms of Dramatic Art, and of the Problems of Adaptation of Stage Plays into Films.* London: Associated UP, 1979.

Miller, Jordan Y., ed. *Twentieth Century Interpretations of A Streetcar Named Desire: A Collection of Critical Essays.* Englewood Cliffs, NJ: Prentice-Hall, 1971.

Staggs, Sam. *When Blanche Met Brando: The Scandalous Story of 'A Streetcar Named Desire.'* New York: St. Martin's, 2005.

*A Streetcar Named Desire.* Dir. Elia Kazan. DVD. Warner Brothers, 1951.

Van Duyvenbode, Rachel. "Darkness Made Visible: Miscegenation, Masquerade and the Signified Racial Other in Tennessee Williams's *Baby Doll* and *A Streetcar Named Desire.*" *Journal of American Studies* 35.2 (2001): 203–15.

Williams, Tennessee. *A Streetcar Named Desire. Tennessee Williams: Plays 1937–1955.* Eds. Mel Gussow and Kenneth Holditch. New York: Library of America, 2000. 467–64.

———. "A Streetcar Named Success." *New York Times.* 30 Nov. 1947.

# *SUMMER AND SMOKE*

## READING TO WRITE

I N 1948, with the debut of *Summer and Smoke,* Williams presented a work that captured the essence of a major philosophical dilemma—namely, the difficulty of reconciling body and spirit. Using this single theme as your focus, you should be able to come up with countless topics for your own essay. You might choose to anchor your essay to an exploration of how this philosophical topic is reflected in the characters, their interactions, and their development throughout the play. The main characters, John Buchanan, Jr., and Alma Winemiller, are depicted as representatives of the physical and spiritual realms, respectively. Alma, whose name translates to "soul" in Spanish, is a reverend's daughter who resists John's physical advances and trembles when John's knees so much as touch her own. John, meanwhile, is a doctor's son, a wild young man who shuns responsibility and refuses the possibility of anything that cannot be explained away by science. Love seems to be, for him, a biological entity, little more than a chemical reaction, while for Alma love remains, indisputably, a matter of the soul. As we approach the end of the play, the characters are transformed, and each comes to some understanding of their counterpoints, with Alma realizing a sexual awakening and John tapping into his spiritual self, but it is too late; the two have traveled too far to the opposite extreme, leaving no possibility of their uniting in the middle. If you were awestruck by the failure of the characters to find balance and realize their love even after their dramatic transformation, then unrealized love or the danger of extremes could be perfect topics for your essay, with particular attention paid to the ending of the play. *Summer and Smoke* concludes with Alma and John trading roles rather than coming together—a con-clusion that, if it were not so tragic, would come off as farce. The ending of the play should raise some questions that can be used to help you develop ideas for your essay: Why does Williams conclude the play in this fashion? What does the ending tell us about the reconciliation of body and spirit? How does this conclusion relate to the endings of his other plays, and what does it say about larger thematic concerns? Do you think that the play would have had greater success if Alma and John reconciled in the end? As you begin forming answers to these questions, you should be able to settle on an area of focus and begin drafting an outline.

Aside from the matter of the ending of the play, which is perhaps foremost in our minds, the opening of the play can serve as an equally dynamic topic to write about and reflect on. Rather than open the play with John and Alma meeting, or reuniting as the case may be, as adults, Williams chooses to include a prologue in which the characters are introduced to us as children. This prologue, though brief, possesses dramatic depth of purpose, and from it one should be able to extract countless topics for exposition. For instance, the scene that follows, which might appear to be a playful take on the impish young boy tug-ging at a young girl's ponytail, is actually one of the most revelatory scenes of the play, for it introduces the primary concerns of this work, while giving us tremendous insight into Williams's own development as a writer. Once you have gone back to the text with these ideas in mind and have formed your own conclusions, either of these subjects— the primary thematic concerns of *Summer and Smoke* or what the play reveals about Williams's development as a writer—could be developed into the central topic of your essay. Remember that the prologue is only a place to start, and you will need to draw connections between the significance of the passages you are discussing in the prologue and the rest of the text. Consider the start of the prologue. First, the passage introduces us to both John and Alma:

> *In the park near the angel of the fountain. At dusk of an evening in May,*
> *in the first few years of this Century.*
> *Alma, as a child of ten, comes into the scene. She wears a middy blouse*
> *and has ribboned braids. She already has the dignity of an adult; there is*

*a quality of extraordinary delicacy and tenderness or spirituality in her,*
*which must set her distinctly apart from other children. She has a habit of*
*holding her hands, one cupped under the other in a way similar to that of*
*receiving the wafer at Holy Communion. This is a habit that will remain*
*with her as an adult. She stands like that in front of the stone angel for a*
*few moments; then bends to drink at the fountain.*

*While she is bent at the fountain, John, as a child, enters. He shoots a*
*peashooter at Alma's bent-over back. She utters a startled cry and whirls*
*about. He laughs. (571)*

Here Alma debuts as a refined, spiritual being beyond her years, while
this single action from John paints a picture of a carefree imp who could
not be more opposite his scene-mate. Once the matter of becoming
acquainted with the main characters is taken care of, the prologue introduces us to the central theme of the play—the difficulty of reconciling
body and spirit. It is not coincidental that it is here in the prologue where
Williams both first presents the angel Eternity that will maintain a con-
sistent presence throughout the play and where Williams first reveals
Alma's and John's positions on matters of body and spirit:

**ALMA.** Do you know the name of the angel?

**JOHN.** Does she have a name?

**ALMA.** Yes, I found out she does. It's carved in the base, but it's all worn
away so you can't make it out with your eyes.

**JOHN.** Then how do you know it?

**ALMA.** You have to read it with your fingers. I did and it gave me cold
shivers! Go on! Read it with your fingers! . . .

*John grins indulgently and turns to the pediment, crouching before it and*
*running his fingers along the worn inscription. . . .*

**JOHN.** Eternity?

**ALMA.** *Eternity!*—Didn't it give you the cold shivers?

**JOHN.** Nahh.

**ALMA.** Well, it did me!

**JOHN.** Because you're a preacher's daughter. Eternity. What is eternity?

**ALMA.** (*in a hushed wondering voice*). It's something that goes on and on when life and death and time and everything else is all through with.

**JOHN.** There's no such thing. (573)

By becoming acquainted with the past selves of the main characters and their most intimate thoughts, we are exposed to what we can be certain is their true nature. This affirmation that their views on body and spirit were ingrained even as children makes their ultimate transformations that much more spectacular and also lends much greater significance to their few meetings as adults. Already there is more than enough information stemming from the prologue to start you on your way to a number of interesting essays focusing on theme, character, or symbolism as a point of takeoff.

For those who may be interested in considering *Summer and Smoke* from a wider perspective, within the context of the whole of Williams's oeuvre, for instance, there are other notable attributes of the prologue to consider. For example, careful readers will note that Alma and John's initial meeting and discussion from the prologue are essentially duplicated later in the play. When Alma and John reconvene as adults, John gets Alma's attention not with a peashooter but with a firecracker; he throws one in Alma's direction, and when he pretends to come to her aid, they have the following conversation:

**ALMA.** You're planning to stay here and take over some of your father's medical practice?

**JOHN.** I haven't made my mind up about anything yet. . . .

**ALMA.** . . . And bacteriology—isn't that something you do with a microscope?

**JOHN.** Well, partly. . . .

**ALMA.** I've looked through a telescope, but never a microscope. What . . . what do you—see?

**JOHN.** A universe, Miss Alma.

**ALMA.** What kind of a universe?

**JOHN.** Pretty much the same kind that you saw through the lens of a telescope—a mysterious one. . . .

**ALMA.** Oh, yes. . . .

**JOHN.** Part anarchy—and part order!

**ALMA.** The footprints of God!

**JOHN.** But not God. (580–81)

Although the repetition of Alma and John's meeting and the repetition of the revelation of their contrasting views on science and spirituality is certainly not the first instance of duplication in Williams's work, following *Summer and Smoke*, the process of duplicating actions and dialogue would become more prominent in Williams's plays, becoming an undeniable part of the composition of his next major work, *The Rose Tattoo*. The repetition of action and dialogue in *Summer and Smoke*, and in Williams's other works, would not only compel readers to take notice of the underlying meaning of particular scenes, it would also make his readers more conscious of the passage of time—a major theme of Williams's works and, notably, a major challenge for the characters in most of Williams's plays. This effect of duplication would also tie in with the more immediate concerns of Williams's work. Within the context of *Summer and Smoke*, duplication would serve as reinforcement for the concept of the doppelganger, which is introduced to us with some sarcasm by John later in the play. Duplication would also serve as a variation of Williams's treatment of pairs—child and parent, husband and wife, doctor and reverend—which would also become more prominent as Williams turned to an exploration of paradoxes in his next few works. Therefore, this concept of duplication as a literary device could be explored in your essay within the limited context of this one play or within the context of Williams's entire body of work. These are just some of the ideas for essay topics that could result from a close reading of the prologue.

If you feel overwhelmed by a text such as *Summer and Smoke* that takes a philosophical or ethical dilemma as its primary focus, try approaching the work from a slightly more external perspective. Consider, for example, how others envisioned and understood the text. In other words, explore the critical reception of the work. Consider how it was received by both critics and popular audiences. Was it well received? If not, where does the work's failure lie? Remember not to simply focus on whether or not a work was popular; explore why the work received the reception that it did. This will demand, again, that you focus on an inspection of the formal elements of the text, but taking this approach means that you will be examining the text armed with some opinions about the text that you can then set out to support or refute. In other words, other people's criticism or praise will provide some direction, a starting point, for your own exploration of the text. *Summer and Smoke* was not Williams's most popular work; it failed to garner the same success as *A Streetcar Named Desire,* and the loftiness of its concerns and the suggested narrowness of its thematic range made it a poor candidate for popular entertainment. Writers who are interested in the critical reception of the work should avoid presenting a recap of the criticism itself and focus on the significance of how the work was received. If it was poorly received, was its reception the result of problems with the formal elements of the text? Or are societal or cultural factors to blame? If you choose the latter, this will allow you to focus on historical and contextual elements of the text. Consider when the work was written and what issues were prevalent at that time. How would this have shaped people's perception of the work? Would the reception of the work be different today? In the case of *Summer and Smoke,* you might also choose to consider Williams's own criticism of the play. After all, Williams chose to revise *Summer and Smoke,* reworking it and presenting it as *The Eccentricities of a Nightingale* some years later. This should raise questions for readers—why did Williams feel it was important to revise the text? What changes were made to the work and why? Is the text better served by these changes? And, finally, what does this revision reveal about the process of Williams's work? An answer to any of these questions, supported by examples from the text, could become the base of your essay.

It is important to note that, while *Summer and Smoke* may not have achieved critical success, it allowed Williams to reach beyond his own lexicon as a writer. In addition to allowing Williams to experiment with duplication, the farcical elements of the text—the young John shooting Alma while she is bent over, the adult John throwing firecrackers in Alma's direction, the over-the-top Rosa Gonzales, and the dopey Roger Doremus—also foreshadowed another turn in Williams's work—namely, the injection of comical elements into tragedy, the beginning of the use of a mixed genre form in Williams's plays that would find its true realization in the playwright's next major work, *The Rose Tattoo.* This topic would allow you to write about a less-explored aspect of *Summer and Smoke*: its heavy influence on Williams's future work. Perhaps, you would argue that the writing of *Summer and Smoke* was a turning point in Williams's development as a writer. On the other hand, you might argue that, while the text did allow Williams to change the course of his style, it was the beginning of a downward trend in the quality of his work, because it was a departure from those elements that made his work successful. No matter your opinion, either of these topics could make fine essays as long as you use the text to support your argument.

## TOPICS AND STRATEGIES

In the sections that follow, you will find a variety of suggested topics accompanied by questions and observations to assist you in the task of writing successfully about *Summer and Smoke.* Remember that this is not a comprehensive list of topics, and the statements and questions that appear after each suggested topic are merely a guide to help spark your own ideas about the work. A successful paper will present a strong thesis based upon your own original ideas and will be supported by relevant examples resulting from close readings of the text. A wide variety of interpretations will be possible as you consider each topic. Use the strategic questions and observations to stimulate your own thoughts about the text and to assist you in developing a strong thesis. Remember to read through the text more than once, making note of those elements of the text that support your argument. It will be equally important to make note of those elements that contradict your thesis, as this will help you to refine your argument and create a stronger case.

## Themes

As indicated above, the major theme of *Summer and Smoke*—the problem of the reconciliation of body and spirit—is a philosophical matter. This means that if you choose to write about this topic you will be working with abstract ideas. Consider how Williams gives shape to these abstract ideas through his use of symbolism and characters and through the action revealed in the plot. How do his settings also tie in to this theme? And does the structure of the play give us any information about this theme? In fact, how Williams gives form to abstract ideas in *Summer and Smoke* or in his plays at large could be a successful essay topic itself, but it will require a thorough exploration of all of the formal elements of the work.

Recalling our discussion of ways to address the thematic concerns of the text, another approach might be to consider and respond to the following: Critics have frequently commented on the narrowness of the thematic range of *Summer and Smoke*. It has been cited as one of the major flaws of the work. Paired with the absence of any redemptive closure between Alma and John, many fail to relate to or enjoy the work. While Williams's earlier plays such as *The Glass Menagerie* and *A Streetcar Named Desire* have prominent central themes that serve as a bridge to a myriad of other thematic concerns, some would contend that *Summer and Smoke* remains idle, stuck on a single philosophical issue that fails to resonate with readers and viewers because it is so constricting and because it provides no redemptive closure. In previous chapters, we addressed how to approach works with limited physical action or minimalistic plots such as *The Glass*

*Menagerie. Summer and Smoke* provides the opportunity to consider how to write about a work that has sufficient action but limited thematic concerns. An explanation of your viewpoint on the matter of the allegations mentioned at the beginning of this paragraph can serve as the start of a good essay. Use the suggestions below to formulate your own ideas about this issue. Is a focus on a single theme inherently problematic for a work of literature? Depending upon your opinion, you might compare *Summer and Smoke* to another work of literature that seems to support this notion or that refutes this point.

## Sample Topic:

1. **Reconciling spirituality and physical desire:** *Summer and Smoke* seems to revolve around the interplay between Alma and John as representatives of the physical and spiritual realms. Is it fair to assert that the play is an allegory about the challenge of reconciling spirit and body? Or does this kind of categorization go too far?

   If you agree with the notion that the play can be classified as an allegory about the challenge of reconciling body and spirit, explain why. How does the conflict between the characters represent a universal concern? Consider how Williams presents this philosophical dilemma. You will also need to consider if the work has other thematic concerns. If so, are they unique or are they simply variations of the aforementioned theme? If you believe that they are variations of the single theme noted above, explain whether this works to Williams's advantage or not. How does the focus on a single theme serve the work? Alternatively, you might argue how it betrays the work by isolating readers. In this instance you will want to use examples from the text (or other texts) to show how the work would be better served by presenting a wider range of themes.

## Character

Although an analysis of the individual characters in a work functions as a kind of go-to, no-fail option when choosing an essay topic, *Summer and Smoke* presents some other good options. The play presents an interesting connection between each of the characters and their parents. Consider Alma's relationship to her father, Reverend Winemiller, or John's relationship to his father, Doctor Buchanan. What about the issue of the main characters' relationship to their mothers? Alma's mother has had a nervous breakdown, and the family sees her as their cross to bear, while John has grown up without a mother, as the prologue reveals that his mother has been dead for some time. Aside from the main characters, this topic could extend to characters like Nellie Ewell, whose mother is known as a merry widow, and Rosa Gonzales, whose father owns the Moon Lake Casino. If this topic interests you, you could compare the relationships of the parents and their children in *Summer and Smoke* to the parent-child relationships evidenced in Williams's other works such as *The Glass Menagerie* or *The Rose Tattoo.* How do the characters' relationships with their parents affect their own development or hinder their development? Why does Williams put so much emphasis on these relationships in *Summer and Smoke* and his other works? Are the sons and daughters very different from their parents? Or does Williams create parallels between them as individuals? How does this create a link between past and present? What information is revealed through these relationships that we might not have access to otherwise? Any of these topics could be utilized to create a strong and interesting essay.

## Sample Topics:

1. **Alma Winemiller:** Analyze this character.

   Consider how Williams presents Alma. What significance does her name have? And what about her gestures and her personality? What are her strongest character traits? How does she change throughout the play? What is it that compels her to change? Are these changes good or bad?

2. **John Buchanan, Jr.:** When John reappears as an adult, he is introduced as a Promethean character. What does Williams mean by this and why is it an important description?

   Prometheus was a Titan deity in Greek mythology who stole fire from Zeus and gave it to the mortals. First you will need to refer to some versions of the original Prometheus myth to become acquainted with the nuances of this myth and explore Prometheus's character. What traits does John share with Prometheus? Where do their characters diverge?

The figure of Prometheus was also frequently appropriated in the literature of the romantic period during the 18th and early 19th centuries. Therefore, an examination of this topic might allow you to segue into an essay on how John functions as a romantic character, or how John serves as an example of the resurrected Prometheus myth in literature. If you choose to explore this, consider why the Prometheus myth has been retold so many times. What does John, in particular, bring to this role?

3. **Nellie Ewell:** Of all of the female characters presented in the play, why do you think that Nellie Ewell ultimately wins John's heart?

In order to answer this question, it will be necessary to compare Nellie to the other female contenders for John's heart, such as Alma and Rosa Gonzales. What traits separate Nellie from the other women? Why is this desirable? Alternatively, what does she share in common with these women?

4. **Rosa Gonzales:** Analyze this character.

Consider Williams's presentation of Rosa. Why does she wear feathers and jewels? What image is Williams trying to create? What purpose does Rosa serve in the play? Do we learn anything about the other characters by her presence that we might not otherwise know? What about her personality? Are we able to get a sense of her true character or do we learn anything intimate about her? In other words, should Rosa be considered a flat character or a round character? If she is a flat character, what is her function in the play and what does she represent?

## History and Context

Despite writing the play during the 1940s, Williams chose to set the play at the turn of century. This setting allowed Williams to work comfortably with themes such as love and sexuality and to address the myth of hysteria or mental illness as a female condition. These issues, which biographical (and autobiographical) sources show were important concerns in Williams's own life, also happened to be prominent issues at the turn of the century. You might choose to write about these issues from a biographical standpoint. How did Williams's own life inform his treatment of these topics? As you consider how these topics were perceived at the turn of the century, consider how our views on these topics have changed today.

## Sample Topics:

1. **Hysteria and mental illness as female conditions:** Is it fair to say that the play presents hysteria and mental illness as distinctly female conditions? If so, what do you believe Williams's intentions were for presenting this idea in *Summer and Smoke*?

   First you will need to refer to the text and consider if there are any instances where hysteria or mental instability are applied to a male character. If not, consider why Williams limited this affliction to his female characters. If so, is Williams's work condoning this view or condemning it? Consider Williams's real-life experiences with mental illness and the treatment of mental illness as experienced in the case of Williams's sister, Rose. Are the female characters truly mentally unstable or is their condition really due to some other affliction? How does John's diagnosis of Alma present us with another view of what might really be plaguing these women?

2. **New ideas of love and sexuality:** Were the notions of love and sexuality presented in the play realistic for the time period the play is set in? Or are they more contemporary models applied to a historical setting?

   You might choose to consider how the notions of love and sexuality in *Summer and Smoke* compare to those presented in literature written at the turn of the century. Choose a work written at the beginning of the 20th century. Are the models of love and romance in this work similar to those presented in *Summer and*

*Smoke*? How do they differ? Do not simply state the similarities and differences. Explain why these factors are significant.

## Philosophy and Ideas

In addition to its presentation of the problem of the reconciliation of body and spirit, Williams's play also dabbles in other abstract concepts, such as the ethical dilemma of responsibility versus self-satisfaction and fulfillment, and the notion of the doppelganger. As discussed above, consider how Williams uses the formal elements of the text to give shape to these abstract ideas.

### Sample Topics:

1. **Responsibility versus self-satisfaction:** What message does *Summer and Smoke* promote when it comes to responsibility versus self-satisfaction? Is one more important or more dominant than the other?

   Consider instances in the text where characters are forced to choose between being responsible or choosing some form of self-satisfaction. What do they choose and what are the consequences of these decisions? Do these consequences form a general statement about which is dominant over the other? Can the two be reconciled, or does self-satisfaction necessarily require the abandonment in some way of responsibility? Likewise, does being responsible mean repressing one's own desires and needs? Whatever your view, explain how the characters evidence this.

2. **Doppelganger:** Why does John tell Alma that she has a doppelganger? What does he mean by this?

   Revisit the passage where John "diagnoses" Alma with a doppelganger. Begin by giving some definition to this term. Do not simply rely on the explanation given in the text. You will need to consult some reliable reference books such as *Merriam-Webster's Collegiate Dictionary* and the *Oxford English Dictionary*, which define this word. You may find that the definitions vary slightly, with some sources indicating that the concept of a doppelganger is a supernatural phenomenon, while others approach it from a psychological point of view. One idea for your essay might be to consider the various interpretations or definitions of this term and present your argument as to which definition John had in mind when he diagnosed Alma. Is Alma's reaction to the diagnosis significant? Do you believe that Alma interprets the concept of the doppelganger in the same way that John does?

You might also give consideration to the idea of a doppelganger as a catalyst for discussion of issues of identity. How well do the characters know themselves? Do they have other selves that they are not fully aware of? Does John's ability to diagnose Alma with this condition indicate that he has a greater sense of self-awareness?

3. **Anarchy versus order:** Williams addresses the notion of anarchy versus order literally within the dialogue and also uses it as a motif within the play. Why is anarchy-versus-order an important motif? Does the play present the view that one ultimately rules over the other?

First, consider the dialogue between Alma and John that refers to this concept. How is this idea reflected more generally in the play? Consider plot, setting, and symbolism. Is Williams's treatment of this dichotomy evenhanded? Consider how various elements of the text would fall under either heading. Is one of these elements ultimately dominant?

## Form and Genre

The form of *Summer and Smoke* provides an example of how a play's structure can support its greater themes, and this single topic can provide a good start to an essay on the significance of form as it pertains to *Summer and Smoke*. Williams breaks the play down into two acts. The first takes place in the summer, and the second takes place in the winter. The seasons mimic the inner states of the characters. This use of seasons and weather to create atmosphere and give us further insight into the characters can also be evidenced in Williams's other works. For example, you might choose to write an essay that compares the use of seasons and weather in *Summer and Smoke* to the use of weather and seasons in *The Glass Menagerie* to shape the work. Why is this link between the characters and the natural world important? Could this be considered a romantic notion?

## *Sample Topics:*

1. **Structure:** Williams breaks the play down into two parts, one that takes place in the summer and one that takes place in the winter. Why are these seasons significant and how does the form of the play reflect the key aspects of the story?

   Examine the structure of the play. Think generally about what we associate with each season. How does this tie in to the action that takes place in each section? How do the seasons serve as metaphors for the state of the characters in each section? Consider how the two acts also signal change and a passage of time.

2. **Evolution of the work:** Several years after its publication and production, Williams revised *Summer and Smoke* and rereleased it as *The Eccentricities of a Nightingale.* How do the two works differ, and why do you believe Williams wanted to revise *Summer and Smoke*? Explain which version you think is more successful and why.

   Begin by considering the changes that Williams made to the play. Remember to consider all of the formal elements of the text rather than simply noting changes to plot. Next you will want to make some assertions about why you believe Williams made these choices. How do the changes help or hinder our ability to relate to and understand the play?

## Language, Symbols, and Imagery

If you are unsure of what the important symbols of a work are, try to locate imagery that is repeated throughout the work. Often this is a good indicator of what is most significant. In *Summer and Smoke* there are many images that are carried throughout the work, such as the angel, the sky, birds, and smoke, and any of these symbols could be a point of exploration for your essay.

## Sample Topics:

1. **Setting:** Williams chooses to have the major portions of the play take place either at the rectory or at the doctor's office, but some scenes also take place at the arbor and the fountain. Why does Williams employ these sites and how do they function symbolically?

   The rectory and the doctor's office serve as symbols of the spiritual realm and the physical realm, just as Alma and John serve as representatives of these realms. Meanwhile, the arbor and the fountain are natural sites, and there the spiritual and the physical can be reconciled. The concept of the reconciliation of the physical and the spiritual through nature is a key theme in works of the romantic period. Consider the actions that take place at each site. Why does Williams set them accordingly? What relevance do these sites have?

2. **Big sky:** In Williams's production notes he emphasizes the importance of the sky as part of the set. Why is this so? What great significance does the sky hold in *Summer and Smoke*?

   Consider the sky in its various contexts, both literal and symbolic—as a source of weather and as a symbol of a spiritual realm. The sky is also frequently equated with flying and with freedom. Like the arbor and the fountain, it could be considered the bridge between two realms. Now consider all instances where the sky is referenced in the text. Why is its constant presence relevant? What should it remind us of?

3. **Chart of anatomy:** This particular symbol was once adopted for the play's working title before it was renamed *Summer and Smoke*. What is the significance of the chart of anatomy?

Consider any scenes in the play where this chart of anatomy is referenced. Does it hold any symbolic significance? Do we associate the chart of anatomy with any particular character or theme?

4. **Angel:** The image of the angel at the fountain is repeated throughout the play, and Williams is careful to make sure that it is visible during key scenes. Why? What does the angel represent and how does this tie in with the thematic concerns of the play?

Begin by considering the scene where the angel debuts and the other scenes where the angel is present. What does the angel represent? Why does Williams choose to name it Eternity? What significance does this have? Consider the characters' responses to this name. How does this symbol tie in with the greater theme of the work?

5. **Birds:** Williams uses the imagery of birds and plumage throughout the play. Why is Williams preoccupied with birds as symbols in this work?

Consider all the instances of Williams's use of birds or bird-related imagery in the play. Alma is often compared to a nightingale, while Roger Doremus is likened to a sparrow. What does this metaphor tell us about each character? Rosa is described as being decked out in feathers, while Mrs. Winemiller steals a hat with a plume and hides it. How does Williams also utilize the concept of the bird metaphorically—for instance, where does he present the metaphor of the caged bird?

6. **Smoke:** The title contains the image of smoke, imagery that is also present in the play. What does smoke signify and why did Williams choose this as a symbol?

You will need to examine any scenes in the play that reference smoke. Who speaks of smoke and in what context is it spoken of? What do we associate with smoke, and how does this tie in to Williams's own use of smoke as a symbol and his treatment of theme?

# Compare and Contrast Essays

*Summer and Smoke* provides countless options for compare and contrast essays. You can begin by modifying some of the topics addressed in other sections. For example, instead of examining the relationships between parent and child, you could actually compare and contrast a character with one of their parents. You might also find that it is easy to note similarities or glaring differences between the characters in *Summer and Smoke* and those in Williams's other plays. The play also shares thematic concerns and symbolism found in other works. Your essay might focus on one of these elements or might treat the subjects more broadly. What can we learn by studying these similarities and differences?

## Sample Topics:

1. **Mrs. Winemiller and Blanche:** Compare and contrast Mrs. Winemiller and Blanche DuBois of *A Streetcar Named Desire*.

    Begin by considering what these two characters have in common. Why are their commonalities significant? How are they different? Consider their full characters, including their ways of speaking and their mannerisms. Do they suffer from the same affliction? Consider, for instance, how both characters revert to an irretrievable past.

2. **Alma and her mother:** Are Alma and her mother so different as we are led to believe, or is it possible that Alma's mother is in some way her doppelganger?

    Consider Williams's references to Alma's lost childhood and Mrs. Winemiller's regression to a childlike state. Mrs. Winemiller often mimics Alma, but is it also true that she sometimes says those things that Alma seems incapable of saying? Likewise, is it possible to see some of her mother's flaws in Alma at times?

3. **Alma and Laura from *The Glass Menagerie*:** Compare and contrast these two characters.

    Consider how Williams presents these two characters to us. What methods does he use? Consider not only their physical similarities, but also the similarities between the inner selves of the two characters. How do they evolve throughout the plays? What is their response to love and romance?

4. *Summer and Smoke, The Glass Menagerie,* and *A Streetcar Named Desire* as a trilogy: These three plays are often grouped together as a southern trilogy. Is it accurate to link them thus? Or is this classification problematic?

If you believe that the three plays can be classified accurately as a trilogy, explain why. You will need to reference commonalities in the texts. What unites the works? Do they share a common theme or message? Are the characters similar or the plots? If you believe this is a faulty classification, explain why by contrasting the plays. Are the differences mechanical, thematic, or both?

## Bibliography and Resources for *Summer and Smoke*

Adler, Thomas P. "Before the Fall—and After: *Summer and Smoke* and *The Night of the Iguana.*" *Cambridge Companion to Tennessee Williams.* Ed. Matthew C. Roudané. Cambridge: Cambridge UP, 1997. 114–27.

Brooking, Jack. "Directing *Summer and Smoke*: An Existential Approach." *Modern Drama* II (1960): 377–85.

*The Eccentricities of a Nightingale.* Dir. Glenn Jordan. 1976. DVD. Kultur Video, 2002.

Kramer, Richard E. "*Summer and Smoke* and *The Eccentricities of a Nightingale.*" *Tennessee Williams: A Guide to Research and Performance.* Ed. Philip C. Kolin. Westport, CT: Greenwood, 1998. 80–89.

Speidel, Susan. "Paper Mill Playhouse Education and Outreach Study Guide: Summer and Smoke." 12 Dec. 2008. <http://www.papermill.org/_media/outreach/SUMMER%20AND%20SMOKE%20sg.pdf>.

*Summer and Smoke.* Dir. Peter Glenville. 1962. VHS. Paramount, 1998.

Williams, Tennessee. *The Eccentricities of a Nightingale.* New York: Dramatist's Play Service, 1998.

———. *Summer and Smoke. Tennessee Williams: Plays 1937–1955.* Eds. Mel Gussow and Kenneth Holditch. New York: Library of America, 2000. 565–643.

# THE ROSE TATTOO

## READING TO WRITE

A LTHOUGH *THE Rose Tattoo* possesses many of those same qualities that are attributable to the whole of Williams's work, including a treatment of existential themes, a southern setting, and dynamic
round characters who serve as representatives of a diverse, struggling
working class, the play, which debuted in 1951 and was adapted for film
in 1955, represented a significant departure from Williams's previous
work. Readers who are acquainted with Williams's earlier plays such as
*The Glass Menagerie* and *A Streetcar Named Desire* may be surprised
by the tone of *The Rose Tattoo*, which strays from the serious, sad voice
of tragic realism that dominated his earlier works and moves in the
direction of comedy. Do not be daunted by this change in tone. As you
prepare to write about a semicomic play like *The Rose Tattoo*, you can
apply the same tactics that you would apply when writing about any
tragedy. In fact, a work's most distinguishing characteristics—those
traits that separate it from the rest of an author's oeuvre—often serve
as captivating essay topics.

As you consider what to write about *The Rose Tattoo*, or any text
that diverges from an author's conventional repertoire, a good way to
begin is by looking for motifs. Motifs are simply elements that recur
throughout the text. A motif can be a trait that is accentuated in a
character through repetition or a trait that is duplicated in more than
one character. It could be a certain repeated use of color, light, or
music; or it might be an image that surfaces and resurfaces throughout
the text. Observing these repetitions in the text will provide you with
some sense of what is significant information, allowing you to zero in

on those items that the author wanted us to take notice of. To better understand this concept, let us consider some examples of well-known motifs from Williams's other plays. In *The Glass Menagerie*, for instance, the symbol of glass is used generously throughout the text. We recognize glass as a symbol of fragility and transparency, and we are aware of its properties of reflection and diffraction of light. Next, take what you know about this motif and ask yourself how these concepts relate to the text. In the case of *The Glass Menagerie*, we know that the characters, particularly Laura, seem to be quite fragile. Transparency could be, for instance, a symbol of our ability to see into the inner selves of the characters. Finally, the relationship of glass and light could be symbolic of a number of things—the inner light of the characters, truth, and even illusion, if we consider the distorting effects of a prism. In other words, when motifs are considered as metaphors, these associations reveal important information about the true nature of the characters and help us to recognize the central themes of the play. The motif can also help to create a sense of atmosphere that enhances our recognition and understanding of these themes. In *A Streetcar Named Desire*, the same is true of desire, although in this instance the motif consists of the repeated suggestion of a more abstract notion, which is suggested quietly via symbolism but which is also presented much more forcefully in the revelation of the relationships between the characters and in the dynamic action of the plot. Like the motif of glass in *The Glass Menagerie*, the repeated reference to desire reveals information about the characters and the central themes of the play. These two examples also reveal another helpful hint. *The Glass Menagerie* and *A Streetcar Named Desire* both demonstrate how one might begin by referring to the title of a work for assistance in identifying important motifs. In the case of both of these plays, the title references a key motif, which can then be explored more fully by considering its presence in the text. In the case of *The Rose Tattoo*, the title presents us with the image of the rose. When paired with the image of the tattoo, the rose becomes something that is marked on the body and something indelible. We can loosely conclude that the rose is symbolic then of something that is a part of us. With these observations from the title in mind, you should move on to the text, keeping in mind the following question: Why is the image of the rose so important that Williams chose to incorporate it in the title of the play? The text will provide you with an answer to this question.

In the first act, we are introduced to Serafina, and Williams presents us with the following image:

> Serafina looks like a plump little Italian opera singer in the role of Madame Butterfly. Her black hair is done in a high pompadour that glitters like wet coal. A rose is held in place by glittering jet hairpins. Her voluptuous figure is sheathed in pale rose silk. On her feet are dainty slippers with glittering buckles and French heels. It is apparent from the way she sits, with such plump dignity, that she is wearing a tight girdle. She sits very erect, in an attitude of forced composure, her ankles daintily crossed and her plump little hands holding a yellow paper fan on which is painted a rose. Jewels gleam on her fingers, her wrists and her ears and about her throat. Expectancy shines in her eyes. (657)

A careful reader will note that the image of the rose has appeared several times within a single paragraph. This passage does not yet give us enough information to decipher what meaning the rose has in the context of the play, but it confirms that the rose is a prominent and important symbol. Of course, as we proceed with the text, we can confirm that the rose is, in fact, the most prominent symbol in *The Rose Tattoo*. It is repeated obsessively not just in this one passage but throughout the entirety of the play. At this point you will need to consider all other instances where the symbol appears after its initial introduction in the title and in the paragraph containing Serafina's debut. As you think about what, specifically, you want to assert about the use of a rose as a symbol in your essay, consider where the symbol appears and how it is used in the text. What is the rose associated with and who is it associated with? Close readings of these passages will provide you with enough information to begin speculating about the symbolic meaning of the rose in this play. For example, in the first scene where Serafina talks with Assunta as she awaits her husband's return, the following exchange takes place:

> **SERAFINA.** Senti! That night I woke up with a burning pain on me, here, on my left breast! A pain like a needle, quick, quick, hot little stitches.

> I turned on the light, I uncovered my breast!—On it I saw the rose
> tattoo of my husband!
>
> **ASSUNTA.** Rosario's tattoo?
>
> **SERAFINA.** On me, my breast, his tattoo! And when I saw it I knew I had
>     conceived . . . (659)

The passage reveals that Serafina's husband has a rose tattooed on his body. From this we can draw the conclusion that the rose is not simply linked to females; it is attributable to males as well. This allows us to hypothesize that the rose functions in the play as more than a simple symbol of femininity or female sexuality. In fact, a close reading of the text reveals that the rose is linked to many of the characters in the play—Serafina, Rosario, Rosa, Alvaro, and even Estelle. From here you might extrapolate that the rose is associated with something universal, perhaps a basic part of human nature. Furthermore, in this passage the rose is depicted as a symbol of fertility; Serafina recognizes it as a sign of her conception. This use of the rose is duplicated later in the text when Serafina talks again about her pregnancy, telling us that "in [her] body another rose was growing" (659). Here the rose becomes a symbol of life. These are just a few examples of the use of a single symbol. When Estelle Hohengarten arrives, the rose is used in other contexts. She sees Rosa and calls her a "twig off the old rose-bush" (662); she presents Serafina with a piece of rose-colored silk; and when she learns that Rosario has died, she shows up to view the body holding a bouquet of roses. By examining passages like these, you should be able to make further judgments about what the rose symbolizes. Does it have a single meaning or is its significance more widespread?

The overabundant use of the rose as a symbol in *The Rose Tattoo* should also inspire some other questions: Why did Williams repeat the symbol so frequently? Was his overuse of the symbol intentional? What effect does this have on us as readers? Certainly, the great consensus is that Williams knowingly chose to repeat the symbol of the rose. When you think about why this is, you might ask yourself what effect this intense repetition has on the overall tone of the play. You may note that the overabundant presence of the rose in the text creates a sense of the absurd; it becomes ridiculous. The rose is used to signify emotion. It is used to indicate color and texture and to suggest a quality of light. It appears as a scent in the form of hair oil (used by men), and it even appears plainly as the flower itself, singly in the hair of the young class-mates of Rosa and as a bouquet tossed to the ground. It is also dupli-cated in the names of two significant characters: Rosa Delle Rose and her father Rosario Delle Rose. If, upon closer inspection, you agree that Williams's use of the rose in the text creates a sense of the absurd, this might lead you to an exploration, for instance, of one of the most dis-tinguishing characteristics of the text—the semicomedic or tragicomic tone. In this instance, the repetition of the rose could be the central focus of your paper, or you might choose to write about the symbolic use of the rose as just one example of an element employed by Wil-liams to create a semicomical or tragicomic atmosphere built upon the repetition of absurdities and farce. If you find that this second option is most appealing to you, you might begin looking for other elements in the play that indicate farce, studying, for example, the fight scenes between Serafina and the priest or Serafina, Bessie, and Flora; the chase scene between Alvaro and Serafina; the indication of clownlike char-acters such as Alvaro Mangiacavallo, Bessie, and Flora; or Serafina's pursuit of the goat. You will also want to make note of where Williams instructs that a scene "should be played with the pantomimic lightness . . . of an early Chaplin comedy" (733). Another consideration is Wil-liams's absurd stereotypical treatment of Italians in the play. Exploring these elements might bring you to a discussion of how the tone serves the greater themes of the work or how it indicates a departure from Williams's past work and why this is significant.

Keep in mind, however, that an element does not need to be repeated endlessly or referred to as overtly as the rose to be a worthy subject for your paper. You might consider, alternatively, to focus on a more abstract or philosophical concept—one that is not laid out literally but that is revealed to us in the formal elements of the text. For instance, as you look for motifs in *The Rose Tattoo,* you may note that Williams references time as a key subject. The passage of time (and one's abil-ity to come to terms with it) is undoubtedly a central theme of *The Rose Tattoo,* and this theme surfaces in many of Williams's other works as well. With this motif in mind, you will want to refer back to the text, as we did above, revisiting passages that reference this subject in some way. Any one of Williams's symbols of the passage of time could serve as the primary subject for your essay, or you might choose to explore the symbols as a whole. For one, there is Serafina's gift to her daughter—a wristwatch, which she is planning to give Rosa upon her graduation. Consider also important scenes, such as the scene where Serafina attempts to dress herself for her daughter's graduation: "She snatches a long-neglected girdle out of a bureau drawer and holds it experimentally about her waist. She shakes her head doubtfully, drops the girdle. . . . She gasps with astonishment when she catches sight of herself . . . snatches a girlish frock off a dummy. . . . But she discovers it won't fit over her hips" (675). This scene is much more than the depiction of a woman's trouble finding the right outfit. It is symbolic of her realization of the loss of her youth. In addition to this revelation, Williams also references the life cycle throughout *The Rose Tattoo* by pairing opposites, such as children and adults and the dummy in bridal garb and the dummy in widow's clothes. Close readings of the play also reveal that the play begins with death and ends with the suggestion of new life. Consider also how Williams uses Rosa to address this theme, providing a counterpoint to the aging Serafina or how the play presents Rosa's graduation as well as her coming-of-age.

Ultimately, you may want to ask yourself what Williams is saying about the passage of time and our relationship to time. Williams himself suggested that the artist can surmount time through his or her creation of works of art. How is this sentiment paralleled in the play? Look at the following passage where Rosa talks about the relationship of love and time. She says, "No, the clock is a fool. I don't listen to it. My clock is my heart and my heart don't say tick-tick, it says love-love! And now I have two hearts in me, both of them saying love-love!" (661). You might use this passage to show how the play suggests that love can allow us to surmount or survive the passage of time.

These are just a few examples of how to begin an essay by recognizing and exploring motifs. These motifs will reveal the text's most important features and most distinguishing characteristics. Be vigilant of repetition, as it is an indicator of what is most significant in the text. This holds true not only for Williams's work or for a particular genre but for any work of literature.

# TOPICS AND STRATEGIES

In the sections that follow, you will find a variety of suggested topics accompanied by questions and observations to assist you in the task of writing successfully about *The Rose Tattoo*. Remember that this is not a comprehensive list of topics, and the statements and questions that appear after each suggested topic are merely a guide to help spark your own ideas about the work. A successful paper will present a strong thesis based upon your own original ideas and will be supported by relevant examples resulting from close readings of the text. A wide variety of interpretations will be possible as you consider each topic. Use the strategic questions and observations to stimulate your own thoughts about the text and to assist you in developing a strong thesis. Remember to read through the text more than once, making note of those elements of the text that support your argument. It will be equally important to make note of those elements that contradict your thesis, as this will help you to refine your argument and create a stronger case.

## Themes

While *The Rose Tattoo* can be placed in a different genre than that of Williams's past works, the themes are still familiar. They are themes that have inhabited Williams's earlier works and that appear commonly throughout literature, and as themes that address the human condition, they are themes that we can all relate to and understand. Williams uses *The Rose Tattoo* to begin a dialogue about desire and passion, illusion and reality, and the passage of time, much as he does in the plays that preceded this one. However, just as *The Rose Tattoo* represents a different form and genre, one could argue that Williams's revelations about these themes also present a departure from what he had suggested in works of the past. For example, the theme of desire, which appeared in all of the works we have previously addressed, is also evident in *The Rose Tattoo,* but consider how it is treated in this text. In *A Streetcar Named Desire* and other plays, we noted that there seemed to be a relationship between desire and death or desire and loss or self-destruction. Does this apply to *The Rose Tattoo* as well? Your own response to this question could form the core of your essay. Many critics have argued that *The Rose Tattoo* reverses this pattern, while others have noted that this is not a completely accurate conclusion to draw. While there is sufficient scholarship to support a proposal that *The Rose Tattoo* reverses the desire/death or desire/self-destruction relationship presented in his previous works, after performing close readings of the text, you may feel that the text provides evidence to the contrary, suggesting that it is a mistake to conclude that passion is a redeeming force in *The Rose Tattoo*. Either point of view could serve as the core of a successful essay, so long as you use the text to support your own ideas. If Williams's variations on a singular theme cause you confusion, keep in mind that Williams may not necessarily be presenting a single, conclusive point of view or a fixed commentary on these themes. Consider how he uses varied methods to open up a larger dialogue about these subjects. Are both sides of this view well represented? You may find that the answer is yes. Great writers of fiction are able to present us with more than one point of view. They inform us and then trust us to give appropriate consideration to the subject, drawing our own conclusions.

### Sample Topics:

1. **Passion:** Can we conclude that passion is presented as a redeeming force in *The Rose Tattoo*? Why or why not?

   Consider passages in the play where passion is represented. You could examine the passion between Rosa and her boyfriend, Jack, or Serafina and Alvaro. You might also consider passion that is suggested in the text rather than actually depicted, such as the passion between Serafina and Rosario or Estelle and Rosario. Consider and analyze the effect of passion on these characters. Does this passion have a positive effect or a negative one? Or both? Support your opinions with examples from the text.

2. **Illusion versus reality:** Why does Rosa seem to be incapable of accepting the reality of her husband's infidelity? How does she deal with this reality?

   Answering this question could become a variation of the topic presented above. You might suggest that Serafina is blinded by love and passion, which makes her unable to see the truth. Where do we see examples of this in the text? Or do you feel that Serafina was already aware of her husband's infidelity and used her boasting about their relationship to hide this pain? Why does she continue to deny the truth even after it has been fully revealed?

3. **The passage of time:** How is time represented in the play and what does the play tell us about our relationship to time?

Look for symbols and motifs that reference time and suggest that it is a key theme. For instance, we know that Serafina wants to give her daughter a wristwatch for a graduation present. What significance might Serafina's gift of the wristwatch hold? Why do you think that Williams makes it so that Rosa never actually receives the watch? Is he suggesting that she has no use for a watch because time is of no concern to her? Is this because she is young and in love? Consider Serafina's remarks on the relationship between love and time in the first act. Consider also how the play presents the life cycle through the development of the characters and through symbolism. What is Williams trying to tell us, or what questions is he trying to raise about the nature of time and our relationship to it?

4. **Pride:** How is Serafina affected by pride?

It is obvious that Serafina is proud of the love she believes was shared between her and her husband, but how does this pride affect Serafina? Does it have negative consequences? Is it fair to say that pride is Serafina's tragic flaw? Is her display of pride only a way for her to cover up her true feelings? Consider the exchange between the doctor and the priest in scene 3. What message does this exchange about pride present about the effects of pride on faith?

## Character

While an examination of any individual character could work well for an essay, Williams creates an interesting portrait of Italian Americans in *The Rose Tattoo*. Consider Williams's depiction of the Italian characters as a whole. How does his presentation of these characters contribute to the semicomic tone of the play? Consider also how the other characters relate to the Italian characters. What does this interaction tell us about social biases? And about human nature? A discussion of these considerations will allow you to extend your range by focusing on the formal element of character from a historical or philosophical perspective.

## *Sample Topics:*

1. **Serafina:** How does Williams want us to react to Serafina? Do you feel that the play elicits the response that Williams was seeking?

   Consider all aspects of Serafina's character, including the way that she speaks, her manner of dress, and her gestures and actions. Does Williams want us to sympathize with Serafina, or is she meant to be a comical character? Consider how she relates to the other characters. What is their response to Serafina? Does Williams's comment in his production notes that he presents the view of her house's content "with sentiment and humor in equal measure" (654) also apply to his approach with Serafina's character? If so, was he successful in achieving this balance?

2. **Rosario:** Although Rosario never appears in the text, can he be considered a central character? If so, why?

   We come to know Rosario only through Serafina's recollection of him and what the other characters reveal to us about him. Although he never actually appears, how does he affect the other characters and drive the dramatic action of the play? Explain. Would it have been more effective to have actually presented him in the play? Or is his absence more revealing?

3. **The doctor and the priest:** In the third scene of the first act, Williams pairs up a doctor and a priest, who engage in a dialogue about Serafina's reaction to her husband's death. Why is this pairing significant?

The doctor is a man of science, and the priest represents the world of faith and religion. How does their interaction serve as a metaphor for the tension between body and spirit, science and faith? You might choose to use this section of the text to engage in a larger consideration of the problem of reconciling faith and body or science and spirituality as presented in Williams's works. One idea would be to compare this subject to its presentation in Williams's *Summer and Smoke*.

4. **The children:** In the background of many scenes, we hear children playing. When the play begins, we are presented with children rather than with the main character. Why does Williams choose to include children throughout the play even though they are not central to the plot?

Refer to the sections of the text where the children appear. The debut of Bruno, Salvatore, and Vivi at the start of the play might seem superfluous, but what might Williams have had in mind when he chose to begin the play with the presence of youth? How does the presence of youth create a contrast with other elements of the play? Does it compel us to consider the life cycle? If so, explain how this ties in with the larger concerns of the play.

5. **Italian Americans:** How does Williams present Italians in general in the play? How do the other characters in the play treat the Italian-American characters? What does this tell us about ethnic bias in America at this time?

Consider Williams's presentation of Italian characters such as Serafina, Rosario, and Alvaro Mangiacavallo. How are they depicted? Consider their manner of dress, their way of speaking, and their other characteristics, including the contents of their homes and their beliefs. Why do Rosario and Alvaro share so much in common? Are the characters unique, or is Williams presenting us with a stereotype? Or is he able to achieve both—round characters who also function as archetypes? If you feel that Williams is presenting a stereotype, why do you think he chose to do this? Does he agree with this view of Italians, or does his use of a stereotype serve some other purpose? As you think about answering these questions, give consideration to the tone of the play.

6. **The Strega:** Who is The Strega, and what might she symbolize?

*Strega* is the Italian name for "witch." Consider all of the scenes where The Strega appears. Is her name appropriate? Is she really a witch? How does Serafina perceive this character? How does Rosa's perception differ? Does The Strega somehow tie in to the themes of the play? Why is she presented in a procession with a goat and a child?

## Philosophy and Ideas

Through the interchange between characters like Assunta and Serafina, and the doctor and the priest, *The Rose Tattoo* is able to enter into a dialogue about complicated issues such as faith and superstition, love, and the nature of the human spirit. As you sit down to write, consider how Williams is able to use comedy to engage us in these deeper issues. Is the use of comedy more successful than the use of tragedy?

*The Rose Tattoo* is also quite well-known for its reflection of the Dionysian elements of life. While scholars often talk about the play serving as a celebration of the Dionysian aspects of life, many fail to note that the story itself is actually, in many ways, a recreation or adaptation of the myth of Dionysus. This topic alone could serve as a very engaging essay topic, but it will require significant research. This might also inspire you to write about a broader topic such as evidence of the influence of classical Greek literature in *The Rose Tattoo* or in Williams's works as a whole.

### Sample Topics:

1. **Faith and superstition:** What view does the play present on matters of faith and superstition? Are faith and superstition generally accepted or are they considered foolish?

Consider Assunta, Serafina, the doctor, and the priest. How do their beliefs differ when it comes to matters of faith and superstition? Examine the first scene of the play where Assunta and Serafina interact. Assunta comes bearing magic powders, but it is Serafina who seems to have a sense of what is imminent. Also, examine the description of Serafina's religious relics and instances in the play where she turns to or abandons her faith. Alternatively, consider examples of superstition in the text, such as Serafina's fear of The Strega. Is it suggested that these beliefs are cultural or linked to a certain generation? Why is Rosa able to see The Strega as a deformed old woman while her mother believes that she is evil? What can we ultimately learn about faith and superstition from the play?

2. **The Dionysian myth:** Many scholars have focused on the Dionysian elements of *The Rose Tattoo*. Why do you believe that Williams chose to apply this concept to a modern play?

Dionysus is a god in Greek mythology. In some versions of the myth, he was born to Zeus and a mortal woman. According to this telling of the myth, Zeus's wife Hera learned of the affair before Dionysus was born and tricked Dionysus's mother into demanding proof that Zeus was indeed immortal. Zeus eventually complied, but since mortals are unable to survive the revelation of his immortal powers, Dionysus's mother died upon the revelation that Zeus was indeed a god. How does this myth compare to Serafina's own story, including the revelation of her husband's affair? A treatment of this topic might serve as the core of your essay, or you might choose to look at different versions of the myth and approach the symbolic use of Dionysian elements in the play. In this case, consider how these characterizations of Dionysus relate to the larger concerns of the play. How does the genre and overall tone of the play lend itself to a comparison to this myth?

## Language, Symbols, and Imagery

With some works of literature it can take some effort to uncover symbolism and locate important imagery, as it may be well disguised, set carefully within the text. Some authors may prefer to be more subtle than others. Likewise, it may not be immediately obvious what language is most important. *The Rose Tattoo* dispels these problems and makes it easy to isolate these elements, as Williams has taken an over-the-top approach in the presentation of all three elements. Do not simply locate and list these symbols, characteristics of language, and imagery in your paper, however. Consider why Williams took this approach. Examining why he took this approach, using repetition to make these elements stand out, could lead to a variety of interesting essay topics that can conclude with interesting and unexpected revelations about the play.

## Sample Topics:

1. **The rose:** The rose is indisputably the most prominent and oft-repeated symbol of the play. What does the rose symbolize? Does it have more than one meaning? How does Williams's use of the rose tie in with the thematic concerns of the work?

If you choose to undertake this topic, you will need to examine all instances in the text where the rose appears. Who is it associated with? Is the rose associated with one gender or both? Why is this significant? What contexts is it used in? What does its use in the title indicate? Remember that, if you decide to write about such a prominent symbol, your conclusion needs to do much more than simply point out that the rose is an important symbol. You will need to engage in a detailed discussion of how we know this and what it reveals to us about the themes of the play and the text as a whole.

2. **Clothing:** How does Serafina's relationship to clothing reflect the themes of the play?

This question could be approached in many different ways. You might first consider Serafina's profession as a seamstress. Look also at the scenes where she dresses in a corset. How does it fit? Why does she remove the corset? Since we already know that Serafina is plump, what symbolic value might this action hold? Consider also the scene where Serafina attempts to dress for her daughter's graduation. What is the significance of this scene? Consider how the clothes fit. Is she able to find something suitable to wear? What about other examples of Serafina's relationship to clothing in the play—her appearance in the dirty slip after the death of her husband, the clothes that she saves for her daughter's wedding day, the rose-colored silk shirt that she makes for Estelle?

3. **The goat:** Throughout much of the play, Serafina tries to catch the goat that is loose in her yard. What is the result of this pursuit and what might it symbolize?

Today we tend to recognize the goat as a symbol of stubbornness. While this interpretation can certainly be applied in consideration of *The Rose Tattoo*, the goat has other symbolic significance as well. Research some meanings of the goat in Italian culture. The goat functions traditionally as a symbol of sexuality, fertility, and lust, and in the past the goat represented joy and a lust for life, but in modern Italian culture it is also symbolic of infidelity. How does this inform or change our understanding of the symbolic significance of these chase scenes? Consider all of the passages where the goat appears. Who is ultimately able to tame the goat? Why is this significant?

4. **Treatment of language:** Since Williams has already identified his characters as Italian Americans, why does he choose to incorporate Italian language into the play?

In answering this question, you could travel in many different directions. For instance, answering this question could lead you to a discussion of authenticity—how the language helps to make the characters more believable and relatable. Alternatively, you might talk about how Williams uses language as an element of farce. Would the play have the same effect on us if there was no use of the Italian language and the characters' grammar was perfected? Would we view the characters in the same way? How would this affect the tone of the play and our understanding of the themes?

## Compare and Contrast Essays

As we discussed in the preceding chapter, as Williams progressed as a writer, his work began to show evidence of a greater interest in pairs and duplication, ultimately manifesting itself as a concern with paradoxes in later works. *The Rose Tattoo* presents us with evidence of these concerns. The work is a hybrid of two genres—comedy and tragedy. It raises issues of life and death, old age and youth, science and faith, and presents dual relationships—Serafina and Alvaro and Rosa and Jack. Because of this duality in the text, the play lends itself very well to the compare-and-contrast method. You could compare and contrast any elements within the text, or you might compare the play to Williams's other works. You could address shared themes or character traits between works. In contrast, you could answer an important question: What does *The Rose Tattoo* offer that Williams's other plays do not?

### Sample Topics:

1. **Lighting:** Consider the lighting of the play. Does the lighting match the set appropriately? Is Williams really concerned with presenting a romantic view as he suggests in his production notes, or is he using the lighting as parody?

   Return to Williams's production notes where he describes his vision of the lighting at the start of the play. What does it seem his intentions were? Is Williams trying to create a sense of the romantic? Or is his choice of lighting over-the-top and ridiculous? Depending on your view, you might use this to enter into a larger dialogue about themes of romance and love in the work or, alternatively, to focus on the play as a work of comedy.

2. **The relationship between Serafina and Rosa and the relationship between Amanda and Tom of *The Glass Menagerie*:** How do the relationships between Serafina and her daughter and Amanda and her son compare? How do these relationships inform us about the thematic concerns of each work?

   An examination of the texts will suggest that Amanda and Serafina are both mothers concerned for the welfare of their children. But are they overbearing and driving their children away? Or are their feelings warranted? Where do their concerns stem from? How do their histories compare? Consider all scenes where the children interact with their mothers. How do the children respond to their mothers' styles of parenting? Do we learn anything about the inner selves of the characters as a result of their interactions? Would you say that Serafina is finally able to change the way that she interacts with her daughter, while Amanda remains unable to change?

3. **Models of love and romance as evidenced by Serafina and Rosario and Stella and Stanley in *A Streetcar Named Desire*:** In *A Streetcar Named Desire*, Williams seemed to present a new model of "love" and "romance." How does this compare to the model of love and romance presented in the relationship between Serafina and Rosario in *The Rose Tattoo*?

Although Rosario does not actually appear in the text, refer to what you know about his relationship with Serafina from Serafina's point of view and from external perceptions of the relationship. You will also need to spend some time characterizing Stella and Stanley's relationship. How do the two relationships compare? Why do Serafina and Stella value the physical part of the relationship as much as they do? Does it impair their ability to decipher between fantasy and reality?

## Bibliography and Resources for *The Rose Tattoo*

Durham, Leslie Atkins, and John Gronbeck-Tedesco. "*The Rose Tattoo*." *Tennessee Williams: A Guide to Research and Performance*. Ed. Philip C. Kolin. Westport, CT: Greenwood, 1998. 90–99.

Parker, Brian. "Multiple Endings for *The Rose Tattoo (1951)*." *Tennessee Williams Annual Review* 2 (1999): 53–68.

———. "Provisional Stemma for Drafts, Alternatives, and Revisions of Tennessee Williams's *The Rose Tattoo*." *Modern Drama* 40.2 (1997): 279–94.

———. "*The Rose Tattoo* as Comedy of the Grotesque." *Tennessee Williams Annual Review* 8 (2005): 1–8.

*The Rose Tattoo*. Dir. Daniel Mann. 1955. DVD. Paramount, 2004.

Styan, John. *The Dark Comedy: The Development of Modern Comi-Tragedy.* Cambridge: Cambridge UP, 1968.

*Tennessee Williams's "The Rose Tattoo": A Study Guide from Gale's: "Drama for Students."* Vol. 18. Ch. 9. PDF. June 20, 2003.

Thompson, Judith J. "Symbol, Myth and Ritual in *The Glass Menagerie, The Rose Tattoo,* and *Orpheus Descending." Tennessee Williams: Thirteen Essays.* Ed. Jac Tharpe. Jackson: U of Mississippi P, 1980. 139–71.

Tischler, Nancy. "'Sentiment and Humor in Equal Measure': Comic Form in *The Rose Tattoo." Tennessee Williams: A Tribute.* Ed. Jac Tharpe. Jackson: UP of Mississippi, 1977. 214–31.

Williams, Tennessee. "The Meaning of *The Rose Tattoo." Where I Live: Selected Essays.* Eds. Christine R. Day and Bob Woods. New York: New Directions, 1978. 55–57.

———. *The Rose Tattoo. Tennessee Williams: Plays 1937–1955.* Eds. Mel Gussow and Kenneth Holditch. New York: Library of America, 2000. 645–739.

———. "The Timeless World of a Play." *Where I Live: Selected Essays.* Eds. Christine R. Day and Bob Woods. New York: New Directions, 1978. 49–55.

# CAMINO REAL

## READING TO WRITE

WHEN WILLIAMS'S *Camino Real* debuted in 1953, it was poorly received by critics, and dismayed audience members walked out on performances of the play, demanding that they receive a full refund. *Camino Real* abandoned the realism of Williams's previous works; the action of the plot was often illogical and nonsensical, and the audience may have had trouble recognizing many of the characters who were taken primarily from European literature. The setting was simply a fantastical place in the Spanish-speaking world, a site that closely resembled a military state where citizens are fearful of being shot by police or carted away by street sweepers who function as giggling grim reapers. The only bit of familiarity for audiences in the 1950s might have been the inclusion of a piece of American popular culture reflected in the creation of the character named Kilroy. Kilroy allowed Williams to bring to the play the famous World War II slogan "Kilroy was here," a graffiti phrase that had appeared mysteriously, and repeatedly, at impossible locations throughout the world during and after the war. The phrase gained tremendous notoriety, with people everywhere hypothesizing about who had begun leaving this mark. In *Camino Real,* Kilroy is not an American soldier but a different kind of fighter—a champion boxer just past his prime who also happens to be a romantic with a heart as big as the head of a baby. Not long after his arrival on the scene, Kilroy is robbed of everything but his golden boxing gloves, a belt that bears the word *Champ,* and a picture of his one true love, a blonde who is said to resemble Greta Garbo. In the dark world of the Camino Real, Kilroy is a bright spot. He represents an innocence and romanticism that seems to be lost to the other characters.

Kilroy, however, is just one of the many inhabitants of the Camino Real, and even his familiarity was not enough to allow audiences to take hold and accept the play.

Although theatergoers in the 1950s had nothing to go on except the action they witnessed onstage, today we have the benefit of scholarship that breaks the work down into digestible parts and provides us with clues about the significance of the text. Even with this help, writing about *Camino Real* can be difficult, especially challenging for those acquainted primarily with the straightforwardness of American realist drama, which dominated this period. While you may, after an initial reading, approach some works of literature with a general notion of what you are setting out to write about and ideas that you are prepared to examine more thoroughly, in the case of a work like *Camino Real,* which strays from realism, you might find it helpful to approach the work with questions instead. In fact, writing down some of your questions and returning to the text for answers may be the best way to begin. As you begin seeking answers to these questions, you may find that one question leads you to the next, and in the process of asking these questions and uncovering answers, you will begin to locate topics that can form the base of your essay. You may also find that, while the play is difficult to understand, there are other familiarities in the text besides the American ideal projected in Kilroy. Like Williams's other works, *Camino Real* deals with existential themes and basic human concerns. And while the characters are fantastical, we can approach them with the same careful eye that we would any other character. In fact, the borrowed characters come with some benefit, as we can always refer back to the texts in which they originally appeared for clues to their characters.

If you feel confused by the text, consider the play first as a whole. Try to identify the source of your confusion. What is it that makes this text different from the others you have encountered? What elements present a challenge? Clearly, the form and genre of the play present a challenge for most readers and viewers. We know that *Camino Real* is not a work of realism, so you might begin by jotting questions such as these: How do we know that *Camino Real* is not a work of realism? What elements provide the clues that reveal this? What does Williams hope to achieve by abandoning realism? Does this more fantastical approach suit his goals?

Remember that all fiction is actually a work of fantasy. Therefore, when writing about works categorized within the genre of fantasy or magical realism, such as *Camino Real* or some of Salman Rushdie's or Gabriel García Márquez's works, for example, you can apply the same tactics that you would apply to any other works of fiction.

Once you have asked some general questions about the play, such as those cited above, return to the text and begin examining the formal elements such as symbolism, plot, and language. Try to work systematically through the text, remembering to also consider the title. Make note of important motifs, pieces of dialogue, and significant actions as you go along. If you are not immediately certain of their significance, you can always return to these passages later. In the case of *Camino Real*, it may be helpful to begin by focusing on one of the most remarkable features of the play—its cast of characters. Williams employs a very large cast of characters from a variety of backgrounds. In fact, as noted above, most of the characters are taken from European works of literature such as *Don Quixote, The Hunchback of Notre-Dame,* and *La Dame aux Camélias.* Williams also mixes in characters from real life, such as the poet Lord Byron and the infamous adventurer and lover Casanova. This should compel you to ask: Why would Williams want to set these characters in his own text? Why does he choose to mix the real and the surreal? Your paper might center on this very topic, or you might simply use these questions to lead you to another topic.

Readers often tend to gravitate toward an examination of plot first, but in the case of *Camino Real,* the plot can be difficult to understand, and a study of the dialogue between characters is really the best way to understand what is happening. Instead of struggling to make sense of what is happening in the play, go back to the opening of the play, choose a section of dialogue that seems to be important, and perform a close reading of the text. What does the exchange reveal about the larger concerns of the play? Try to look for information about important themes. The first exchange, for instance, takes place between Don Quixote and Sancho Panza, characters borrowed from the classic novel *Don Quixote.* The dialogue between these two characters provides us with enough information to make sense of the title of the play, gives us revealing information about the setting, and introduces key themes of the play:

QUIXOTE. Forward!

SANCHO. Aw, naw. I know this place. (*He produces a crumpled parchment.*) Here it is on the chart. Look, it says here: "Continue until you come to the square of the walled town which is the end of the *Camino Real* and the beginning of the *Camino Real*. Halt here," it says, "and turn back, Traveler, for the spring of humanity has gone dry in this place and—"

QUIXOTE. (*He snatches the chart from him and reads the rest of the inscription.*): "—there are no birds in the country except wild birds that are tamed and kept in—" (*He holds the chart close to his nose.*)—*Cages*!

SANCHO. (*urgently*): Let's go back to La Mancha!

QUIXOTE. Forward! . . .

SANCHO. *I'm* going back to La Mancha! (*He dumps the knightly equipment into the orchestra pit.*). . . .

QUIXOTE. (*looking about the plaza*):—Lonely . . . (*To his surprise the word is echoed softly by almost unseen figures huddled below the stairs and against the wall of the town. Quixote leans upon his lance and observes with a wry smile—*). . . . Yes, I'll sleep for a while, I'll sleep and dream for a while against the wall of this town . . .—And my dream will be a pageant, a masque in which old meanings will be remembered and possibly new ones discovered, and when I wake up from this sleep and this disturbing pageant of a dream, I'll choose one among its shadows to take with me in the place of Sancho . . . (751–52)

Sancho's reading of the parchment helps us to head into the play with an understanding of the title, which might otherwise remain a mystery without some instruction regarding its proper translation. Sancho's emphasis on certain syllables tells us that he and Don Quixote are leaving the Royal Road and are heading to the Real Road. We know that it is not a pleasant place, for the parchment also says that in the Camino Real "the spring of humanity has dried up" (751). This notion is supported by the insight that the inhabitants of the Camino Real are like caged birds. The fearful Sancho abandons Don Quixote and heads back to La Mancha. The single word that Don Quixote uses to describe the situation he finds himself in is notable, for after he utters it, the text reveals that it is a sentiment shared by the other people on the Camino Real. Next Don Quixote goes to sleep, but not before indicating that his dream will be a kind of "pageant" or allegory, another allusion that we should keep in mind as we continue with the text, as it summarizes the atmosphere of the play. From the information presented in this single passage, you should be able to come up with countless topics for your essay—an exploration of the title of the play, isolation and loneliness as key themes, a study of Williams's use of characters from other literary works and an explanation of how they enlighten us, or how *Camino Real* functions as allegory, for instance. Close readings of the dialogue that follows this exchange and a thorough examination of symbolism will provide you with the information to support your assertions and build a strong argument.

## TOPICS AND STRATEGIES

In the sections that follow, you will find a variety of suggested topics accompanied by questions and observations to assist you in the task of writing successfully about *Camino Real.* Remember that this is not a comprehensive list of topics, and the statements and questions that appear after each suggested topic are merely a guide to help spark your own ideas about the work. A successful paper will present a strong thesis based upon your own original ideas and will be supported by relevant examples resulting from close readings of the text. A wide variety of interpretations will be possible as you consider each topic. Use the strategic questions and observations to stimulate your own thoughts about the text and to assist you in developing a strong thesis. Remember to read through the text more than once, making note of those elements of the text that support your argument. It will be equally important to make note of those elements that contradict your thesis, as this will help you to refine your argument and create a stronger case.

## Themes

It can be difficult to locate the themes of *Camino Real*, but an exploration of the dialogue reveals that the play deals with themes common to Williams's work. The situation that the characters find themselves in presents a portrait of isolation and loneliness. They seem to exhibit difficulty in accepting the passage of time, and they struggle to find escape and to make sense of love. Characters like Don Quixote, Kilroy, and, it might be argued, Camille and Casanova inform us about the redeeming properties of romance and love and the necessity and power of romanticism. Any of these thematic concerns might become the topic of your essay. Remember not to simply present a theme. Your essay should note how the theme is revealed in the work, why Williams might have utilized these methods in presenting the theme, and why the theme is significant.

### *Sample Topics:*

1. **Isolation:** How does *Camino Real* address isolation as a key theme? Are the characters really alone, or are they somehow united? If so, how?

   Examine passages in which there is a sense of isolation and loneliness. Which characters does this apply to? Is it associated with a single character or the cast of characters at large? Camille explains that any romance she would share with Casanova would truly be nothing more than their coming together because of their isolation as caged birds. What does this say about the link between love and loneliness? Consider what is plaguing each of the characters. Do they share similar problems? Does this mean that they are not really alone? Are they drawn together in their predicament and unified by their flaws and by their wants and needs? Analyze Don Quixote's remarks that "it would be inexcusably selfish to be lonely alone" (752). Is Williams trying to make a broader statement about the human condition?

2. **The passage of time:** The characters in the play all seem to be dealing with a confrontation with the passage of time, their passing youth, and their looming irrelevance. Are any of the charac-

ters able to better handle this problem than others? If so, what greater message is Williams trying to present about our confrontation with time and our ability to deal with our faded youth?

Although Williams chooses to borrow characters who had represented youth and sexuality in other works of literature, in *Camino Real* these same characters are often haggard and worn. Consider how each of the characters deals with his or her fading youth. Do Kilroy and Don Quixote approach this dilemma the same way that the other characters do? How do Camille and Casanova deal with this issue? Are any of the characters more accepting of their fate than others? If so, explain what it is that makes these characters better able to adapt and accept change.

3. **Romance and romanticism:** The play seems to present some dialogue about love and romance, and it also references romanticism. What statement does the play ultimately make about these themes?

   Consider first how love and romance are presented in the play. Look at how Casanova and Kilroy reference love. How does Camille view love? Does her view change throughout the play? Does Camille and Casanova's relationship change by the end of the play? What does the conclusion of the play, including Kilroy's exit, tell us about the possibility of the survival of love, romance, and romanticism?

## Character

As noted above, most of the characters in *Camino Real* are borrowed from other famous works of literature or from real life. An examination of this single attribute of *Camino Real* could serve as a successful topic for your essay. Does Williams remain true to the original depiction of these characters? If not, how are they different in *Camino Real*? Explain why these changes are significant. By placing these characters together in a fantastical work, do the characters serve as archetypes? Do they create a greater sense of fantasy when they are assembled together in one location? While it is helpful to consider the dialogue that takes place between the characters in *Camino Real,* another focus for your essay could be to analyze the relationships between the characters. For instance, why do Kilroy and Casanova seem to bond while other characters maintain their distance from each other? How does their fate in the play compare? Another interesting relationship in the play is that between Camille and Casanova. How can the relationship of Camille and Casanova be characterized? Consider also how Williams wanted us to respond to the characters. Are we meant to sympathize with Camille? Or should we be critical of her? If you choose to write about the intended reception of a character, be sure to explain why you believe Williams wanted to elicit this response.

## Sample Topics:

1. **Kilroy:** Who is Kilroy and what does he represent? Why is he able to escape the Camino Real while others who have been there much longer fail to find a way out?

   The expression "Kilroy was here" is borrowed from American pop culture. The phrase appeared as graffiti in various locations throughout World War II and after the war ended. Although there was speculation about the source of this graffiti, its origins remain a mystery. In the play, Williams references this bit of popular culture by creating a character by the name of Kilroy. Kilroy is not a soldier but an American boxer who used to be a champion. He has a heart the size of a baby's head. Consider Kilroy's introduction to the Camino Real and his response to it. How do we learn about Kilroy? For instance, consider if Williams simply describes Kilroy or if we learn more from Kilroy's dialogue and actions. How might Kilroy represent the lost American spirit? Or does he represent something even more universal?

2. **Camille:** Who is Camille and what does she reveal to us about love? Does her view of love change throughout the course of the play? What significance does this change, or lack of change, hold?

You will need to refer to Alexandre Dumas fils's *La Dame aux Camélias* to study how Camille is originally presented in literature. How does she compare in Williams's play? Does she maintain the same nature, the same physical and emotional attributes? Consider her interaction with Casanova and her comments on love. She implies that love is an illusion, nothing more than two people coming together in desperation as a result of their shared entrapment. Does her view on love change by the end of the play? Williams is rather vague when it comes to answering this question. You will need to depend on your own understanding and interpretation of the text and the final scene to answer this question. Finally, conclude by explaining why Camille's view of love is significant.

3. **The appropriation of literary characters:** Why does Williams borrow characters from other works of literature and insert them into his own work? What purpose does this serve? Is it effective?

Consider the characters that Williams borrowed from literature. Some may be more familiar to you than others. Do these characters share anything in common? Using the text, explain how they inform us about larger themes through dialogue and interaction. How would our view of the text be different if these were original characters? Would it alter the tone of the play?

## Form and Genre

While Williams is better known for his works of realism, *Camino Real* allowed Williams to experiment with other genres and forms. With this play, he abandoned the form that was most familiar to him (and to audiences of the day). The play was broken into blocks rather than divided traditionally by scenes and acts. Paired with the other formal elements of the text, a fantasy was generated. This was a surprising departure for a playwright who had expressed an interest in dealing exclusively with reality, but Williams had never suggested that fantastical forms could not address reality. In fact, years before *Camino Real* debuted, Williams had suggested that fantasy, or any departure from realistic forms, should only serve to strengthen our understanding of reality. As you write about *Camino Real*, keep this in mind. If you decide to write about genre and form, you will need to explain how these elements of *Camino Real* serve, or attempt to serve, this greater purpose. Ultimately, you might decide that Williams failed to accomplish what he set out to do. It is fine to present this point of view, as long as you support this assertion with examples from the text. In this instance, you might choose to strengthen your argument by presenting some comparison to works that you feel were more successful because they took a different approach to genre and form.

## Sample Topics:

1. **Magical realism:** With *Camino Real*, Williams temporarily abandoned his use of realism, employing fantasy instead. Is it fair to say that *Camino Real* fits into the genre of literature known today as magical realism? How does the work compare to the works of Salman Rushdie or Gabriel García Márquez, for instance?

   If you choose to write about this topic, you will need to begin by providing some explanation of how magical realism can best be characterized. What characteristics do works of magical realism share that allow us to group them together accordingly? Cite some examples. Next you will need to explain how *Camino Real* shares these characteristics or, alternatively, how it lacks these characteristics. You might choose to isolate one work of magical realism and compare it to *Camino Real*, or you might want to talk about magical realism from a wider perspective, citing examples from various texts. It may be helpful to consult some reference books that provide information about magical realism as a movement and then refer to an anthology such as Keith Hollaman and David Young's *Magical Realist Fiction: An Anthology*. Consider Williams's comments from the production notes to *The Glass Menagerie*: "When a play employs conventional techniques, it is not, or certainly shouldn't be, trying to escape its responsibility of dealing with reality, or interpreting experience, but is actually or should be attempting to find a closer approach, a more penetrating and vivid expression of things as they are" (395). Where is this concept evidenced in *Camino Real,* or how does it fail to accomplish this? Do Williams's approach in *Camino Real* and the approach taken in other works of magical realism give us better insight into reality?

2. **Blocks:** In the final version of the play, why does Williams choose to break the play up into "blocks" rather than scenes or acts?

Consider the form of the play. First you will need to explain how the form of *Camino Real* differs from the form presented in Williams's other works. How does the form of the play create a sense of place rather than a sense of time? Why does Williams want to emphasize one over the other? How does this contribute to the fantastic tone of the play? The division of the play into blocks also allows Williams to break up the play into smaller sections. Plays with scenes and acts often have only a few of each, but in the final version of Camino Real, the text is divided into sixteen sections or "blocks." Does the division of the play create a sense of movement or signify a journey? Look for examples of how these notions tie in with the action of the play and the greater themes of the work. Why does Williams want to create a setting that is beyond time? Consider Williams's remarks on timelessness in his foreword to the play.

3. **Allegory:** Does *Camino Real* function as an allegory? If so, how? What can we learn from it?

First you will need to briefly explain what an allegory is. Consider other examples of allegory such as Plato's allegory of the cave, Aesop's fables, or Dante's *Divine Comedy.* How do the formal elements found in *Camino Real* lend themselves to this form? Are the characters flat or round? Do they represent something beyond themselves, some universal quality? Look for universal themes and universal lessons presented in the text. What moral, religious, social, or political significance does the text have?

4. **Freedom in form:** Williams often noted that, despite its critical failure, *Camino Real* remained one of his favorite works because it allowed him to express complete freedom. Does this freedom of form create a stronger work or is it inherently problematic?

   Examine and discuss the form of *Camino Real*. You will need to explain how this form reflects complete artistic freedom. Next you will need to decide whether or not you think this expression of freedom is problematic. If you feel that it is problematic, support your argument by explaining how this freedom alters the elements of the text in a way that isolates readers and viewers or prevents them from comprehending the text. If you do not believe it was problematic and feel that this freedom strengthened the work, explain why. Use examples from the text to show how this freedom helps the play. You might also choose to explain how the exhibition of freedom in *Camino Real* reflects an important milestone in Williams's development as a writer.

5. **Versions of *Camino Real*:** There are actually several different versions of *Camino Real* available for study. There is an early one-act draft entitled *Ten Blocks on the Camino Real* and another later version entitled *Sixteen Blocks on the Camino Real*. There is also a third version that includes revisions implemented after the play's debut. What can we learn from an examination of these versions?

   There are several different approaches available to you if you choose to write about this topic. You might compare two of these versions or you might choose to consider the works as a whole. How does the play change throughout revisions of the text? Which formal elements were revised and which remained untouched? How do these changes alter our under-standing of the work? You could also explain what a study of these versions reveals about the process of Williams's writing and his development as a writer.

## Language, Symbols, and Imagery

*Camino Real* is filled with strong imagery imbued with symbolic meaning. In fact, many scholars and critics would contend that the play itself functions as a symbolic story or allegory. Consider how the formal elements of the text lend themselves to this form.

### Sample Topics:

1. **Kilroy's boxing gloves:** What do Kilroy's boxing gloves represent?

   Consider the passages where Kilroy refers to his boxing gloves. Why are they golden? Why does he resist pawning the gloves after he is robbed? Why does he change his mind later in the play? Is this a smart choice? Explain what this action tells us about his character.

2. **The title:** Without some suggestion of how it should be translated, the title of the play remains open to interpretation. What does the title of the play mean and what information does it give us about the action and thematic concerns of the play?

   *Camino Real* can be translated to "royal road" from Spanish or, if only the first word is translated into English, it becomes "real road." Look at the passage where Don Quixote's companion Sancho Panza speaks of the Camino Real. How does this dialogue confirm the dual meaning of the title? Once we know that the title has dual meanings, what does this tell us about the concept of the play? Is it a journey? Explain how the play represents a movement from a symbolic royal road to a real road. Why is this journey significant?

3. **Birds:** *Camino Real* contains several references to birds. Examine these examples and discuss their significance. Why does Williams choose to use birds as a motif in this play?

First you will need to cite examples of the use of birds as a metaphor in the text. Consider the repeated references to Jacques Casanova as "hawk-like." Likewise, Camille often refers to the citizens of Camino Real as caged birds, and the parchment that Sancho Panza reads from duplicates this notion. What associations do we apply to the bird and how does this relate to the use of the bird as a metaphor in *Camino Real*? Besides their ability, or inability as the case may be, to take flight, what else is notable about birds: Are birds hearty creatures or fragile creatures?

4. **Resurrection and restoration:** The play addresses resurrection and restoration in various contexts. Explain how Williams addresses these themes in *Camino Real*. What message does *Camino Real* provide about the possibility or impossibility of resurrection and restoration?

First you will need to locate and describe the passages where Williams addresses resurrection and restoration. How does he depict the restoration of the gypsy daughter Esmerelda's virginity, for instance? Is her virginity truly restored, or is this restoration only a trick? Look for other references to resurrection in the text. Do not just look for literal references to resurrection and restoration. Consider, for instance, how Camille and Casanova resurrect parts of themselves via their romance. How does Kilroy resurrect or restore parts of himself? Is restoration and resurrection a spiritual notion bestowed by God, or is it something that can be self-generated?

5. **The Fugitivo:** What is the significance of The Fugitivo?

Although everyone seems to be wishing for an exit from the Camino Real, rather than seek a way out, many seem to simply hope for the arrival of The Fugitivo, an illusive, impromptu flight that will carry them away. Consider the passage where The Fugitivo arrives. Is The Fugitivo the only way out of the Camino Real? Is the infrequency of The Fugitivo holding the characters back? If not, you will need to explain what other choices the characters have. Is it possible that The Fugitivo simply symbolizes a happy opportunity that can help us to escape a difficult situation but which is not wholly dependable? Explain by supporting this notion with examples from the text.

6. **The death of the Survivor:** Shortly after his debut in the text, the Survivor is shot and killed. What symbolic significance does the death of the Survivor hold?

Examine the passage which presents the debut of the Survivor. Is the Survivor a flat character or a round character? Now consider the scene that presents the death of the Survivor. What other characters appear in this scene? What are their roles? You will need to explain what the relationship is between the Survivor and the Dreamer, for instance. Why is the word brother exchanged between them so powerful that it would be forbidden? What social or political significance might this passage have? Explain the significance of Gutman's phone call to the Generalissimo on the Survivor's being shot. Why does Williams create a scene similar to the Pieta with the Madrecita? Does this passage convey something about religion or faith?

## Compare and Contrast Essays

Now that we have broken the play down into its various components, you can turn any of the subjects above into an essay by simply comparing or contrasting them or you might choose to address elements that were not already cited above. For instance, consider the two "narrators," for instance, Kilroy and Gutman, or compare and contrast Jacques Casanova and Kilroy. You might also choose to compare elements found in *Camino Real* to those of other texts written by Williams. What comparisons can we draw between *Camino Real* and Williams's other texts? You could write about how the works address shared themes or how their forms differ. By contrasting *Camino Real* and one or more of Williams's other texts, you might enter into a discussion of Williams's evolution as a writer. Comparing *Camino Real* to the work of another author, such as an author of magical realism, is another good option. Aside from making obvious comparisons, try comparing the play to a classical work of literature. How does *Camino Real* compare to Dante's *Inferno*, for example?

Like many of Williams's works, *Camino Real* was adapted for film. You might choose to compare and contrast the film version with the play, organizing your essay around an examination of how Williams's fantasy translates to the screen. How does this adaptation compare to other film adaptations of Williams's works?

Any of these subjects could serve as the topic for your essay, as long as you remember to go beyond presenting a simple list of similarities or differences. Remember that your essay needs to explain what we can learn from these similarities and differences.

## Sample Topics:

1. ***Camino Real* and Dante's *Inferno*:** Williams uses a quotation from Dante's *Inferno* to introduce *Camino Real*. Why does he choose to use this quotation as a precedent to his play? What do these works have in common?

   How does Dante's description of the straight way being lost apply to the characters of *Camino Real*? Although you can interpret the general meaning of Dante's quotation from an isolated reading of this quotation, you should consult a copy of *Inferno* to get a better understanding of Dante's story. Explain what it shares in common with *Camino Real* and why these similarities are significant. How do the formal elements of both texts—such as characters, theme, plot, and narration—compare? Your essay could explain why the elements of the *Inferno* can still be applied in a modern work like *Camino Real*.

2. **Camille and Blanche from *A Streetcar Named Desire*:** Compare and contrast these two characters.

   First, you will need to refer back to characterizations of Camille and Blanche in their respective texts. How are they described? You will need to be thorough in explaining how they are similar. Aside from physical attributes, what else do the two women share in common? How do they view love and romance? What about their relationship to time or age?

3. *Camino Real* **and Samuel Beckett's** *Waiting for Godot:* Compare and contrast these two plays.

*Camino Real* and *Waiting for Godot* both debuted in 1953. Both plays were subject to wide interpretation on cultural, social, and religious levels. Why is this so? Examine the formal elements of the play and explain how the texts compare and where they diverge. Is the broad interpretation of both plays the result of shared formal characteristics?

## Bibliography and Resources for *Camino Real*

Alighieri, Dante. *The Divine Comedy: Volume 1: Inferno.* Trans. Mark Musa. New York: Penguin, 2002.

Balakian, Jan. "*Camino Real*: Williams's Allegory about the Fifties." *Cambridge Companion to Tennessee Williams.* Ed. Matthew C. Roudané. Cambridge: Cambridge UP, 1997. 67–94.

Byron, George Gordon. *Lord Byron: The Major Works.* Oxford: Oxford UP, 2008.

Casanova, Giacomo. *The Story of My Life.* Ed. Gilberto Pizzamiglio. Trans. Stephen Sartarelli. New York: Penguin, 2001.

Cervantes, Miguel de. *Don Quixote.* Trans. Edith Grossman. New York: Harper Perennial, 2005.

Dumas, Alexandre. *Camille.* New York: Signet, 2004.

Faris, Wendy B., and Lois Parkinson Zamora, eds. *Magical Realism: Theory, History, Community.* Hillsborough: Duke UP, 1995.

Fisher, James. "*Camino Real.*" *Tennessee Williams: A Guide to Research and Performance.* Ed. Philip C. Kolin. Westport, CT: Greenwood, 1998. 100–08.

Hollaman, Keith, and David Young, eds. *Magical Realist Fiction: An Anthology.* Oberlin, OH: Oberlin College P, 1984.

Hugo, Victor. *The Hunchback of Notre-Dame.* New York: Signet, 2001.

Neumann, Claus-Peter. "Tennessee Williams's Plastic Theatre: *Camino Real.*" *Journal of American Drama and Theatre* 6.2–3 (Spring/Fall 1994): 93–111.

Pagan, Nicholas. *Rethinking Literary Biography: A Postmodern Approach to Tennessee Williams.* Rutherford, NJ: Fairleigh Dickinson UP, 1993. 17–34.

Parker, Brian. "Documentary Sources for *Camino Real.*" *Tennessee Williams Annual Review* 1 (1998): 41–52.

Saddik, Annette J. *The Politics of Reputation: The Critical Reception of Tennessee Williams' Later Plays.* Madison, NJ: Fairleigh Dickinson UP, 1999.

*Ten Blocks on the Camino Real.* Dir. Jack Landau. 1966. DVD. Kultur Video, 2002.

Williams, Tennessee. *Camino Real. Tennessee Williams: Plays 1937–1955.* Eds. Mel Gussow and Kenneth Holditch. New York: Library of America, 2000. 749–842.

# CAT ON A
# HOT TIN ROOF

## READING TO WRITE

A FTER RELEASING a string of plays that failed to achieve critical or popular acclaim, Williams returned on the scene with *Cat on a Hot Tin Roof*, a southern gothic drama that depicted a family in crisis and that resurrected Williams's preoccupation with interpersonal relationships, truth, and questions of existence. The play possessed many of the qualities of Williams's earlier (and most successful) work. It began as a short story entitled "Three Players of a Summer Game" and was published in *The New Yorker* in 1952. After being subjected to Williams's typical process of revision and restructuring, it was released in 1955 as a dramatic work. The play, which won a Pulitzer Prize that same year, marked a return to realism, depicting gritty issues such as alcoholism, failed romance, homosexuality, and social conduct in the South with a straightforward approach devoid of fantasy and structural tricks. The play allowed Williams to rekindle his working relationship with director Elia Kazan, who directed the initial Broadway run of the play. Audiences responded favorably. Like many of Williams's works, *Cat on a Hot Tin Roof* was later adapted for film. Of all of the film adaptations of the play, it was the 1958 film directed by Richard Brooks that had the most success, rivaling the popularity of Elia Kazan's 1951 film adaptation of *A Streetcar Named Desire*. The film, which cast Burl Ives as Big Daddy, Elizabeth Taylor as Maggie Pollitt, and Paul Newman as Brick Pollitt, was hugely successful, earning its main actors Academy Award nominations and *Cat on a Hot Tin Roof* a place in popular culture.

In addition to its ability to serve as popular entertainment, the play had great social significance. It continued to address historical and cultural concerns that had revealed themselves to Williams in the course of his own life. In the play's allegorical reference to the death of the Old South via the imminent death of Big Daddy and the decomposition of the Southern family, *Cat on a Hot Tin Roof* returned to themes found in Williams's early works such as *The Glass Menagerie* and *A Streetcar Named Desire*, continuing a social conversation that extended beyond the realm of popular entertainment. The play also adopted other weighty themes that Williams chose to reveal primarily by way of the exchanges that took place between characters. In this way, the play presented a series of psychological portraits, which provided Williams with a format to pose philosophical questions about existence, truth, and self-knowledge.

In writing about *Cat on a Hot Tin Roof,* there are several ways to approach the most significant aspects of the play, noted above. First, you might choose to analyze the central actions of the play and explain their significance by performing close readings of the text. Second, you might look at one of the more understated and overlooked aspects of the play—the set—to consider how this element works in line with the thematic concerns of the play, giving weight to the information that is revealed to us through the characters. Third, you might choose to focus on the ending of the play, a variable conclusion that Williams revised several times throughout his career. Of course these are only a few of the options that are available to you, but any one of these options will work well, giving you room to consider the themes of the play and the play's ultimate significance through an evaluation of the formal elements of the work.

If you choose the first option—analyzing the central actions of the play and explaining their significance by performing close readings of the text—you will need to begin by examining the form of the play. The play is broken down into three acts that each have a central action. By analyzing each of these acts and the actions that are central to each, you can begin to identify important themes of the play. This will help you to choose a topic, prepare a thesis, and begin gathering evidence to support your claims. In the first act, for example, an introductory reading will reveal that the major action lies in the interaction between Maggie Pollitt and her husband Brick. In fact, their interaction fills most of the first act, accented only by brief interruptions from Mae, Big Mama, and Dixie. By examining passages that relate to the interaction of Brick and Maggie, we can begin to gain an understanding of their relationship and the dramatic tension of the play. Consider, for example, the following exchange:

MARGARET. . . . Why are you looking at me like that?

BRICK (*whistling softly, now*). Like what, Maggie?

MARGARET (*intensely, fearfully*). The way y' were lookin' at me just now, befo' I caught your eye in the mirror and you started to whistle! I don't know how to describe it but it froze my blood!—I've caught you lookin' at me like that so often lately. What are you thinkin' of when you look at me like that?

BRICK. I wasn't conscious of lookin' at you, Maggie.

MARGARET. Well, I was conscious of it! What were you thinkin'?

BRICK. I don't remember thinking of anything, Maggie.

MARGARET. Don't you think I know that—? Don't you—?—Think I know that—?

BRICK (*coolly*). Know what, Maggie?

MARGARET (struggling for expression). That I've gone through this— *hideous!—transformation*, become—*hard! Frantic!* . . . Of course, you always had that detached quality as if you were playing a game without much concern over whether you won or lost, and now that you've lost the game, not lost but just quit playing, you have that rare sort of charm that usually only happens in very old or hopelessly sick people, the charm of the defeated. . . . [O]ne thing I don't have is the charm of the defeated, my hat is still in the ring, and I am determined to win!

(*There is the sound of croquet mallets hitting croquet balls.*)

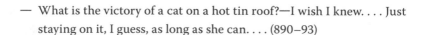 

— What is the victory of a cat on a hot tin roof?—I wish I knew. . . . Just staying on it, I guess, as long as she can. . . . (890–93)

The passage presents countless possible topics for your essay—an analysis of one of the characters, an examination of the title metaphor, or some exposition on the thematic concerns of the play and their significance, to name only a few. This single passage not only reveals Maggie's and Brick's true characters—Maggie as a frustrated wife who has become "hard" and "[f]rantic" (890), and Brick as a detached man with "the charm of the defeated" (892); it also reveals several themes of the play—isolation, failed relationships, and mendacity. The passage also references the title of the work, and an entire essay could be formed around an examination of this metaphor. Any of these topics could form the basis of a thesis that can then be supported by performing close readings of other sections of the text that deal with these same topics.

The same tactic can be applied with each act. Consider, for instance, the second act, which takes as its central action a strained dialogue between Brick and Big Daddy. Like the passage cited previously, the exchange between Brick and Big Daddy that fills the second act also presents the option of analyzing characters, examining the title metaphor, or writing about the thematic concerns of the play and their significance. A passage from the second act might serve as your starting point, or the information it yields could be combined with your observations about the previous citation from act 1 to begin building the argument of your essay. For instance, if you choose to analyze a character or compare and contrast characters in the play, the dialogue reveals much about Brick and Big Daddy and their relationship. It seems to expose the best and worst features of each character—the honesty and sincerity that both are capable of but also their inability to communicate and to truly connect with those who love them and their failure to refrain from that which disgusts them. Therefore, you could use this part of the passage to begin an essay analyzing Brick or Big Daddy or comparing and contrasting the two. In this case, you would continue on by evaluating other places in the text where Brick and Big Daddy make an appearance.

If you choose to evaluate the title metaphor of the play, you would consider its appearance in the following passage:

**BIG DADDY.** That woman of yours has a better shape on her than Gooper's but somehow or other they got the same look about them.

**BRICK.** What sort of look is that, Big Daddy?

**BIG DADDY.** I don't know how to describe it, but it's the same look.

**BRICK.** They don't look peaceful, do they?

**BIG DADDY.** No, they sure in hell don't.

**BRICK.** They look nervous as cats?

**BIG DADDY.** That's right, they look nervous as cats.

**BRICK.** Nervous as a couple of cats on a hot tin roof?

**BIG DADDY.** That's right, boy, they look like a couple of cats on a hot tin roof. It's funny that you and Gooper being so different would pick out the same type of woman.

**BRICK.** Both of us married into society, Big Daddy.

**BIG DADDY.** Crap . . . I wonder what give them both that look?

**BRICK.** Well. They're sittin' in the middle of a big piece of land, Big Daddy, twenty-eight thousand acres is a pretty big piece of land and so they're squaring off on it, each determined to knock off a bigger piece of it than the other whenever you let it go.

**BIG DADDY.** I got a surprise for those women. I'm not gonna let it go for a long time yet if that's what they're waiting for. (924–25)

Consider Brick's use of the metaphor in this passage. To whom or what does this metaphor apply? What does Big Daddy contribute to this part of the conversation? Likewise, you could combine this information with your observations about the appearance of the title metaphor in the first act and go on to explore its other manifestations in the text. This passage indicates that Mae and Maggie are like cats on a hot tin roof, but other close readings may indicate that other characters can be compared in this manner as well. You would need to conclude by explaining why the title and the methods that Williams uses to convey its importance are significant.

As an alternative, if you choose to focus on the thematic concerns of the play and their significance you will want to focus on a later portion of the dialogue that builds up to a literal revelation of a central theme of the work: mendacity. Consider the following exchange between Brick and Big Daddy:

> **BIG DADDY.** I'll make a bargain with you. You tell me why you drink and I'll hand you one. I'll pour the liquor myself and hand it to you.
>
> **BRICK.** Why do I drink?
>
> **BIG DADDY.** Yea! Why? . . .
>
> **BRICK.** I'll tell you in one word.
>
> **BIG DADDY.** What word?
>
> **BRICK.** DISGUST! . . . Have you ever heard the word "mendacity"?
>
> **BIG DADDY.** Sure. Mendacity is one of them five dollar words that cheap politicians throw back and forth at each other.
>
> **BRICK.** You know what it means?
>
> **BIG DADDY.** Don't it mean liars and lying?
>
> **BRICK.** Yes, sir, liars and lying.
>
> **BIG DADDY.** Has someone been lying to you? . . . Who's been lying to you, has Margaret been lying to you, has your wife been lying to you about something, Brick?

BRICK. Not her. That wouldn't matter.

BIG DADDY. Then who's been lying to you, and what about?

BRICK. No one single person and no one lie. . . .

BIG DADDY. Then what, what then, for Christ's sake?

BRICK.—The whole, the whole—thing. . . .

BIG DADDY. . . . What do you know about this mendacity thing? Hell! I
could write a book on it! Don't you know that? I could write a book on
it and still not cover the subject? Well, I could, I could write a goddam
book on it and still not cover the subject anywhere near enough!!—
Think of all the lies I got to put up with!—Pretenses! Ain't that mendacity? Having to pretend stuff you don't think or feel or have any idea
of? (939–41)

Mendacity is a theme that is verbalized by Brick in this passage,
expounded upon by Big Daddy, and, further, reflected in the interactions of the characters throughout the entire course of the play. From
this passage we know that both Brick and Big Daddy struggle with dis-
honesty in the world, but their dialogue elsewhere in act 2 reveals that
both also allow it to seep into their own lives, with Brick unable to own
up to the truth of his relationship with Skipper and Big Daddy lying
to his wife and refusing to deal properly with the realization that he
despises the woman he has lived with for most of his life. You might
choose to make note of these observations and then return to the first
act to consider how the interaction between Maggie and Brick also references this theme. You would continue to look for evidence of this
theme throughout the play and would conclude with your thoughts
on what the play is telling us about mendacity and why this is significant. These are only a few of the topics that could be utilized using this
method. Consider what other information is revealed to us by considering the central action of each act and use the same methods of close
reading, identification, and exposition to shape your own observations
into a strong essay.

If you prefer to consider a more subtle aspect of the play, you may choose the second suggested topic—an examination of the importance of the set in *Cat on a Hot Tin Roof.* In addition to our own observations of how the set is presented in the text, Williams provides his own "Notes for the Designer," which explain thoughts on how the set should be treated in staged versions of the play. You might begin by making note of your own observations about the set from the text and then return to Williams's notes. Consider his explanation of the physical aspects of the set such as furniture and props:

> Two articles of furniture need mention: a big double bed which staging should make a functional part of the set as often as suitable, the surface of which should be slightly raked to make figures on it seen more easily; and against the wall space between the two huge double doors upstage: a monumental monstrosity peculiar to our times, a *huge* console combination of a radio-phonograph (Hi-Fi with three speakers) TV set *and* liquor cabinet . . . This piece of furniture (?!), this monument, is a very complete and compact little shrine to virtually all the comforts and illusions behind which we hide from such things as the characters in the play are faced with. . . . (880–81)

Here Williams identifies the bed and the television/liquor cabinet as the two most important props in the play. Consider why this is and return to the text again, looking for examples of where these items appear in the play and how they function as symbols. You may also want to consider Williams's intended use of light and the implied history of the home among other symbols. Do not simply rely on Williams's own comments on these matters. Make note of what else the text itself reveals to us about the set and, consequently, what the set reveals to us about the play.

Finally, you may find that the conclusion of the play is most appealing to you. Williams actually created three different versions of the final act: the original version, a version that was revised for the Broadway debut of the play, and a third version that was drafted for a 1973 revival of the play. You may wish to compare and contrast two of the versions or all three. You can prepare for the start of your essay in much the same way that was outlined for the topics above. Perform close readings of important passages from the versions you have chosen, making note of similarities and differences. You will need to conclude by giving some insight into why these similarities and differences are important and what they reveal about the play.

# TOPICS AND STRATEGIES

In the sections that follow, you will find a variety of suggested topics accompanied by questions and observations to assist you in the task of writing successfully about *Cat on a Hot Tin Roof.* Remember that this is not a comprehensive list of topics, and the statements and questions that appear after each suggested topic are merely a guide to help spark your own ideas about the work. A successful paper will present a strong thesis based upon your own original ideas and will be supported by relevant examples resulting from close readings of the text. A wide variety of interpretations will be possible as you consider each topic. Use the strategic questions and observations to stimulate your own thoughts about the text and to assist you in developing a strong thesis. Remember to read through the text more than once, making note of those elements of the text that support your argument. It will be equally important to make note of those elements that contradict your thesis, as this will help you to refine your argument and create a stronger case.

## Themes

Although mendacity is often identified as the central theme of the play, no doubt because it is a theme that is spelled out literally for us in the dialogue, the play has many other themes for consideration. Aside from having to deal with truth and deception, the characters also struggle with isolation and loneliness. The play is also built around the characters' greedy attempts to gain control of the Pollitt plantation in light of the imminent death of Big Daddy. An exploration of any of these themes can serve as a good start for your essay. Ask yourself what Williams is saying about these topics and why these revelations are significant.

### *Sample Topics*:
1. **Mendacity:** When Big Daddy asks Brick why he is an alcoholic, Brick tells him that he drinks because of disgust. He is, he says, disgusted by mendacity. What is mendacity and how is this

theme treated in the play? What is the relationship of each of the characters to this theme?

You will want to begin by considering the passage referenced above. How do the characters define mendacity? Although Brick and Big Daddy indicate that they are fed up with mendacity, are they the only characters entitled to feel this way? Consider if their own actions also indicate mendacity. In other words, are their views on mendacity hypocritical? You will need to go beyond this one passage, considering instances of mendacity in the other acts. Brick indicates that the only way to live with mendacity is to drink. Big Daddy also seems to suggest that there is no other escape from mendacity. Are they correct?

2. **Isolation:** Although the characters in the play are never alone, there is a distinct atmosphere of isolation throughout the play. How does Williams create this sense of isolation and why is it significant?

As mentioned above, you should note that throughout the play as characters attempt to have private dialogues, they are often interrupted repeatedly by other members of the family. Knowing that Williams does not present the characters as literally, physically isolated, you will need to determine how he creates a sense of isolation in the play. Consider the formal elements of the text such as symbolism, for one. Also, consider the characters and their development or lack of development. What do we know about the emotional state of the main characters? How do we know that they feel isolated? What formal elements provide us with this information? Consider also what causes their isolation and why this is significant. Is Williams attempting to present some larger statement about society or about human nature?

3. **Greed:**  Much of the play is devoted to the characters' struggle to win their share of the Pollitt inheritance. Is it fair to say that

the characters are driven by greed? Or is there something else at work? Do any of the characters have better intentions?

Consider all of the scenes that reference the characters' struggle to win their share of Big Daddy's estate. Who is interested in the estate and who is not? Can we determine anything about the motivations of the characters? For instance, we know that Mae and Maggie are desperate to inherit his estate, but why? Are they motivated by greed? You may feel that they are, or you may feel, given what we know about their current situations and their backgrounds, that they are driven by other forces. For instance, how does Maggie's background contribute to her desire to inherit the Pollitt estate?

# Character

*Cat on a Hot Tin Roof* provides endless possibilities for writing about character. The play consists of strong characters who consistently clash, leaving little need for symbolism. The play is, ultimately, a series of portraits of individuals, relationships, and the family as a whole. You might choose to analyze a single character or compare and contrast several characters. You could also focus on the relationship between two or more characters such as Maggie and Brick or Brick and Big Daddy. It could also be rewarding to examine the presentation of the Pollitt family as a whole. In all cases you will want to consider everything we know about the characters. Consider what drives each of the characters to act as they do. How do they react to each other? How self-aware are the characters? Make note of how the characters change—or fail to change—throughout the play.

## Sample Topics:

1. **Maggie the Cat:** How does Williams want readers and audiences to respond to Maggie the Cat?

   Your answer to this question may vary depending upon which version of the play you choose to address, or you might choose to center your issue on an examination of the various versions of the play and how Maggie is presented in each. Consider how

Maggie is presented to us. What do we know about her history as well as her current predicament? Does Williams's treatment of this character elicit sympathy? Can she be categorized as a strong character or is she really a weak character? Either view may be supported using examples from the text.

2. **Brick:** Analyze this character.

Begin by considering all of Brick's attributes. His name suggests strength and solidity, but is this in line with his character? We also know that Brick was a football hero. He is also depicted as the favorite son of Big Daddy and Big Mama. How is this portrait contradicted by his true state? What is the symbolic significance of Brick's crutch?

3. **Big Daddy:** Analyze this character.

Although Big Daddy may be characterized as a simple, coarse character, the dialogue of the play reveals that he is a very complex person. Consider how Big Daddy is presented in the play. How does this image change when he appears in act 2 with Brick? What do we learn about him, his emotions, his views on existence from these passages?

## History and Context

Like *The Glass Menagerie* and *A Streetcar Named Desire*, *Cat on a Hot Tin Roof* references a specific time in American history, when the ways associated with plantation life were being lost amid industrialism and urbanization. Consider how the play addresses this theme. Specifically, you may want to consider how Big Daddy functions as a symbol of plantation life. On the other hand, you may also want to consider how the other characters represent the new industrialized society. Is their greed symptomatic of a modern society?

*Sample Topic:*

1. **The death of the Old South:** Like Williams's early works, *Cat on a Hot Tin Roof* seems to point to the death of the Old South,

although this concept is never revealed literally. What methods does Williams employ in order to address this theme?

In order to address this topic, you will want to consider not only literal references to the Old South such as the set, which is a plantation in the South, but also the interaction between the characters in the play. How, for instance, does the decay of the Pollitt family serve as a symbol of the decay of the Old South? You may also want to focus on Big Daddy. The other characters note that he is the biggest planter in the South, but the play also reminds us that he is not infallible. Like all others, he also must face death. Consider also what role the other characters have in this metaphor. Are they perhaps representative of something that is replacing the ways of the Old South? Does the play suggest that industrialism is the cause of the decay and death of the Old South, or does it suggest rather that immorality and greed are the primary culprits? Are these simply symptoms of modern society, or are we able to separate the two? It may be helpful to compare Williams's treatment of the death of the Old South in *Cat on a Hot Tin Roof* to the treatment of the death of the Old South in *The Glass Menagerie* and *A Streetcar Named Desire.* Alternatively, you could compare the treatment of the death of the Old South in this play with the death of the Old South in other works of literature, such as William Faulkner's "A Rose for Emily."

## Philosophy and Ideas

Death is presented as a major theme in the play as is self-knowledge, or the denial of self. The play also addresses questions of existence, truth and illusion, and our options for living with disappointment and difficulty. The question seems to be: What comes of our confrontation with topics of mortality and existence? Consider what view or views the play presents on these matters.

### *Sample Topic:*

1. **Death and self-knowledge:** Does the play present the view that a confrontation with mortality generates self-knowledge or self-

awareness? If so, is this presented as a positive effect or is it rather something that we are plagued with?

Consider the scenes in the play that reference death or mortality. Which of the characters seem to struggle with this issue? Of course we know that Big Daddy has to face his mortality, but how does Skipper's death affect Brick? Do the characters seem to come to a greater understanding of themselves through a consideration of death? Is this necessarily a good thing? To go beyond a typical treatment of this topic, you may wish to also consider how the play references symbolic deaths. For instance, consider how the death of the relationship of Maggie and Brick affects Maggie. What about instances in the play that reference the death of a dream? Consider Maggie's and Brick's remarks on this subject.

## Form and Genre

Like many of Williams's plays, *Cat on a Hot Tin Roof* is a family drama. All of the action of the play pivots on the interaction among the family members and the family's reaction to the terminal illness of the patriarch, Big Daddy. This genre, which has its roots in classical drama, became popular in American theater during this time period. Consider why the family would have been a topic important enough to drive an entire genre of literature. You will want to consider how the American family could be categorized and how the idea of the family was shifting during this time. An examination of genre will therefore allow you to work from a historical or contextual standpoint or a philosophical one.

If you decide to address the form of the play, you will want to begin by considering its structure. The play is broken down into three acts, and each act has a central action. These actions—dialogues, primarily—are easily identified because they dominate the act and are only briefly interrupted by other characters. You may choose to consider the major actions of each act, looking for key themes or elements that stand out. The third act may present more of a challenge because it has been variable, with Williams revising the ending twice. This variable should not be viewed as a problem. In fact, it could become the topic for your essay.

## *Sample Topics:*

1. **Multiple endings:** Williams composed several different endings for *Cat on a Hot Tin Roof.* Which ending do you feel is most successful? Explain why.

   Williams created several different endings to the play. Two versions, the original ending and the ending created for Elia Kazan's film, are included in the Library of America printing of the play that we are using in this book. In addition to these two versions, there is also one other ending that Williams drafted later. Compare two or more of these endings. What do they share in common and what elements did Williams change? How do these changes affect our understanding the play? For instance, does the reappearance of Big Daddy significantly impact the way we perceive the play? Do the endings change our response to the individual characters? Conclude by explaining which version you feel is most successful and why.

2. **Family drama:** Analyze the play as a work of family drama.

   The play presents the breakdown of a southern family. Consider what themes Williams is able to address by working in this format. Is the breakdown of the family symbolic in any way? What do we learn from the interaction between the characters? What causes the conflicts that drive the family apart? In addition to considering the Pollitt family as a whole, you may wish to examine the other families that comprise it—Gooper, Mae, and the children; Brick and Maggie; or Big Mama and Big Daddy. You might also choose to compare the Pollitt family to another family in literature or in American theater, such as the Tyrone family in Eugene O'Neill's *Long Day's Journey into Night* or the Loman family of Arthur Miller's *Death of a Salesman.* What message do the plays give us about the state of the modern family? If you choose to compare the play to *Death of a Salesman,* you will also want to consider how the play presents the image of the patriarch. What message does the play share with *Cat on a Hot Tin Roof,* and why is this significant?

## Language, Symbols, and Imagery

The most prominent symbol of the play is, of course, the metaphor of the cat on a hot tin roof, which Williams uses for the title of the play. It is referenced throughout the play, noted in the interactions and private commentaries of Brick, Big Daddy, and Maggie. Not all of Williams's symbols are this overt, but close readings of the text will reveal that there are countless other examples of symbolism that you might use to begin your essay. Consider, for example, Brick's crutch. How does the crutch function as a symbol of his true self? In addition to making his physical shortcomings apparent, what does it indicate about his mental or emotional well-being? Consider the scenes that reference his crutch. How do these scenes impact our interpretation of Brick? Does the crutch make us more sympathetic to his character, or does it simply reinforce what we already know about Brick?

### *Sample Topics:*

1. **The title:** Why do you feel that Williams named the play *Cat on a Hot Tin Roof*? Does the title accurately reflect the major concerns of the work?

   Begin by considering the title outside of a reading of the text. In other words, note what you think of when you read this title. What images come to mind? Refer back to the text and make note of all passages that address the idea of a cat on a hot tin roof. For instance, Maggie and Brick often refer to this idea, and later in the play, Brick and Big Daddy discuss this notion as well. Although Maggie identifies herself as the cat and Brick and Daddy liken Maggie and Mae to cats on a hot tin roof, does this metaphor apply to only these two characters or does it also refer to the condition of other characters in the play? Consider how this metaphor reinforces the thematic concerns of the play.

2. **The imminent death of Big Daddy:** The play centers on the looming death of Big Daddy. What symbolic value does this imminent death hold? And what themes is Williams able to address by suggesting the imminent death of Big Daddy as a metaphor?

Consider what information we are presented with regarding the imminent death of Big Daddy. You will need to ask yourself who Big Daddy is and what he represents. Then consider how his death might be symbolic. In addition to revealing social or cultural themes, how does his looming death allow Williams to present philosophical concerns?

3. **The set:** Preceding the play, Williams provides detailed notes regarding the proper design of the set. Analyze the set of *Cat on a Hot Tin Roof* and explain what significance these details have.

Consider Williams's "Notes for the Designer" and consider his instructions regarding the set. How do props such as the bed and the television/liquor cabinet create a sense of the thematic concerns of the play? What about the features of the plantation, the house, and the huge double doors? What significance does the lighting have? You will need to return to the text and look at where these parts of the set are apparent and what effect they have on us as readers.

## Compare and Contrast Essays

If you choose to write a compare and contrast essay, you will find that the play presents many unlikely topics for comparison. For example, a comparison of Big Daddy and Brick may reveal that the characters are more alike than it first appears. The same is true of the female characters of the play who seem to constantly clash but who have much in common. Whether you treat characters, themes, or other formal elements, consider how information is revealed from elements that seem to be in opposition.

## Sample Topics:

1. **Big Daddy and Brick:** Compare and contrast these characters.

   Although Big Daddy and Brick appear to be very different characters at first glance, there is much they share in common as well. Consider descriptions of their characters, their speech, and their manner. You will also want to consider how each of the characters is perceived by the other characters in the play. It will be particularly useful to examine their exchange in act 2 of the play. How do the characters interact with each other and what does this reveal to us about them?

2. **Children in *Cat on a Hot Tin Roof* and *The Rose Tattoo:*** Both plays employ children throughout the play. What function do they serve and why is this significant?

   Consider all instances where children appear in these plays. What are the children doing when they make an appearance? Do they engage with the main characters in any way or are they primarily flat characters? Consider how the appearance of children is in harmony with the thematic concerns of the play. Does the presence of the children give us any insight into the main characters of these plays? Consider if the children hold any symbolic value. What might the children represent?

3. **The film and the play:** Compare and contrast the play with a film version or compare and contrast multiple film or television adaptations.

   The best-known film version of *Cat on a Hot Tin Roof* is the 1958 version, which featured Burl Ives as Big Daddy. Why do you think that this is the most well-known adaptation of the play? Is it true to Williams's own vision of the themes and characters? If not, what is different and how does this impact the way we interpret and react to the play?

If you choose to compare and contrast multiple film or television adaptations, you will need to note similarities in the different versions. What do they share in common and why is this important? Why do you believe that all of the versions treated this element or these elements in the same way? You will also need to note variations in the versions and explain why these differences are significant. Were the changes due to structural concerns or concerns with the formal elements of the play? Or were they dictated by social constraints such as censorship? How do these variations, and their causes, change our interpretation of the play? If you locate changes that are due to social constraints, you might choose to organize your essay around an exploration of this topic, comparing its impact on this play to its impact on other Williams plays or examples of censorship in other works of literature.

4. **Brick and Blanche from *A Streetcar Named Desire:*** Compare and contrast these two characters.

Brick and Blanche are both troubled characters, plagued by events of the past. First you will need to explain what evidence we have to support the claim that Brick and Blanche are troubled characters, plagued by events of the past. What do we know about them and their past? How are these events revealed to us in the texts? How are the events similar? What impact do they have on Brick and Blanche? You will want to explain how each character responds to these events. Compare Brick's alcoholism and his search for the click that will bring him peace to Blanche's alcoholism and the polka that is followed by a gunshot. Are either of the characters able to surmount the problems associated with their tragic histories? Also, how does the theme of mendacity apply to each character?

5. **The women of *Cat on a Hot Tin Roof:*** Compare and contrast the female characters in the play.

Although the female characters in *Cat on a Hot Tin Roof* are usually at odds, they share much in common. Consider the similarities between Maggie, Mae, and Big Mama. What are their roles in the family? What are their motivations? How are they impacted by their relationships with their husbands? You may also want to consider Brick and Big Daddy's likening of Mae and Maggie to cats on a hot tin roof. Does this characterization also apply to Big Mama?

## Bibliography and Resources for *Cat on a Hot Tin Roof*

Bloom, Harold, ed. *Tennessee Williams's Cat on a Hot Tin Roof.* Modern Critical Interpretations. Philadelphia: Chelsea House, 2001.

*Cat on a Hot Tin Roof.* Dir. Richard Brooks. 1958. DVD. Warner, 2006.

Crandell, George W. "*Cat on a Hot Tin Roof.*" *Tennessee Williams: A Guide to Research and Performance.* Ed. Philip C. Kolin. Westport, CT: Greenwood, 1998. 109–25.

Davis, David A. "'Make the Lie True': The Tragic Family in *Cat on a Hot Tin Roof* and *King Lear.*" *Tennessee Williams Annual Review* 5 (2002): 1–11.

Devlin, Albert J. "Writing in 'A Place of Stone': *Cat on a Hot Tin Roof.*" *Cambridge Companion to Tennessee Williams.* Ed. Matthew C. Roudané. Cambridge: Cambridge UP, 1997. 95–113.

Kullman, Colby H. "Rule by Power: 'Big Daddyism' in the World of Tennessee Williams's Plays." *Mississippi Quarterly* 48 (Fall 1996): 667–76.

Palmer, R. Barton. "Elia Kazan and Richard Brooks Do Tennessee Williams: Melodramatizing *Cat on a Hot Tin Roof* on Stage and Screen." *Tennessee Williams Annual Review* 2 (1999): 1–11.

Parker, Brian. "Bringing Back Big Daddy." *Tennessee Williams Annual Review* 3 (2000): 91–99.

Williams, Tennessee. *Cat on a Hot Tin Roof. Tennessee Williams: Plays 1937–1955.* Eds. Mel Gussow and Kenneth Holditch. New York: Library of America, 2000. 873–1,005.

# ORPHEUS DESCENDING

## READING TO WRITE

I N 1957, Williams presented *Orpheus Descending,* a play that told the story of the tragic culmination of the relationship between an outsider who finds himself an outcast in a small southern town and a woman who has lost herself to a tragic past, whose husband is teetering on the brink of death. The play was, unfortunately, a critical failure in its day; the biggest criticism of the work had to do with familiarity. Critics and scholars argued that the fault of the play lay in its propensity toward redundancy, with Williams recycling themes, characters, and elements of plot that were already explored thoroughly in his other works. It is true that there are many similarities between *Orpheus Descending* and Williams's other plays and, as a result, the greatest challenge of writing about *Orpheus Descending* may be the difficulty of overcoming these familiarities. Although a comparison of the play to Williams's other works can be informative, it is a subject that has its limits, and the play does have its own unique features that present some more attractive (and less constricting) alternatives for those choosing to write about the play. There are two attributes of *Orpheus Descending* that perhaps stand out among all the rest, and a consideration of either topic could be a perfect starting point for an engaging and truly revelatory essay. First, there is the matter of the long, slow evolution of the play. The work that we know as *Orpheus Descending* is actually a rewrite of an early Williams play entitled *Battle of Angels,* which debuted in 1940. After a poor reception instigated the cancellation of the remaining performances of *Battle of Angels,* Williams went back to work. He continued to work on the play for almost two decades, releasing the new version known as *Orpheus Descending* in 1957. In his essay "The Past, the Present and the Perhaps," which precedes the play in the Library of America version of the text that we are using in this book, Williams talks about his reasons for sticking with the play: "Why have I stuck so stubbornly to this play? For seventeen years, in fact? Well, nothing is more precious to anybody than the emotional record of his youth, and you will find the trail of my sleeve-worn heart in this completed play that I now call *Orpheus Descending*" (4). It is not as easy as one would think to see what Williams refers to as "the emotional record of his youth" (4) in the play. *Orpheus Descending* does not immediately seem to present the same thinly disguised characters and clear autobiographical bent as a play like *The Glass Menagerie*, for instance, and yet, Williams saw enough of himself in the play to continue working on it for 17 years.

The intense process of revision evidenced in *Orpheus Descending*, in fact, became a signature of Williams's work. While many authors subject themselves to this same drawn out process of revision, we are not typically privy to anything other than the final draft, so Williams's texts are gifts that give us insight into a private and personal process. Of the new draft, Williams stated that "it now [had] in it a sort of emotional bridge between those early years . . . and [his] present state of existence as a playwright" (7). The play merged past and present, creating a work of literature that ultimately spoke of the future, or what Williams referred to in his essay as "the perhaps." It served as an example of a new model for American drama, all the while addressing classical themes, adapted for our own interpretation and understanding.

Finally, the lapse in time between the original presentation of *Battle of Angels* and the later production of *Orpheus Descending* also serves as evidence that there are many themes that remain relevant long after they are put on paper. In fact, this is the secret of all great literature—the possession of a kind of timelessness, a universal significance that remains steadfast even as cultures, people, and trends change. A consideration of these themes or the "timelessness" of the play could be very rewarding topics for your consideration.

The second notable feature of the play also has much to do with the merging of past and present. The play is heavy with the influence of Greek mythology. It is, as the title suggests, a modern retelling of the Orpheus myth. In the characterization in particular, and in passages such as the final scene where Val goes back for Lady, especially, one finds the refreshed tale of Orpheus and Eurydice. The appropriation of the story of Orpheus allowed Williams to create a work that functioned as a hybrid of classical and modern elements, allowing Williams to work with classic themes such as love and revenge while creating a dialogue about more contemporary concerns such as racism and intolerance.

By beginning with some consideration of this second feature of the play, you open yourself up to a wide range of possible essay topics. You could use *Orpheus Descending* to discuss the overall influence of Greek literature on Williams's work. Certainly the presence of the influence of Greek mythology in *Orpheus Descending* could easily be compared to an exhibition of the influence of Greek mythology in other works by Williams, such as the Dionysian elements of *The Rose Tattoo*. Another idea is to approach the topic of the influence of Greek mythology by examining genre—the classification of the work. It can be tricky to write about genre because, often, it appears to be a self-explanatory subject. We might think that the play is what it is, so to speak, but genre is not so simple. As we see from Williams's previous works, and as evidenced in literature as a whole, our definitions of genre are subject to change. Our notions of romance, family drama, and fantasy, for instance, evolve as time passes and cultures change, and often genres are combined as we saw, for example, in *The Rose Tattoo*, which merged comedy and tragedy. Therefore, the following question (although it may seem straightforward) is a valuable and complex one: How does *Orpheus Descending* function as tragedy? A better question, perhaps, is as follows: How does the play redefine tragedy, making it relevant and reflective of our own concerns in today's world? Seeking an answer to these questions offers countless possibilities for explication. For instance, these questions could lead you to enter into an examination of Williams's work within the context of modern American drama. You might compare *Orpheus Descending* to the works of some other great American playwrights such as Eugene O'Neill and Arthur Miller. How, for instance, does *Orpheus Descending* compare to O'Neill's *Long Day's Journey into Night* or Miller's *Death of a Salesman*? How do these works challenge traditional conceptions of tragedy and the way that we consider genre? Another interesting idea would be to compare and contrast Williams's appropriation of myth with the appropriation of myth in the works of other authors. How does Williams's Orpheus, for instance, compare to the Orpheus presented in Margaret Atwood's poem by the same name? What does the play have in common with Atwood's *The Penelopiad*? What can we learn from a comparison of Williams's play to Salman Rushdie's *The Ground Beneath Her Feet,* Thomas Pynchon's *Gravity's Rainbow,* or Alice Munro's "The Children Stay" (other works inspired by the Orpheus myth)? A consideration of the recurring appearance of this single myth throughout literature should raise questions about why we find these myths so interesting and relevant today. Is the appropriation of myth simply a trend or something more? You should now be able to see how, from identifying only two attributes of the play, you can uncover countless possibilities for exploration. Once you have chosen an appropriate topic, refer back to the text and perform close readings, analyzing the formal elements of the text for information that supports your thesis.

In addition to refining an argument about either of the two broad topics suggested above, *Orpheus Descending* presents many other options. Although the play might seem kitschy to those familiar with representations of "the rebel" in 1950s culture, the play is deeply philosophical. While the characters are described in such a manner that we are led to believe that they are closed off and guarded, we actually become voyeurs who witness the revelation of their most intimate thoughts. The characters reveal their thoughts about love, their regrets, those things that plague them, and their secrets. Through the intimate exchanges between characters, the play addresses interesting and complex issues such as intolerance, revenge, desire, and love. Look, for instance, at the exchange that takes place between Val and Lady in the second act, where Val offers his view of love:

> VAL. *Listen!*—When I was a kid on Witches Bayou? After my folks all scattered away like loose chicken's feathers blown around by the wind?—I stayed there alone on the bayou, hunted and trapped out of season and hid from the law!—Listen! All that time, all that lonely time, I felt I was—waiting for something!
>
> LADY. What for?

VAL. What does anyone wait for? For something to happen, for anything to happen, to make things make more sense. . . . It's hard to remember what that feeling was like because I've lost it now, but I was waiting for something like if you ask a question you wait for someone to answer, but you ask the wrong question or you ask the wrong person and the answer don't come. Does everything stop because you don't get the answer? No, it goes right on as if the answer was given, day comes after day and night comes after night, and you're still waiting for someone to answer the question and going right on as if the question was answered. And then—well—then. . . .

LADY. Then what?

VAL. You get the make-believe answer.

LADY. What answer is that?

VAL. Don't pretend you don't know because you do!

LADY. Love?

VAL *(placing hand on her shoulder)*. That's the make-believe answer. It's fooled many a fool besides you an' me, that's the God's truth, Lady, and you had better believe it. (43)

Consider how this view of love as a "make-believe answer" to a long-asked question is challenged throughout the play. Look, for example, at the conclusion of the play. Does it suggest that his view of love has changed? This could also lead you into an examination of character development in the play. How do Val and Lady change throughout the course of the play? Do their philosophical views and values change? Characters are not stagnant creatures; they often learn and grow (or regress, as the case may be) in the course of a story. Also, remember that while the interaction of Val and Lady is central to the story, there is valuable information in other areas of the play. Consider, for instance, the passages that contain The Conjure Man and Carol Cutrere's reaction to him. How can we use the information from these scenes to talk about ideas of otherness and intolerance? This presents the chance to consider the work from a social or historical point of view. If you are interested in addressing the artist, religion and spirituality, or definitions of intimacy, consider Val's exchanges with Vee, such as the one included here:

> VEE.—Oh I—tell you!—since I got into this painting, my whole outlook is different. I can't explain how it is, the difference to me.
>
> VAL. You don't have to explain. I know what you mean. Before you started to paint it didn't make sense.
>
> VEE. What—what didn't?
>
> VAL. Existence!
>
> VEE (slowly and softly). No—no it didn't . . . existence didn't make sense. . . . (She places canvas on guitar on counter and sits in chair.)
>
> VAL (rising and crossing to her). You lived in Two River County, the wife of the county Sheriff. You saw awful things take place.
>
> VEE. Awful! Things! . . . How do you—?
>
> VAL. Know? I been a witness, I know!
>
> VEE. I been a witness! I know!
>
> VAL. We seen these things from seats down front at the show. (He crouches before her and touches her hands in her lap. Her breath shudders.) And so you begun to paint your visions. Without no plan, no training, you started to paint as if God touched your fingers. (He lifts her hand slowly, gently from her soft lap.) You made some beauty out of this dark country with these two, soft, woman hands. . . . (58–59)

The exchanges between Vee and Val offer us something different to consider, an emotional or spiritual intimacy in stark contrast to the reaction that Val seems to elicit from other women as the subject of their desire. Some exploration of this topic could be the start of a unique and original essay.

## TOPICS AND STRATEGIES

In the sections that follow, you will find a variety of suggested topics accompanied by questions and observations to assist you in the task of writing successfully about *Orpheus Descending*. Remember that this is not a comprehensive list of topics, and the statements and questions that appear after each suggested topic are merely a guide to help spark your own ideas about the work. A successful paper will present a strong thesis based upon your own original ideas and will be supported by relevant examples resulting from close readings of the text. A wide variety of interpretations will be possible as you consider each topic. Use the strategic questions and observations to stimulate your own thoughts about the text and to assist you in developing a strong thesis. Remember to read through the text more than once, making note of those elements of the text that support your argument. It will be equally important to make note of those elements that contradict your thesis, as this will help you to refine your argument and create a stronger case.

### Themes

In addition to addressing some of the thematic concerns evidenced in Williams's other works, *Orpheus Descending* deals with many themes that traditionally appear in classical Greek mythology such as desire, love, and revenge. Choose a theme and explore how it is treated in the text. How is the treatment of this theme different from its treatment in classical literature? How do the formal elements of the play reveal these themes? Does Williams present clear-cut views on these topics? Or does he leave them open for our interpretation?

### *Sample Topics:*

1. **Desire:** Is desire presented as a positive force or a negative force in the play? Or is the nature of desire contingent on the person who desires and the object of that desire? Explain.

Although it is initially suggested that Lady desires Val, this idea is not confirmed until we are deep into the play. What effect does this desire have on Val and on Lady? How does it change Lady's life? You may feel that Lady's relationship with Val is restorative and allows her to access a part of herself that was lost in a loveless marriage to Jabe. In this case, you will need to present examples that demonstrate that she had lost a part of herself and show how her interactions with Val restored those lost parts. Alternatively, you may feel that Lady's unbridled desire is what ultimately leads to the tragedy at the conclusion of the play. Either of these viewpoints can work well in your essay as long as you provide examples from the text to give weight to your own opinions.

2. **Revenge:** One of the central themes of *Orpheus Descending* is revenge. This is exhibited in various incarnations: Lady's attempt to recreate her father's vineyard by working on the confectionery even as her husband is dying, the conversation between Lady and the nurse in which we learn that Lady would like to kill her husband, the sheriff's attack on Val, Jabe's attack on Val and Lady, and, arguably, Lady's confession to David Cutrere. What message does the play ultimately present about revenge?

Begin by examining passages where revenge is represented. How does each character's desire for revenge affect him or her? Can Lady's confession to David Cutrere be considered an act of revenge? How does she ultimately feel after this confession? Is anything gained (or lost) by it? Does the play make any connections between revenge and karma? Consider, for example, if the text suggests any relationship between Jabe's illness and his relationship to the killing of Lady's father or his confession of his part in the killing. What about Lady's conversation with the nurse in which she suggests that she would like to kill her husband? Is there any relation between her wish for revenge and her own death at Jabe's hands? Ultimately, you will need to explain if you feel that the play presents desire as self-destructive or as an attempt at self-restoration. Perhaps, it may be both. Use examples from the text to support your assertions.

3. **Redemptive power of art:** Some of the most intimate scenes in the play take place between Val and Vee in verbal exchanges about art. What message do these scenes impart about the power of art?

Consider Val and Vee's conversations about art. Do these exchanges present art as a powerful and redemptive force or as a kind of curse? Consider how spirituality is also a dual theme of their conversations. You will want to make note of Val's remarks about how music makes him feel and Vee's explanation of art as a spiritual activity. You might choose to compare the view of art presented in the play with that presented in some of Williams's other texts, such as *The Glass Menagerie* and *The Night of the Iguana*.

4. **Intolerance:** Intolerance is presented throughout the play in many different contexts. What do we learn about intolerance from the play?

First you will need to describe some of the evidence of intolerance in the play. You might consider the ostracized Carol Cutrere, who is banished by her own family; the people's reaction to The Conjure Man; Sheriff Talbot's words to Val upon catching him with his wife; or the use of ethnic and racial epithets throughout the play. What are we to make of Beulah's comment that "[y]ou can't ostracize a person out of this county unless everybody cooperates" (47)? Is intolerance an individual problem or a social problem? Your essay will need to consider who is ostracized and explain why the others react to these characters as they do. Are they not tolerated simply because they are different? Or are there cultural factors to consider? How, for instance, were African Americans treated in the South at the time the play was written? This topic will lead you to an exploration of the historical context of the work.

How does the treatment of intolerance in the play reflect the time period in which the play was written? Is its treatment of intolerance still relevant today?

5. **Love:** In his conversations with Lady, Val reveals a sordid past and indicates that love is nothing more than a trick, the illusion of the fulfillment of something long awaited. Is his perception of love perpetuated throughout the story? Or does the play challenge this view?

This topic might be approached in a variety of ways depending on your opinion on the matter. You might, for example, see Lady and Jabe's relationship as confirmation that love is only an illusion. In this instance, you would also want to pay attention to Beulah and Dolly's insight that "[p]eople can live together in hate" (14) and their notion that couples "hang on together" (14). You could also use the failed relationship of Lady and David Cutrere to help support your argument.

You might prefer instead to support the view that Val's view of love is challenged and that love is not an illusion. In this case you will want to approach the topic by considering Val and Lady's relationship. You will need to use their dialogue and interactions to support the view that this was a positive and redemptive relationship. If you take this approach, pay careful attention to the conclusion of the play and Val's revelation of his feelings for Lady. Has his point of view on the matter of love changed?

## Character

*Orpheus Descending* presents some character types that should be familiar to you if you have studied some of the other plays written by Williams—the outsider, the artist, the woman whose difficult past has led her to the point of hysteria, for instance. Are these characters redundant or does Williams have something new to say with the creation of characters like Val, Vee, and Lady? Are the characters simply archetypes? Another interesting consideration is whether or not the characters fulfill traditional notions of gender. How can we talk about masculinity in

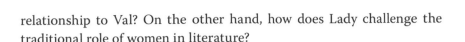

relationship to Val? On the other hand, how does Lady challenge the traditional role of women in literature?

## Sample Topics:

1. **Val:** Can Val be characterized as a typical male character? Does he seem to embody a traditional view of masculinity? How does Williams want us to perceive Val?

Consider descriptions of Val in the play. You will need to look not only at the text that describes him but remember to also look at how the other characters perceive him and react to him. Do the women perceive him differently than the men in the story? What might be the significance of Val's name? Does Val subvert traditional notions of sexuality? You will need to build an argument for how you feel males are traditionally depicted in literature. Then, using examples from the text, explain how Val fits into this mold or how he creates a new definition of masculinity. You may want to compare and contrast Val and a male character from another work of literature or consider how Val compares to Stanley of *A Streetcar Named Desire*. Also, consider how we, as outsiders, view Val. Is he a protagonist or an antagonist? Depending on your opinion, you may want to consider the scene where Val confesses his love for Lady or the scene where he steals the money from the cashbox and disappears. Is it possible to categorize him as either, or does he embody the inherent duality of human nature?

2. **Lady:** Analyze this character.

Lady is a complicated character. She is also a familiar character if you have read works such as *The Glass Menagerie, A Streetcar Named Desire,* or *The Rose Tattoo.* Look at how Lady is presented in the text. How does she interact with the other characters, and how do the other characters perceive her? What are her strengths and weaknesses? Consider how Williams might want us to view Lady. Can we say that she is a strong character? Explain how her character gives us insight into the themes of the play. Does she represent a traditional notion of femininity? Does her name hold any significance?

**3. Vee:** Why does Williams introduce a character like Vee in the text? How does her reaction to Val differ from the other women's, and why is this significant?

First, consider what we know of Vee. How does her self-proclaimed role as a visionary artist allow her to relate to Val? What are we to make of her revelation that she "paint[s] a thing how [she] feel[s] it instead of always the way it actually is" (57)? You might choose to write about Vee as an archetype of the frustrated artist. You could also compare her to other characters in Williams's works who also seem to embody the character of the repressed artist.

Vee also plays a large role in driving the dramatic action of the play. Her emotional intimacy with Val essentially leads to the tragedy that concludes the play. Does this connection suggest that emotional intimacy is more powerful and dangerous than physical intimacy?

**4. The Conjure Man:** Why does Williams include The Conjure Man in the play? What role does he play, and how does he help to reveal the thematic concerns of the play?

First, consider if The Conjure Man is a flat character or a round character. If you believe he is a flat character, explain what he might represent. The Conjure Man appears at various points throughout the text. Consider what is happening when he shows up and who is present upon his arrival. How do these characters react to his presence? Why is Carol Cutrere unafraid of The Conjure Man while the other women hide or exit when he enters the room? Is there any link between Carol and The Conjure Man? You may choose to examine how his character raises issues of identity, intolerance, and superstition. Choose one of these themes and explain how The Conjure Man informs us about this topic. You could also consider what role The Conjure Man has within the context of the myth of Orpheus. What is the symbolic significance of his keeping Val's snakeskin jacket?

5. **The outsider:** How does Williams reprise the role of "the outsider" in *Orpheus Descending*?

This topic will allow you to write about intolerance and otherness through an analysis of the characters in the play. Consider which characters are presented as outsiders. What do they share in common? Why are they considered different and labeled as outsiders? How do they deal with this label? Where else do we find this notion of the outsider in Williams's work? Look for examples of this character type in plays like *The Glass Menagerie, Cat on a Hot Tin Roof,* and *The Rose Tattoo.* What do these characters have in common?

## Philosophy and Ideas

In addition to referencing Christianity through the character Vee, the play also addresses other complex issues of faith and superstition and, also, existentialist themes. How does the play address superstition? What might cause the characters to be superstitious? The play also raises issues about fate and order. Consider the dramatic action of the play. Do the characters create their own fate in a kind of karmic fashion? Or are they simply subject to a disorderly universe? How do their own choices play a part in their fate?

### Sample Topics:

1. **Superstition:** How does superstition play a role in the play?

Consider instances in the play where there is evidence of superstition. For example, Carol comments that she may find love because the heel of her shoe broke off. Look at scenes where The Conjure Man appears. Why do the characters fear him? Does a character's belief in superstition seem to reveal anything about his or her character? Or does it reveal more about social beliefs? Explain.

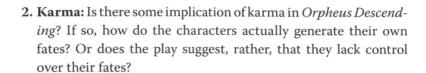 

2. **Karma:** Is there some implication of karma in *Orpheus Descending*? If so, how do the characters actually generate their own fates? Or does the play suggest, rather, that they lack control over their fates?

You may feel that there is a certain implication of karma in the play. For example, Jabe Torrance, who played a part in the killing of Lady's father, is struck with a terminal illness, and when he confesses his part in the killing, he begins to suffer a hemorrhage. Also, shortly after Lady's implication that she wishes to kill her husband, she is shot by Jabe. However, if you choose to focus on the conclusion of the play, you might argue that there is no karma or any sense of order or reason to the actions in the play, as Val and Lady ultimately suffer a tragic fate despite their revelation of love. Does the play simply imply that we live in an unfair universe or is something more at work?

3. **Existentialism:** The main characters seem to be plagued by questions relating to their very existence. How does the play confront the larger issue of existentialism?

Consider what we know about the main characters' views on life. What issues do they struggle with? You will certainly want to look at Val's conversations with Lady. How does Carol's view of life differ from, say, Val's view? How self-aware are these characters? Is there some meaning to the things that happen to them? How do their own views differ from how we perceive their fates?

4. **Duality:** Vee states that we live in "a world of—light and—shadow" (77). Her comment seems to reflect the play's concern with duality. How is duality evidenced in the play and why might this topic be of interest to Williams?

There are many examples of duality in the play: Lady recreates her father's vineyard; Jabe kills twice; Lady becomes pregnant for a second time; The Conjure Man shows up twice at the store. The play also addresses pairings such as good and evil, truth and illusion, body and spirit. What purpose does this duplication have? You will need to consider all examples of duality in the text and think about its effect on you as a reader. How does the presentation of one element inform our perception or understanding of its opposite element? What effect does repetition have on us?

5. **Unanswered questions:** In his essay "The Past, the Present and the Perhaps," which precedes *Orpheus Descending* in the Library of America printing of the play, Williams describes the play as being about "unanswered questions that haunt the hearts of people" (4). What does he mean by this? What questions are the characters dealing with in *Orpheus Descending* and what answers do they receive or fail to receive? How do some characters "continu[e] to ask them" while others accept "prescribed answers that are not answers at all" (4)?

Although the main characters are presented as fairly guarded, closed-off characters, we are privy to their innermost thoughts and secrets. What issues do we know the characters are struggling with? Consider the intimate or revealing conversations that take place between Lady and Val, Carol and Val, and Vee and Val, for instance. How does each character deal with the problem of unanswered questions? Does each character have the same response or present the same view on these matters?

## Form and Genre

We can easily identify *Orpheus Descending* as a tragedy, but what does this mean? How is tragedy defined? If you choose to write about form and genre as it pertains to *Orpheus Descending,* you will certainly be carried into a broader examination of literature. Consider how the idea of tragedy in American theater was changing at the time the play debuted. Were any other playwrights presenting a similar approach to tragedy? You might choose one formal element and explain its function in the play as tragedy. For instance, how do the characters relate to the kinds of characters we typically experience in tragedies and how do they fare? If you feel that there are some redemptive aspects included in the play, does this change our view of the play's classification?

## *Sample Topics:*

1. **Tragedy:** Analyze the play as a tragedy. What elements allow us to categorize it as such? How does it fit the definition of a tragedy or how does it redefine this genre?

   While this may seem like a simple and straightforward topic, keep in mind that definitions of tragedy have shifted throughout the history of literature. For example, the definition of tragedy as we find it in classical Greek mythology is different from the vision of tragedy that we find in modern American drama. Playwrights like Arthur Miller, Eugene O'Neill, and Williams created a new kind of tragedy that encompassed the everyday and made the everyman its central character. How do these changes better serve us as contemporary readers or viewers?

   *Orpheus Descending* is unusual because it is able to combine both classical and modern notions of tragedy. You may address how the play fulfills the concept of tragedy in either context, or you might explain how it takes on attributes of both old and new conceptions of tragedy. Make note of formal elements such as plot, characters, and symbolism that support your assertions.

2. **The appropriation of myth:** *Orpheus Descending* is a modern retelling of the Orpheus myth from classical Greek mythology. What does the play teach us about the significance of myth and the application of myth in modern times?

   Consider all references to the Orpheus myth in the play. Explain how the play recreates the Orpheus myth, and follow up with some explanation of why Williams would have found this myth to be valuable for a modern audience. What themes and cultural or philosophical concerns do we find in this myth that are still relevant today? Can we draw any comparisons between the characters presented in both plays? Use an analysis of the elements of the text to show how myth can be adapted for contemporary use.

## Language, Symbols, and Imagery

Although Williams employs symbolism in the play, the play may not feel as heavily imbued with symbolism as some of Williams's other works. We tend to pick up on symbols that apply directly to the characters, such as Val's guitar and snakeskin jacket, but much of the meaning in the play can be found in the interactions of the characters rather than in objects enlisted as metaphor. In this play, Williams's use of language is less subtle than his use of symbolism. Consider how the characters speak to each other. Many of the supporting characters use racial and ethnic slurs in the course of their everyday conversation. What significance does this have? Does it provide us with information from a social standpoint? Consider how audiences today might react to this language. Do you think that we react the same way that audiences would have reacted at the time the play debuted? If you believe that audiences would react differently, explain why. These questions may compel you to explore the play from a cultural perspective.

### *Sample Topics:*

1. **Language:** Racial and ethnic epithets are often used throughout the play. Why do you believe Williams chooses to use them in his play?

   The epithets used in the play give us a sense of the intolerance that haunted the South during this time period. Consider how the language makes the play more powerful. You might choose to compare the use of this type of language to that of another work of literature—Williams's *The Rose Tattoo,* for example, or Mark Twain's *Huckleberry Finn.* Would our understanding of the work and its themes be the same if offensive language was removed?

2. **Animals:** Williams uses animals as metaphors throughout the play. Why? How do these metaphors inform us about the themes of the play?

Begin by considering examples of the use of animals as metaphor in the play. There is Val's snakeskin jacket; Carol is compared to a wild animal; and later, Val compares Carol to a bird. These are just a few examples of animal imagery implemented in the text. How do these metaphors inform us about the true selves of the characters? And how does this reveal information about the themes of the play? Is Williams appealing to the most basic and instinctual parts of our human nature?

3. **Val's guitar:** What is the significance of Val's guitar in the play? Why does he refuse to allow anyone to touch it?

Aside from being a literal manifestation of Val's status as a musician, the significance of Val's guitar is open for interpretation. It is a prop that was absent in *Battle of Angels*. Consider why Williams added it to *Orpheus Descending*. What social, sexual, or spiritual significance does it have? What are we to make of Val's comment that music "washes [him] clean like water" (34)? Examine the play and consider who is able to touch the guitar. Does this action have some significance?

## Compare and Contrast Essays

Because *Orpheus Descending* is a recreation of a myth, and because it contains many of the same themes evidenced in Williams's other works, it lends itself very well to the compare-and-contrast method. Choose one element of the text—a character, for instance—and compare him or her to the other characters in the play. You might also compare a character from *Orpheus Descending* to the protagonist or antagonist of another work of literature. Because the play has appeared in another form, there is also the option of comparing and contrasting the two versions. Any comparison of any element used in the play can be adapted into a topic for your paper, but be sure not to succumb to the pitfall of simply making a list of similarities. Explain why these similarities and differences are important and how they influence our understanding of the text.

## Sample Topics:

1. **Lady and Serafina of** *The Rose Tattoo:* Compare and contrast these two characters.

   Consider how Williams portrays both women. What characteristics do they share in common? Consider what motivates these women. How is their desire a result of a troubled past? What consequences does this have? How do their relationships with men compare? You may also wish to discuss how you believe Williams wanted us to perceive these characters. Is his treatment of them the same in all respects?

2. **Desire in** *Orpheus Descending* **and** *A Streetcar Named Desire:* How does the treatment of desire in *Orpheus Descending* compare to the vision of desire in *A Streetcar Named Desire?*

   Examine the texts for passages that reference desire (realized or unrealized). In *Orpheus Descending,* this will mean looking at the scenes that contain Val and Lady and the scenes that pair up Val and Carol Cutrere. In *Streetcar,* this will mean looking at the relationship between Stanley and Stella and Blanche's romantic history. How does desire affect the characters in each play? You may choose to narrow the topic by considering the effect of desire on a single character from each play—Lady and Blanche, for instance.

3. *Orpheus Descending* **and** *Battle of Angels: Orpheus Descending* is actually a rewrite of Williams's unsuccessful 1940 play *Battle of Angels.* Compare and contrast the two plays. Which version do you feel is more successful? Why?

   Consider the formal elements of both plays. When Williams rewrote *Battle of Angels,* which elements did he change?

Think about his motivations for these changes—were they structural alterations, or were they changes driven by social constraints? If you feel they were structural changes, you will need to explain why Williams would have wanted to make these changes and how the changes help or hinder the text. If you choose to focus on changes to the text as a result of social constraints, you will need to set up your essay by giving some explanation of the context in which the play was being introduced. How was Williams influenced by these cultural cues? How do the alterations affect our reading of the text?

## Bibliography and Resources for *Orpheus Descending*

Baker Traubitz, Nancy. "Myth as a Basis of Dramatic Structure in *Orpheus Descending.*" *Modern Drama* 19 (1976): 57–66.

Bray, Robert. "*Battle of Angels* and *Orpheus Descending.*" *Tennessee Williams: A Guide to Research and Performance.* Ed. Philip C. Kolin. Westport, CT.: Greenwood, 1998. 22–33.

Clum, John M. "The Sacrificial Stud and the Fugitive Female in *Suddenly Last Summer, Orpheus Descending,* and *Sweet Bird of Youth.*" *Cambridge Companion to Tennessee Williams.* Ed. Matthew C. Roudané. Cambridge: Cambridge UP, 1997. 128–46.

Coronis, Athena. *Tennessee Williams and Greek Culture.* Athens: Kalendis, 1994.

*The Fugitive Kind.* Dir. Sidney Lumet. 1959. DVD. MGM, 2005.

Goldwaite, Charles, Jr. "All Shook Up: Elvis, Bo, and the White Negro in Tennessee Williams's *Orpheus Descending.*" *Tennessee Williams Annual Review* 8 (2006): 95–107.

Kontaxopoulos, Jean. "Orpheus Introspecting: Tennessee Williams and Jean Cocteau." *Tennessee Williams Annual Review* 4 (2001): 1–26.

Minyard, John Douglas. "Classical Motivations in Tennessee Williams." *Classical and Modern Literature* (1986): 287–303.

Segal, Charles. *Orpheus: The Myth of the Poet.* Baltimore: Johns Hopkins UP, 1993.

Strauss, Walter A. *Descent and Return: The Orphic Theme in Modern Literature.* Cambridge, MA: Harvard UP, 1971.

Thompson, Judith J. "Symbol, Myth and Ritual in *The Glass Menagerie, The Rose Tattoo* and *Orpheus Descending.*" *Tennessee Williams: Thirteen Essays.* Ed. Jac Tharpe. Jackson: U of Mississippi P, 1980. 139–71.

Wallace, Jack E. "The Image of Theater in Tennessee Williams's *Orpheus Descending.*" *Modern Drama* 27 (1984): 324–35.

Williams, Tennessee. *Orpheus Descending. Tennessee Williams: Plays 1957–1980.* Eds. Mel Gussow and Kenneth Holditch. New York: Library of America, 2000. 1–97.

———. *Orpheus Descending with Battle of Angels.* New York: New Directions, 1958.

———. "The Past, the Present and the Perhaps." *Tennessee Williams: Plays 1957–1980.* Eds. Mel Gussow and Kenneth Holditch. New York: Library of America, 2000. 3–7.

# THE NIGHT OF
# THE IGUANA

## READING TO WRITE

**I**N 1961, Williams presented audiences with a strange play about a defrocked minister–turned–tour guide who retreats to the Mexican jungle on the verge of a mental breakdown, stranding his all-female tour party. Like many of Williams's works, the play began as a short story and went through a long period of gestation before being released to the public in the form we recognize today. Although the story was drafted as early as 1948, it did not debut in America in its dramatic form on Broadway until more than a decade had passed. When it was finally released, *The Night of the Iguana* was a hit, earning Williams a New York Drama Critics' Circle Award for best play that same year. Today the play is commonly recognized as Williams's last major success. Although he continued to write until his death in 1983, none of Williams's later works were able to achieve the critical or popular acclaim of this play. While *The Night of the Iguana* focused on the plight of outsiders struggling in an inhospitable universe, much like Williams's previous works, the conclusion of the play was unique in that it seemed to allow some room for optimism, something lacking in the endings of plays like *The Glass Menagerie, A Streetcar Named Desire,* or *Orpheus Descending* that conclude tragically with no trace of redemption or suggestion of hope. In *The Night of the Iguana,* the main characters, who are unified in a shared existential struggle, appear ready to help each other in some way. This small detail was enough to secure the attention of critics, scholars, and popular audiences, who responded favorably to the change.

In the past, critics and audiences had struggled with what seemed to be wholly pessimistic themes, representations of immorality, and suggestions of nihilism. Although *The Night of the Iguana* still possessed an air of melancholy, addressing issues such as death, mental illness, and the destructive nature of desire, it broke these stereotypes of Williams's work with its treatment of contrasting themes such as the will to endure, the search for faith, and the camaraderie inherent in human existence. Despite the success of *The Night of the Iguana*, it had also been suggested that the play lacked a clear shape or form, but many responded in Williams's defense, pointing out that the play was not about a single action but rather about the truth of the human condition, a theme that excused it from the conventions of form. In other words, the truth was neither neat nor wholly containable, and the play's existential observations could be presented only in a loose and somewhat chaotic form. Although the play had received these criticisms, critics and audiences recognized that *The Night of the Iguana* represented a major shift in Williams's work, with many hailing the play as Williams's best work ever, the true realization of that which he sought to achieve throughout his career. The play seemed to dismiss the recycled plot that dominated Williams's earlier works—namely, the female in peril searching for a man to rescue her—and it dispensed with the overwrought gestures and cinematic plot twists found in past works, relying instead on pared down revelations of the innermost selves of the characters and their true relationship with one another—a kind of psychological, philosophical, and spiritual intimacy suggested, perhaps, but not fully realized in the works that preceded it.

As you consider how to begin writing about *The Night of the Iguana*, keep in mind that an understanding of the critical reception of a work and an exploration of those elements that distinguish a text from its counterparts can serve as a perfect starting point for your research. Considering how others understood and interpreted the text gives you a point of focus, presenting a viewpoint to support or to challenge while illuminating the most important features of the text. A consideration of the critical reception of a work and the elements that distinguish the text from its counterparts might lead you to write literally about a critical view of the play, either supporting a view with new insights or challenging it, or a consideration of the critical reception of a work could simply lead you on to another topic—an examination of a specific formal element such as theme or character, or a comparison of the play to an earlier work, for example. Most importantly, some consideration of the critical response to a work will allow you to formulate and voice your own thoughts, contributing something new to the dialogue about a work that is synonymous with contributing to others' understanding of the text in the future. Therefore, the most important thing to remember is that, whether you choose to support a critical view or to dispute it, your conclusion should lend something new and original to the discussion.

In order to pinpoint a topic for your thesis and begin piecing together the ideas that will ultimately form your conclusion, you will need to perform close readings of the text, examining those parts of the play that pertain to the viewpoint you seek to bolster or contradict. Let us consider an example. As noted above, some critics have stated that the *The Night of the Iguana* marked a major departure from Williams's earlier works, suggesting that the ending of the play allowed for some positivity—a bit of optimism and a sense of hope absent in previous works. In order to begin, you will want to first consider the endings of some of Williams's previous works. You might choose endings from two or three other plays so that your essay does not become unwieldy and your ideas too numerous to manage and organize. As you approach these texts, you will need to consider the following questions: What happens at the end of each play? How are the characters affected by the events of the conclusion? What do the conclusions of each play share in common? Are the conclusions simply tragic? Or is there some indication of redemption or hope? Once you have reviewed these texts, paying careful attention to how each draws to a close, you should have some clear sense of what you want to hypothesize about the conclusions of these plays. Your interpretations of the various conclusions may lead you to present the view that the endings are simply tragic with no evidence of redemption or hope, or you may feel that this characterization is inaccurate, that there is some indication of redemption, hope, or another positive force. Once you have formed your own view and have taken some preliminary notes on important passages that support your point of view, you are ready to consider the conclusion of *The Night of the Iguana.* You will need to begin by performing a close reading of the conclusion of the play. Again, you will want to ask many of the questions above so that you can make some determination as to the nature and proper characterization of the conclusion of the play. With a good understanding of all the conclusions of the various texts you have chosen to write about, you should now be ready to draft your thesis.

In the next step you should begin gathering specific evidence that supports your thesis. Of course, this evidence may be in line with previous criticism on the subject, or it may refute it. Look for important passages in the text. For example, as you read *The Night of the Iguana,* you should have recognized that the exchanges between Hannah and Reverend Shannon are some of the most significant passages in the play. They reveal intimate details about each character and help to reveal the themes of the play. Take, for instance, the following passage:

HANNAH. Liquor isn't your problem, Mr. Shannon.

SHANNON. What is my problem, Miss [sic] Jelkes?

HANNAH. The oldest one in the world—the need to believe in something or in someone—almost anyone—almost anything . . . something.

SHANNON. Your voice sounds hopeless about it.

HANNAH. No, I'm not hopeless about it. In fact, I've discovered something to believe in.

SHANNON. Something like . . . God?

HANNAH. No.

SHANNON. What?

HANNAH. Broken gates between people so they can reach each other, even if it's just for one night only.

SHANNON. One night stands, huh?

HANNAH. One night . . . communication between them on a verandah
  outside their . . . separate cubicles, Mr. Shannon.

SHANNON. You don't mean physically, do you?

HANNAH. No.

SHANNON. I didn't think so. Then what?

HANNAH. A little understanding exchanged between them, a wanting
  to help each other through nights like this. (408–09)

If you choose to support the notion that the play's conclusion is positive, representing a departure from Williams's previous works, you will
want to focus on the emotional, spiritual, and philosophical intimacy
that seems evident in this exchange. Does the passage indicate a challenge that both characters are facing? Does it, perhaps, indicate a kind
of camaraderie that is characteristic of the human condition? Why is
the fact that Hannah is concerned with emotional intimacy rather than
physical intimacy significant? How does this relationship and this type
of intimacy compare to or differ from the views of relationships and
intimacy presented in Williams's other plays? Continue to examine the
remainder of the exchange for other evidence that supports your view.
For example, consider Hannah's admission that she, too, has struggled
emotionally and spiritually:

HANNAH. Yes. I can help you because I've been through what you are
  going through now. I had something like your spook—I just had a different name for him. I called him the blue devil, and . . . oh . . . we had
  quite a battle, quite a contest between us.

SHANNON. Which you obviously won.

HANNAH. I couldn't afford to lose.

**SHANNON.** How'd you beat your blue devil?

**HANNAH.** I showed him that I could endure him and I made him respect my endurance.

**SHANNON.** How?

**HANNAH.** Just by, just by . . . enduring. Endurance is something that spooks and blue devils respect. (409)

Again, this passage will allow you to support the view that the characters have a shared condition, one that can be overcome, in fact, by endurance and simple human will. Consider if this element or this concept is present in the earlier plays you have chosen to write about. You may conclude that it is a new concept not evidenced in previous works. From here you will want to go on to note other positive elements of the play's conclusion. For instance, Nonno is able to complete his last poem; the iguana is set free; and Shannon recognizes that there are people who care about him and are ready to help him, people who share an understanding of his condition. Ultimately, as your essay draws to a close, you will need to look beyond the conclusion, explaining how the ending of the play serves as the culmination of concepts presented elsewhere in the text, a reflection of positive themes that run throughout the course of the play.

Alternatively, analyzing passages such as those included above may make you feel that the conclusion of the play is, in fact, in the same vein as the conclusions of Williams's previous works. You might believe that the passages cited above indicate widespread cultural problems such as loss of faith and mental instability. You may also feel that the passage indicates that people are actually unable to help themselves or others (despite their best intentions) and are, therefore, isolated in their condition. Again, you will need to go beyond the conclusion to show how the mood of the conclusion is reflected throughout the text. For example, although Hannah suggests that it is possible for one struggling person to help another, you will want to note Shannon's comments to Charlotte Goodall that "[t]wo unstable conditions can set a whole world on fire, can blow it up, past repair" (363) and "the helpless can't help the helpless" (364). From here you would make note of other elements of the conclusion (and the play at large), as we did above, that support your view, such as the death of Nonno, the fact that Hannah is left alone with no one to call for help, the presence of the Nazi party that reminds us of the immense evil and suffering in the world, and the fact that Shannon may stay with Maxine despite an absence of love between them.

Although these views are disparate, either can form the basis of a strong essay as long as you include your own original observations supported by evidence from the text. Remember, however, that your essay should do more than simply agree or disagree with something that has already been said about the play. In fact, the goal of your essay should be to present your own unique interpretation of the text. Furthermore, it is not necessary to subscribe strictly to one view or another. For example, a study of the topic above might lead you to conclude that, while critics have held opposing views either that the conclusion of *The Night of the Iguana* is a departure from the tragic conclusions of his previous plays or perpetuates the dark endings of the works that preceded it, there is something else to consider—the presence of duality and an inconclusive view of existence in this play (and perhaps in Williams's other works, as well). If you choose to write from this point of view, you could use much of the research that you have already completed, but focus on additional passages such as this dialogue between Hannah and Shannon about dual nature:

> SHANNON. Don't tell me you have a dark side to your nature. (*He says this sardonically.*)
>
> HANNAH. I'm sure I don't have to tell a man as experienced and knowledgeable as you, Mr. Shannon, that everything has its shadowy side? . . . Everything in the whole solar system has a shadowy side to it except the sun itself—the sun is the single exception. (409–10)

The dialogue presents the notion of duality, a concept that you will find evidenced more discreetly within the text. Your essay might further demonstrate how the ending of the play presents other evidence of a concern with duality and contradictions: Nonno completes his last poem but dies shortly thereafter; Shannon realizes that there are people who care about him, but it is implied that he will choose to stay with Maxine in the absence of love; Hannah is free from any constraints following the death of her grandfather but has lost her family and now finds herself alone. If you are familiar with Williams's earlier plays, you will also recall that this concept has appeared elsewhere. In this case, you might choose to link the treatment of duality in *The Night of the Iguana* to the treatment of duality in Williams's other plays. To avoid simply pointing out similarities in the text, you will want to assert something about this shared theme. For instance, you might conclude that, although duality is addressed in many of his other works, *The Night of the Iguana* is the clearest presentation of this concept, ultimately fueling the great success of the work.

Of course, addressing a work through an analysis of its criticism is only one approach of many, and you may decide to take another approach, but most importantly, this method should help you to avoid the search for "the right answer," giving you a clear idea of the variety of interpretation that is possible as you consider any work of literature, whether it is a play written by Williams, a Shakespearean comedy, a classic short story, or a contemporary poem.

# TOPICS AND STRATEGIES

In the sections that follow, you will find a variety of suggested topics accompanied by questions and observations to assist you in the task of writing successfully about *The Night of the Iguana*. Remember that this is not a comprehensive list of topics, and the statements and questions that appear after each suggested topic are merely a guide to help spark your own ideas about the work. A successful paper will present a strong thesis based on your own original ideas and will be supported by relevant examples resulting from close readings of the text. A wide variety of interpretations will be possible as you consider each topic. Use the strategic questions and observations to stimulate your own thoughts about the text and to assist you in developing a strong thesis. Remember to read through the text more than once, making note of those elements of the text that support your argument. It will be equally important to make note of those elements that contradict your thesis, as this will help you to refine your argument and create a stronger case.

# Themes

Many of the themes presented in *The Night of the Iguana* may appear to be grim, but consider how Williams's treatment of these themes indicates something positive—a will to protest, to overcome these challenges, to create a dialogue about difficult issues. Also, consider how he treated contrasting themes such as the will to endure, the search for God, and the unity that is an inherent part of human existence. Consider how Williams presents these themes in the text. What formal elements does he use to bring them to our attention? Most importantly, what is he saying about these subjects? As with many of Williams's plays, you may find that it is difficult to pinpoint Williams's own precise views about these themes. As suggested above, you may believe that Williams subscribes to one view or another, but consider also the possibility that Williams is presenting multiple views on a single theme.

## Sample Topics:

1. **Loss of faith:** The characters in the play, especially Reverend T. Lawrence Shannon, seem to suffer from a loss of faith of some kind, whether it is religious in nature or a loss of faith in humanity. Does the play present this problem as an obstacle that can be overcome?

   Consider passages that reflect the characters' loss of faith. What has each of the main characters lost faith in? Is it a loss of faith in God? You will want to look at Shannon's explanation of his loss of religious faith. Also, look at the passages where Shannon begs characters such as Miss Fellowes and Charlotte Goodall not to further disrupt his faith in humanity, his sense of pride. Does Shannon ultimately regain his faith in humanity? In this instance, it will be particularly helpful to consider his interactions with Hannah Jelkes. The other characters have experienced losses of faith as well. In comparison to Shannon, how have the other characters responded to their loss of faith? If they are able to overcome this problem, or fail to overcome it, what does this say about human will and endurance?

2. **Isolation:** Isolation appears as a key theme in the play. How does Williams create a sense of isolation, and what does his treatment of this theme tell us about isolation and the human condition?

Although the characters never actually appear alone in the play, a sense of isolation certainly pervades the play. Consider the formal elements of the text. How does Williams create a sense of isolation, for instance, through symbolism and character? How does the setting contribute to the perpetuation of this notion of loneliness and separation? Does the play ultimately present the view that the characters are truly isolated? Or does it actually seek to dispel this notion? If we are not isolated and alone, what does the play suggest brings us together? Is Williams able, through the characters Shannon and Hannah, to present more than one view of this theme? If so, does the interaction between Shannon and Hannah present a balanced view of isolation, or does one view triumph over the other?

3. **Desire:** How does the play present desire? Is it a positive force or a negative one?

Consider all examples of desire in the play. When it comes to physical desire, for example, there is Maxine's desire for Shannon, Charlotte's desire for Shannon, the men who have desired Hannah, and Hannah's lack of physical desire. The text also reveals that Shannon has previously had problems managing his desire despite his profession. How is each of the characters affected by these desires? Does anything positive come of desire? Or is it, rather, little more than a source of frustration? Consider Shannon's response to Maxine when she asks him why he is interested in young women. How do Shannon's and Maxine's situations mirror each other in this regard? Is desire more than just lust, the manifestation of an existential longing to not be alone? Does this affect the way we perceive the characters and the theme of desire in the play? Does Hannah's lack of interest in physical desire present the idea that she is somehow more evolved, recognizing that other forms of intimacy are more fruitful and meaningful?

You may also wish to consider desire from a broader perspective, as more than just a synonym for lust. Think about what each of the characters desires or wants. Do they attain it?

4. **The will to endure:** In a conversation between Hannah Jelkes and Reverend Shannon, Hannah confesses that she, too, has been on the verge of a breakdown. They subsequently enter into a discussion about the will to endure. What message does the play ultimately present about human endurance?

Again, you may find that the play presents multiple viewpoints on this one subject. Consider the passage referenced above, but look also at implied or symbolic representations of endurance (or a lack of endurance) as well. If you feel that the play presents the will to endure as a triumphant force, explain how. It will be useful, for example, to consider Nonno and his completion of his final poem despite memory problems and other challenges. If, however, you feel that the play presents endurance as only a short term device for temporary escape, explain why.

## Character

Although the characters in the play are from varied backgrounds, the play presents us with the view that they are all in the same boat, so to speak. Reverend Shannon notes that they are all, like the captured iguana, "at the end of [their] rope" (421). Consider what unifies the characters. How does each character respond to their situation?

The play also seems to abandon the idea suggested in earlier works of the woman in peril who needs a man to rescue her. In fact, in *The Night of the Iguana*, it is the women who offer their help to Reverend Shannon. In light of this notion, you might choose to consider how Williams addresses gender roles—does he somehow define (or upset definitions of) masculinity and femininity, or is he more concerned with a treatment of the general human condition? Also, consider how Williams's treatment of this theme reflects a kind of self-revelation stemming from his own past.

## Sample Topics:

**1. Reverend Shannon:** Analyze this character.

> Reverend T. Lawrence Shannon is a very complicated character and many different papers could result from an exploration of his character. In the play Williams is able not only to present a picture of Reverend Shannon's personal condition but to use Shannon as a symbol of a larger cultural problem. As a defrocked minister, Shannon represents the ongoing struggle of faith, complicated by an often inhospitable universe. You could, therefore, analyze his character from a psychological or philosophical standpoint focusing on his own condition, or you could analyze his character from a historical or cultural standpoint, showing how he represents a cultural problem or issues linked to a certain period in world history. How might Shannon's problems reflect the challenges that people faced during the time of World War II? You will also want to consider how Shannon changes or develops throughout the play. Does he remain stunted, or is he able to overcome some of the personal challenges he faces? Consider everything we know about Shannon. How does Williams want us to respond to his character? In considering this question, it will be helpful to also make note of the responses of the other characters. Certainly, Miss Fellowes despises Shannon and sees him as a villain, while Hannah is sympathetic to his situation despite his many flaws. Is Williams purposely creating a balanced view of

Shannon? If so, how does this affect our own interpretation of his character?

2. **Maxine Faulk:** How are we to perceive Maxine Faulk? Does she have Reverend Shannon's best interests at heart? Does Williams want us to be sympathetic to her character?

Consider everything the play reveals about Maxine Faulk. Is she a likable character? Why is she interested in Shannon? Think about her motivations. Is she driven by loneliness or by lust? Or both? How does her character subvert traditional representations of women in literature?

3. **Hannah Jelkes:** Analyze this character.

Think about the roles that Hannah fills in the play. She is a granddaughter, a caretaker, and an artist, to name only a few. You might choose to organize your essay around an exploration of any one of these roles, or you might choose to write about the complexity of her character and how these roles are all related. Consider everything we know about Hannah, including her past, her desires, and lack of physical desire. What do these things tell us about her character? How do the characters in the play see her? Whose perception of Hannah do you feel is most accurate and why?

4. **Jonathan Coffin (Nonno):** Why does Williams include the character Jonathan Coffin, also known as Nonno, in the play? What does he represent, and what themes is Williams able to treat by his inclusion in the play?

In previous plays Williams often included both old and young characters to create a sense of our confrontation with time. Does this seem to be the key motivation behind the inclusion of Jonathan Coffin, or Nonno, as he is known in the play? Although we know that Nonno is a grandfather, his role as a poet seems to be more prominent. How does Nonno tie in with Williams's preoccupation with the artist as an archetype in his works? Why is his struggle to finish his final poem significant? What symbolic value might this act have? Consider what we know about Nonno's own endurance and will to overcome. How do these traits inform our understanding of the themes of the play? Would our interpretation of these themes be different if he was not present in the play?

## History and Context

Williams began writing the story that would become *The Night of the Iguana* in the late 1940s. During this time, the world was in the midst of World War II, and people everywhere were witnesses to horrifying atrocities. The play makes little mention of the war, referencing it only through the presence of a boisterous German wedding party, who sing Nazi songs and cheer upon hearing that London is burning. Although there are no other literal references in the play, consider how *The Night of the Iguana* addresses cultural issues specific to this period of time in world history. Aside from the grotesque comic use of the German characters, consider how the mood of the play and the problems that the characters face symbolize a cultural mood linked to the context in the time in which the play was written. Remember that Williams set the play in the 1940s not in Europe or America but in a Mexican jungle. Consider why this is. Was Williams trying to avoid a direct discussion of the war? Or is it possible that the setting better serves the treatment of relevant social and cultural themes in the play?

### Sample Topic:

1. **The German wedding party:** Some critics have questioned the inclusion of the German wedding party in the play, claiming that these characters are extraneous and add nothing but a bit of ill humor. Do you agree with these claims?

   Consider all of the scenes where the German wedding party appears. If you agree with these claims that these characters would be better left out of the play, explain why you feel that the inclusion of the characters is not significant or detracts from the play. If you do not agree, explain why you believe Williams included them in the play. What greater purpose do they serve? Is their appearance truly comical as it might appear at first glance? Do they reference a specific cultural issue or historical problem? If so, how does their appearance help to create a specific mood that ties in to the greater themes of the play?

## Philosophy and Ideas

*The Night of the Iguana* is a deeply philosophical play. It deals with existentialist themes and difficult questions of faith and human endurance. Consider what questions and issues the characters are struggling with. How do they address these issues? Are they struggling with personal issues, or are their issues universal or characteristic of the human condition? Like many of Williams's other works, the play also addresses psychological issues. Although Shannon promotes the notion that hysteria is a female condition, consider how Shannon's own condition contradicts this view. It will be helpful to consider how hysteria and mental illness were perceived at the time the play was written. Did the play subvert traditional notions of mental illness? Consider how the psychological issues presented in the play tie in with the philosophical concerns of the text.

### Sample Topics:

1. **Hysteria as a female condition:** Shannon tells Hank that "hysteria is a natural phenomenon, the common denominator of the female nature" (340). How does the play support or subvert this notion?

   Although Shannon makes this claim, the play reveals that Shannon himself is struggling with mental challenges. He is, admittedly, on the verge of a mental breakdown. Consider the passage noted above and all passages where Shannon or the other characters talk about his own mental condition. You will ultimately need to make some claim as to what the play is suggesting about the relationship between mental illness and gender. Does the play dismiss any notion that mental illness or instability can be linked to one gender or another? If so, why is this an important statement? How was mental illness viewed at the time the play was written? How does the view presented in the play compare to the social understanding of mental illness during the 1940s?

You may also to choose to address this question by considering Williams's own family history. How might Williams's reaction to his sister Rose's condition have informed the treatment of this theme in *The Night of the Iguana*? Is this in line with his treatment of this theme in his other works? If not, explain how this play presents an alternate view of this theme and why it is a significant change.

2. **The search for God:** Many of the characters in the play seem to be searching for something. Shannon, specifically, notes that he has lost his faith in God, or at least traditional notions of God. What view or views of God does the play present? Where can God be realized?

Although one of the main characters of the play is a defrocked Episcopal priest, the play presents us with several less traditional notions of God and religion. Consider, for instance, Hannah's discussion of how people need something to believe in. Shannon assumes that she must be speaking about God, but Hannah speaks rather of a human bond, good will. Consider also Shannon's view of God. If Shannon dismisses traditional ideas of God, what vision of God does Shannon believe in? How is God also linked to nature? It may be interesting to link this topic to a consideration of the play's presentation of the breakdown of traditional notions of morality.

## Form and Genre

Although the genre and form of the play do not generally stand out (the play is a work of drama broken down into three acts, like many of Williams's other plays), great emphasis has been placed on the interpretation of the conclusion or third act of *The Night of the Iguana*. The conclusion of a work is typically what makes a final and lasting impression on us.

Consider the ending of *The Night of the Iguana*. What impression does it leave us with? Most importantly, do not consider the conclusion as an isolated passage. Ask yourself how the ending of the play ties in with the themes presented in the rest of the work.

## Sample Topic:

1. **The conclusion of the play:** How are we to interpret the conclusion of *The Night of the Iguana*? Is the ending positive or negative? Or is it impossible to categorize it as either? Does it present any resolution of the issues presented in the play?

   Examine the third act of the play. While the ending of the play is somewhat ambiguous, critics and scholars have argued from both sides of the fence, suggesting that the play's conclusion is a departure from the tragedy inherent in the endings of his other works or that the conclusion mimics the conclusions found in earlier works. You may support either viewpoint, or present your own, but be sure to support your view with evidence from the text. You might also present the view that it is impossible to have a singular interpretation of the conclusion, as its ambiguity and evidence of duality leave it open for interpretation. In this instance you will need to explain what parts of the conclusion are ambiguous and where a concern with duality is evident. Remember not to simply point out these places in the text but to explain why you believe Williams wanted the conclusion to function in this way and why it is an important choice. How would an ambiguous conclusion concerned with duality tie in with the themes of the work? Does it lend the work a greater sense of realism?

## Language, Symbols, and Imagery

With *The Night of the Iguana*, Williams seems to present us with a refined text, cleared of repetitive symbolism and overtly dramatic gestures. Instead, Williams chooses to employ a few symbols and gestures that best capture the mood and themes of the play. Of course, the most prominent symbol is the iguana adopted in the title, an animal that comes to symbolize the human condition and becomes a metaphor for the notion of being at the end of one's rope. You might choose to analyze this symbol or consider other less conspicuous symbols, such as Shannon's second profession as a tour guide, the metaphor of the interrupted journey, and the setting itself.

## Sample Topics:

1. **The iguana:** Why do you believe that Williams chose to use the image of the iguana in the title of the play? What does the iguana symbolize?

   Consider the scenes where the iguana appears. How is it treated? How does its predicament compare to the predicament that the characters find themselves in? Shannon suggests that Hannah must be comparing the iguana's situation to her grandfather's situation, but how are the other characters also linked to the idea of the captured iguana? Explain how the iguana functions as a metaphor for the human condition. You will also want to note who is sensitive to the iguana's plight. Your conclusion should analyze the iguana's ultimate fate, explaining what significance this has.

2. **The setting:** Williams sets the play in a primitive Mexican jungle in the 1940s. How does this setting support the thematic concerns of the play?

   Consider the descriptions of Costa Verde and the area surrounding it. It is a setting that is able to provide a tremendous sense of both isolation and freedom. Think about how the jungle has typically been treated in literature. How does the traditional vision of the jungle compare to the vision presented in this play? In this play, is the jungle a source of the characters' troubles or is it, rather, a sanctuary? Who is familiar with this setting, and who is new to it? You will also want to consider smaller details such as why Williams chooses to put the characters in cubicles rather than in rooms and how the weather allows Williams to create a mood that mimics the thematic concerns of the play.

3. **The interrupted journey:** Shannon is conducting a tour when he stops at Costa Verde in the Mexican jungle. How does the interrupted journey serve as a metaphor for his emotional or philosophical condition?

Works of literature frequently utilize the journey as a metaphor for the mental and spiritual development of a character. Consider Shannon's own journey. How does the interruption of his journey reflect his own mental condition or the status of his development? You may wish to compare the use of the journey as metaphor to the similar presentation of journey as metaphor in other texts. You might compare the play, for instance, to Hermann Hesse's *Siddhartha,* Joseph Conrad's *Heart of Darkness,* or Homer's *The Odyssey.*

## Compare and Contrast Essays

Many of the topics suggested herein can be profitably converted into compare and contrast essays. For example, the major themes of the play—isolation and endurance, for example—are evident in Williams's other plays. Compare Williams's treatment of these themes in *The Night of the Iguana* to the treatment of these themes in his other works. Likewise, an examination of these themes will allow you to also focus on similarities between the characters in Williams's plays. How do Hannah and Alma from *Summer and Smoke* compare, for instance? Is there any correlation between Maxine and Serafina from *The Rose Tattoo*? If you wish to work within the single play, you might compare Hannah and Shannon. Any of these topics can form interesting essays if you provide fresh insights using evidence from the text.

### Sample Topics:

1. **The play and the film:** A film adaptation of the play directed by John Huston was released in 1964. Compare and contrast the play and the film.

Consider how the film does or does not support Williams's vision of the play. What elements remain the same and what has the director changed? Is the conclusion of the film faithful to the conclusion of the play? Is our understanding of the characters similar upon consideration of both versions? How does the film change or maintain our perception of the play?

2. **Treatment of isolation in** *The Night of the Iguana* **and** *Orpheus Descending:* Isolation appears as a key theme in many of Williams's works. Compare and contrast Williams's treatment of isolation in *The Night of the Iguana* and *Orpheus Descending.*

Look for literal and figurative references to isolation in the two plays. How does Williams create a sense of loneliness and isolation without literally isolating the characters in a physical sense? What formal elements does he employ to create this sense of isolation? You will want to consider Shannon's remarks about the impossibility of people being helped to Val's remarks about love and isolation. How do the endings of the two plays affect our understanding of this theme? Are the characters in either play able to overcome this sense of isolation? Or does the play present the view that isolation is an existential certainty despite our relationships with others who care about us, or even love us? In order to answer these questions you will need to look not only at plot but also at character development.

3. **Endurance in** *The Night of the Iguana* **and** *Cat on a Hot Tin Roof:* Compare and contrast the treatment of endurance in the two plays.

There seem to be great similarities between Hannah Jelkes's notion of endurance and Maggie's in *Cat on a Hot Tin Roof.* Compare the passages where each character speaks of endurance. Why are these characters concerned with endurance? Are their motivations the same? Are Hannah and Maggie successful in their will to endure? What view does each play present on the matter of endurance—is endurance a means to an end? Or are the characters psychologically stunted? What about Nonno's endurance in *The Night of the Iguana*? Does his character present us with another view of human endurance and its significance?

4. **Maxine Faulk and Serafina of *The Rose Tattoo:*** Compare and contrast these two characters.

Consider the characterization of Maxine and Serafina. Both are women who were recently widowed. What else do the characters share in common? How do the characters deal with their newfound loneliness and their desires? How does Williams characterize their relationships with their husbands? Does one have a more realistic view than the other? How are the characters different, and why are these differences significant?

5. **Hannah Jelkes and Alma from *Summer and Smoke:*** Compare and contrast these two characters.

Consider what we know of Hannah Jelkes and Alma from *Summer and Smoke.* What do the characters have in common? How do they relate to their families? How do they view love and desire? Do their roles as artists (Hannah as a portrait artist and Alma as a singer) have any correlation to their level of sensitivity? Consider how the characters change or develop throughout the course of each play. How do their changes or lack of change compare or differ, and why are these similarities or difference important?

6. **The ability to overcome that which we despise in *The Night of the Iguana* and *Cat on a Hot Tin Roof:*** In *The Night of the Iguana* and *Cat on a Hot Tin Roof* we see evidence of characters struggling to overcome the very things that they despise most. Compare and contrast the presentation of the ability (or inability) to overcome that which we despise in both plays.

While Shannon despises conventional notions of God and chastises his lovers for their sinful actions, Shannon himself also plays a major part in these actions. Likewise, in *Cat on a Hot Tin Roof,* we find that Brick and Big Daddy are disgusted by mendacity; however, both characters seem to be caught up in their own lies and secrets. Consider the scenes where these characters address the object of their hatred and disgust. Are these characters aware that they are a part of the problem that plagues them? Do any of them overcome this problem? Why do you think that they are able or unable to?

## Bibliography and Resources for *The Night of the Iguana*

Adler, Thomas P. "Before the Fall—and After: *Summer and Smoke* and *The Night of the Iguana.*" *Cambridge Companion to Tennessee Williams.* Ed. Matthew C. Roudané. 114–27.

Blythe, David. "*Othello* and *Night of the Iguana.*" *Notes on Contemporary Literature* 27.1 (January 1997): 1.

Crandell, George W. "*The Night of the Iguana.*" *Tennessee Williams: A Guide to Research and Performance.* Ed. Philip C. Kolin. Westport, CT: Greenwood, 1998. 148–57.

Embrey, Glenn. "The Subterranean World of *The Night of the Iguana.*" *Tennessee Williams: Thirteen Essays.* Ed. Jac Tharpe. Jackson: U of Mississippi P, 1980. 65–80.

Levin, Lindy. "Shadow into Light: A Jungian Analysis of *The Night of the Iguana.*" *Tennessee Williams Annual Review* 2 (1999): 87–98.

*The Night of the Iguana.* Dir. John Huston. 1964. DVD. Warner, 2006.

Phillips, Rod. "'Collecting Evidence': The Natural World in Tennessee Williams's *The Night of the Iguana.*" *Southern Literary Journal* 32.2 (Spring 2000): 59–69.

Taubman, Howard. "Theatre: *Night of the Iguana* Opens." *New York Times.* 29 Dec. 1961.

Williams, Tennessee. *The Night of the Iguana. Tennessee Williams: Plays 1957–1980.* Eds. Mel Gussow and Kenneth Holditch. New York: Library of America, 2000. 327–428.

# INDEX